LEGENDARY LOCALS

OF

HOLYOKE

MASSACHUSETTS

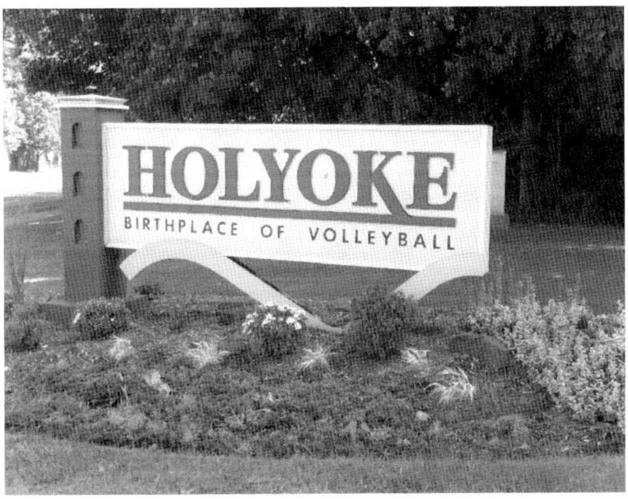

I0805814

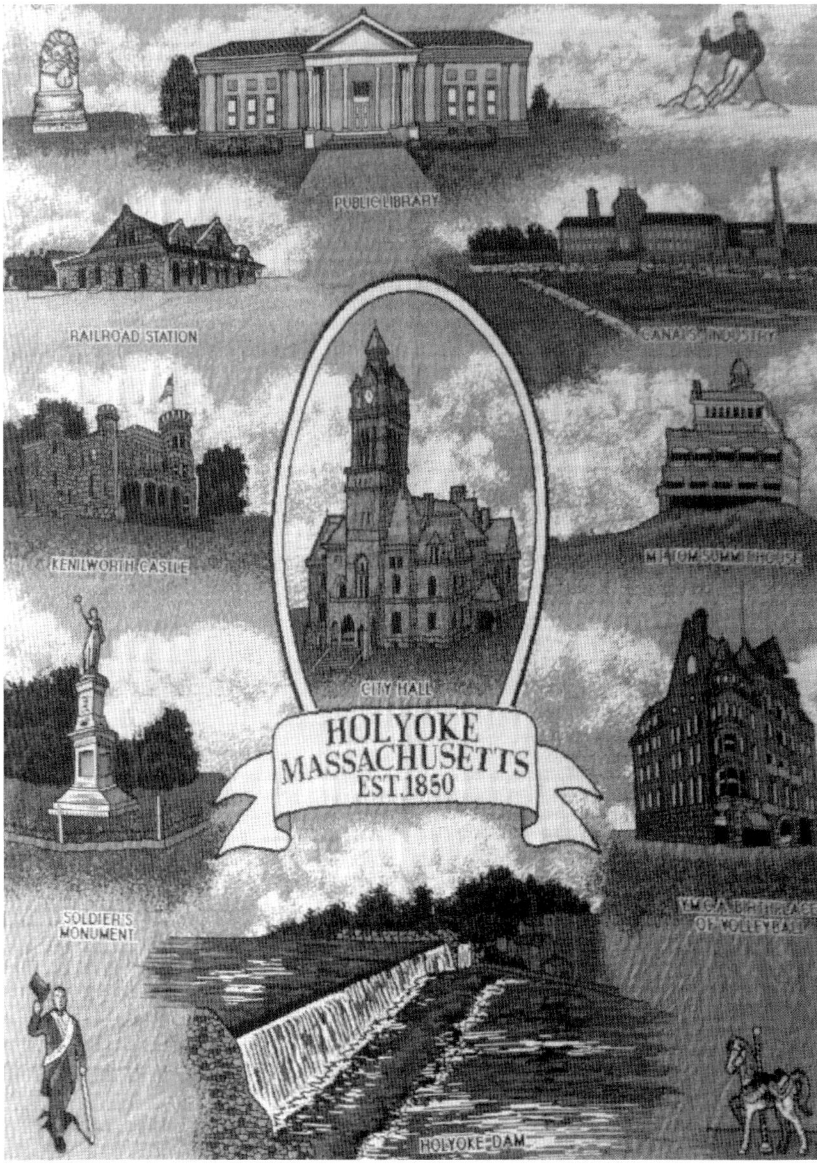

City Landmarks

Pictured is a beautiful afghan portraying some of Holyoke's famous landmarks, such as the Holyoke City Hall, the canal industry, a railroad station, Holyoke Public Library, Kenilworth Castle, Holyoke Soldier's Monument, the birthday place of volleyball, Holyoke merry-go-round carousal horse, Holyoke Dam, Mount Holyoke Summit House, a sentry lion of the Wistariahurst Museum, a Mount Tom Ski Area skier, and a Citizen of the Year marching in the Holyoke St. Patrick's Day Parade. (Courtesy of the Holyoke Public Library.)

Page 1: Welcome to Holyoke

Located on Crosier Field, across the street from the famous Yankee Pedlar Inn, is a "Welcome to Holyoke" sign that proclaims the city as the birthplace of volleyball. (Courtesy of the City of Holyoke.)

LEGENDARY LOCALS

OF

HOLYOKE

MASSACHUSETTS

JACQUELINE M. SEARS

LEGENDARY LOCALS

ISBN 978-1-4671-0181-3

Legendary Locals is an imprint of Arcadia Publishing
Charleston, South Carolina

Printed in the United States of America

Library of Congress Control Number: 2014941771

For all general information, please contact Arcadia Publishing:
Telephone 843-853-2070
Fax 843-853-0044
E-mail sales@arcadiapublishing.com
For customer service and orders:
Toll-Free 1-888-313-2665

Visit us on the Internet at www.arcadiapublishing.com

Dedication

This book is dedicated to the good souls of Holyoke's extraordinary past and to the men and women who will influence its promising future.

On the Front Cover: Clockwise from top left:
Robert Schwobe, historian (Courtesy of Robert Schwobe; see page 103), Barbara Bernard, writer (Courtesy of *Republican* newspaper; see page 100), Elizabeth Towne, wellness writer (Courtesy of the Holyoke Public Library; see page 104), Kathryn "Kay" Burnettt, trailblazer and former music librarian at Smith College (Courtesy of the Mount Tom State Reservation; see page 102), William Skinner, industrialist (Courtesy of the Holyoke Public Library; see page 17), Willma Jennings, teacher and veteran (Courtesy of Henry Jennings; see page 108), Jackie Watson, former comptroller at the Holyoke Gas & Electric Company, and Jimmy Watson, gas and electric technician and community volunteer (Courtesy of Jackie Watson; see page 92), George Ewing, businessman and community leader (Courtesy of the Holyoke Public Library; see page 106).

On the Back Cover: From left to right:
Mount Tom Ski Area (Courtesy of Harry Craven Jr.; see page 107), a view of Holyoke from the Connecticut River (Courtesy of Harry Craven Jr.; see page 8).

CONTENTS

ACKNOWLEDGMENTS

The author would like to thank the following people and organizations: Erin Vosgien, Robert Schwobe, Kate Navarra Thibodeau, Wyatt Harper, Kathleen Anderson, Constance McLaughlin Green, Henry Jennings, Mike Burke, Eileen Crosby, Holyoke Public Library, James Hoar, Harry Craven Jr., James Bronson, Robert E. Barrett Jr., Melissa Boissellee, Wistariahurst Museum, Robert Cahillane, William Beven, Glenn Sullivan, and Olivia Davis Mausel.

INTRODUCTION

Holyokers possess an indefinable quality of open heartedness, frankness, and friendliness that sets them apart from peoples of any other city.

—Howard Conant

The history of Holyoke is a remarkable tribute to American ingenuity, cooperation, and independence. I am the daughter of Rita Hebert and Donald Grenier, members of two hardworking families that have contributed to Holyoke's success. In 2004, I had the opportunity to write about Holyoke's fascinating history in the *Republican* newspaper, so I was delighted when Arcadia Publishing asked me to write about Holyoke's legendary men and women.

Growing up in Holyoke was an extraordinary experience that included meandering through stunning open spaces, like our richly forested parks, pristine reservoirs, the magical Mountain Park, and the Mount Tom Ski area, and of course, attending the annual St. Patrick's Day Parade and the St. Patrick's Road Race.

One thing that Holyoke residents all have in common is our ability to laugh and enjoy each other's company. We have a street-smart, shrewd humor that borders on cynical and yet rests on compassion and acceptance. Of course, our good nature could be the result of our sheer numbers. When I attended the Holyoke Public School System, there were over 40,000 people living in and around the city. Holyoke experienced its heyday from 1890 to 1920, when the population was close to 60,000 people. I was fortunate to have attended school with students of diverse ethnicities.

Prior to the Dutch and English settling in Massachusetts, the Algonquin Indians lived in the Pioneer Valley for about 10,000 years, and the Agawams lived to the south of Holyoke while the Nonotucks lived in northern Holyoke.

One of the original English pioneers to settle in the Springfield area was William Pynchon in 1636. By 1661, Englishman Elizur Holyoke, who was one of Pynchon's son's associates, was appointed deputy to the general court. Eventually, Holyoke was made the rank of captain and, by 1675, was named a selectman and deputy of the general court in Springfield. The area known today as Holyoke did not begin to be developed until the arrival of John Riley and his wife, Grace O'Dea. They emigrated from Ireland in 1634; settled in Hartford, Connecticut; had their children; raised their family; and then moved to the West Springfield area. Holyoke was originally called the "Third Parish," or, as the natives called it, "Ireland Parish." Farming was the mainstay of the community, although gristmills, sawmills, and a tannery were in operation. One successful sawmill was in the Rock Valley, Southampton, and Westfield area. The company cut white oak timbers that were sawed straight, fastened to pine carriers, and floated down the Connecticut River to Hartford, Connecticut, to be used in the shipbuilding industry.

In 1792, the Proprietors of the Locks and Canals built the first navigation canal in the United States on the South Hadley side of the Connecticut River. This unique inclined plane system allowed flatboats to bypass the rapids in South Hadley and Holyoke. In 1842, the Connecticut River Railroad Company came to the valley and reduced the need for the canals.

John Stephen, Warren Chapin, and Alfred Smith managed the first Hadley Falls Company. In 1848, the second and most important Hadley Falls Company developed waterpower on the Connecticut River with a wooden dam and a canal system. It also laid out the industrial, commercial, and residential areas on its 1,100 acres of land in the Ireland Parish area that George Ewing had secured, and encouraged the Hadley Falls Company to build a dam to produce energy to power the mills on a massive scale.

In 1858, Alfred Smith, an attorney from South Hadley and one of the original managers of the Hadley Falls Company, bought the company and sold stock to subscribers. He became the president of the Holyoke Water Power Company, which has successfully provided hydropower to Holyoke citizens for

108 years. The Holyoke Water Power Company also built up an existing wooden dam that had replaced the first ill-fated dam by adding a sloping portion to the downstream side and filling it in with gravel within a year. Fifty years later in the 1900s, a new granite dam was built that withstood the brutal waters of the 1936 flood and still stands strong today.

On May 29, 1873, a city charter was granted to name the town Holyoke due to the ever-growing mill community. In the 1800s, immigrants came to Holyoke to escape tyranny, poverty, and hardships in their motherlands. Hardworking men, women, and children—some under 15 years old—worked in the mills by 1873. Half of Holyoke's workforce by 1880 labored in mills, and 6 out of every 10 workers were female. They manufactured hundreds of products, including textiles, paper, yarn, metal goods, and so much more.

Historically, Holyoke has been called "the Paper City," due to the substantial number of paper manufacturers that produced some of the finest paper in the world, and the city motto is "the power to grow," which is apropos due to the hydropower that the dam produces for companies. The city of Holyoke was incorporated as a town in 1850. As Holyoke developed, immigrants from Ireland, Canada, Italy, and Poland entered the city in droves. The Irish were the first immigrants to arrive. They built the dam and the 4.5 miles of canals by pick and shovel. The mills were built alongside the canals to benefit from the hydropower from massive turbines that were powered by water. The Irish also worked in the mills throughout the city. There was a massive influx of French Canadians around this time, as well as immigrants from Poland, Italy, and Puerto Rico [Puerto Ricans did not come until much later]. By the Civil War, there were three major paper mills: Parsons Paper in 1853, Holyoke Paper in 1857, and Whiting Paper in 1864. In 1865, seven more paper companies were established. By 1873, Holyoke had become a burgeoning city.

This is just a brief example of some of the companies that Holyoke's hydroelectric canal system has supported. Holyoke was at one time a bustling metropolis of opportunity and enterprise. Today, while most of these companies have closed or moved to other regions, a new and emerging force has established itself in the downtown area and throughout Holyoke. The city of Holyoke continues to offer the business community countless advantages due to its convenient location, access to a qualified workforce due to the myriad of colleges and universities in Western Massachusetts, and a cost-effective, reliable green energy source powered by the Holyoke Dam. The greatest asset that Holyoke has always had is its exceptional people and their dedication to each other and the fine city of Holyoke.

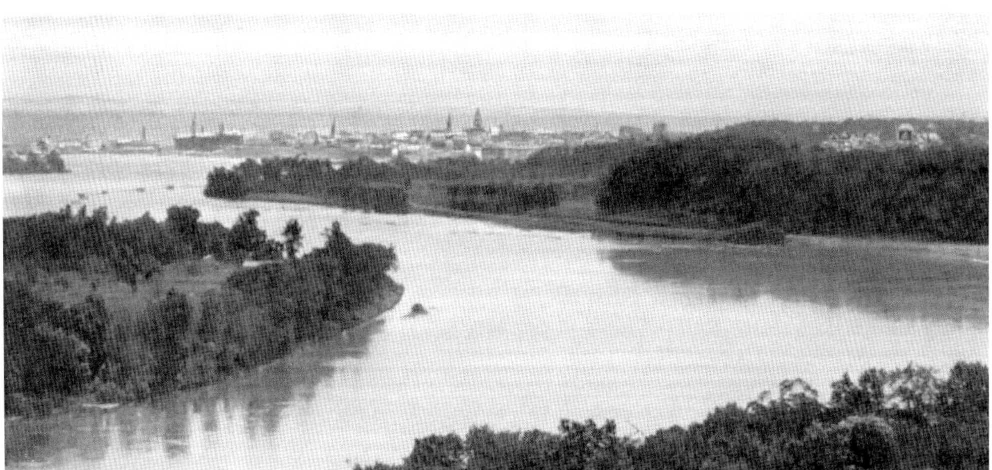

The Paper City
Holyoke is seen from the Connecticut River. (Courtesy of Harry Craven Jr.)

CHAPTER ONE

History Makers

A mere compilation of facts presents only the skeleton of History; we do but little for her if we cannot invest her with life, clothe her in the habiliments of her day, and enable her to call forth the sympathies of succeeding generations.

—Hannah Farnham Sawyer Lee (1780–1863)
The Huguenots in France and America

In 1661, Elizur Holyoke was appointed deputy to the general court, made the rank of captain, and was a selectman and deputy of the general court by 1675. John Riley established the Third Parish, or as the natives called it, Ireland Parish. Later, industrialists purchased the settlers farms to develop Holyoke into a mill town. Parson Rand prepared his students for the future.

The Hadley Falls Company profoundly changed the landscape of Holyoke. William Skinner would rebuild his company in Holyoke utilizing a canal system and a dam that powered his silk mill. William Whiting was a trusted leader for his employees in the Whiting Paper Company, and he served the citizens of Holyoke and Massachusetts. In 1884, William Loomis was the director of the Holyoke Street Railway Company, which eventually developed a park on the Mount Tom Range that would bring great joy and entertainment to the citizens of Western Massachusetts.

In 1853, Joseph Parsons finally opened the famous, long-standing Parsons Paper Company after some discouraging and trying years. Clemens Herschel developed a Venturi meter allowing mills to gauge their water intake. In 1920, Robert E. Barrett and his son skillfully managed the Holyoke Water Power Company. William Street built a hotel on the stunning Mount Tom Range. As the first commissioner of Hampshire County and chairman of the Mount Tom Reservation, Charles W. Bray helped to open up a warming shelter on Bray Lake that was named after him in 1938.

Well-respected professor and veteran Theodore Belsky inspired the community with his historical knowledge and enthusiasm, and John T. Hickey was a dedicated family and company man who encouraged the community to save an important part of their childhood. The Bail family is still striving to make people walk in comfort, while John B. McCormick worked hard on his game-changing turbine that would revolutionize power and improve the lives of countless individuals. Charles Lotspeich, a farmer's son, astutely mastered the story of Holyoke's interesting history so all could understand and relish in the beauty of a technological era it so keenly developed and utilized. John Zwisler researched and documented Holyoke when it was still called the Ireland Parish. Katherine and Ruth Isabel Skinner opened the Skinner Coffee House to help women and their families.

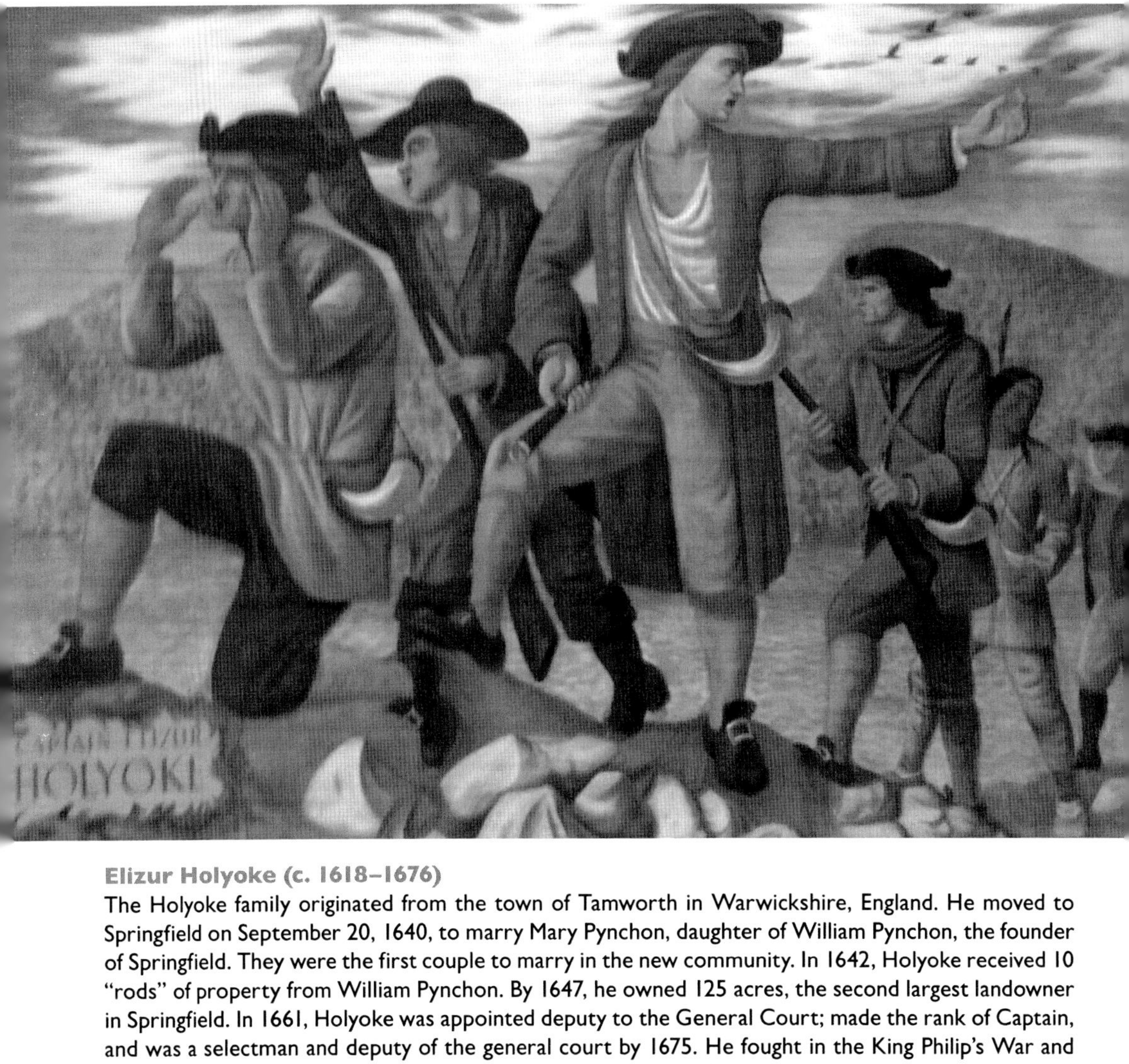

Elizur Holyoke (c. 1618–1676)

The Holyoke family originated from the town of Tamworth in Warwickshire, England. He moved to Springfield on September 20, 1640, to marry Mary Pynchon, daughter of William Pynchon, the founder of Springfield. They were the first couple to marry in the new community. In 1642, Holyoke received 10 "rods" of property from William Pynchon. By 1647, he owned 125 acres, the second largest landowner in Springfield. In 1661, Holyoke was appointed deputy to the General Court; made the rank of Captain, and was a selectman and deputy of the general court by 1675. He fought in the King Philip's War and was killed by Indians on February 5, 1676. Holyoke's grandson Rev. Edward Holyoke (1689–1769) was the president of Harvard, and his great-grandson Dr. Edward Augustus Holyoke (1728–1829) founded the Massachusetts Medical Society. (Courtesy of the Holyoke Public Library.)

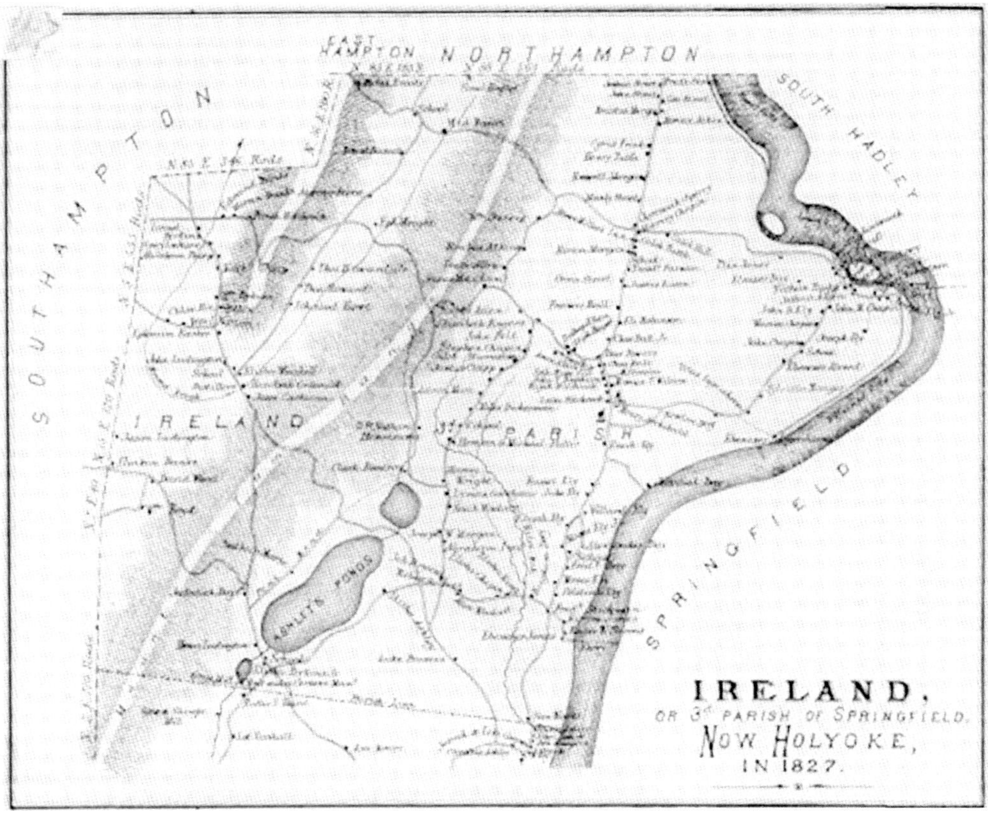

John Riley (c. 1664–1714)
Riley and his wife, Grace O'Dea, from Ireland purchased 28 acres north of West Springfield, near today's Riverdale Road. The area was called Third Parish as well as North Parish, but the Native Americans called it Ireland Parish. Riley and his wife braved the rough terrain and unpredictable environment, all the while trying to survive in a foreign country. (Courtesy of the Holyoke Public Library.)

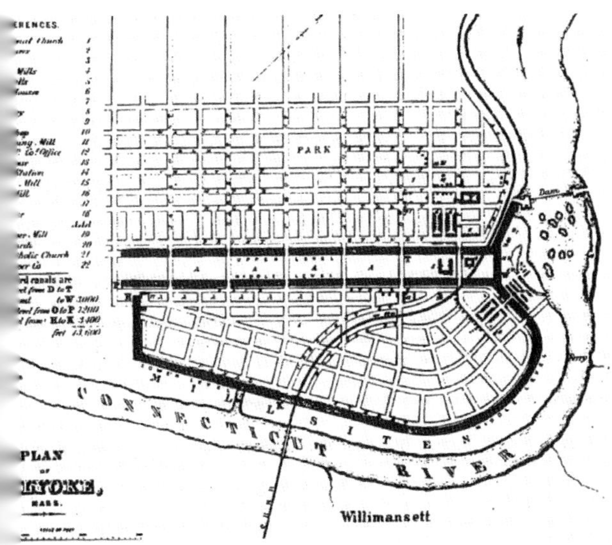

Hadley Falls Company
The first Hadley Falls Company was organized in 1827 by John Stephen, Warren Chapin and Alfred Smith. They procured legislative authority to build a wing dam that extended up the Connecticut River to run its looms in the Hampden Mill Company. The second Hadley Falls Company laid out industrial, commercial, and residential areas on its 1,100 acres of land for future development. In 1859, the company went into receivership and was auctioned off for $325,000 to Alfred Smith, who in turn sold the company to the Holyoke Water Power Company. (Courtesy of the Holyoke Public Library.)

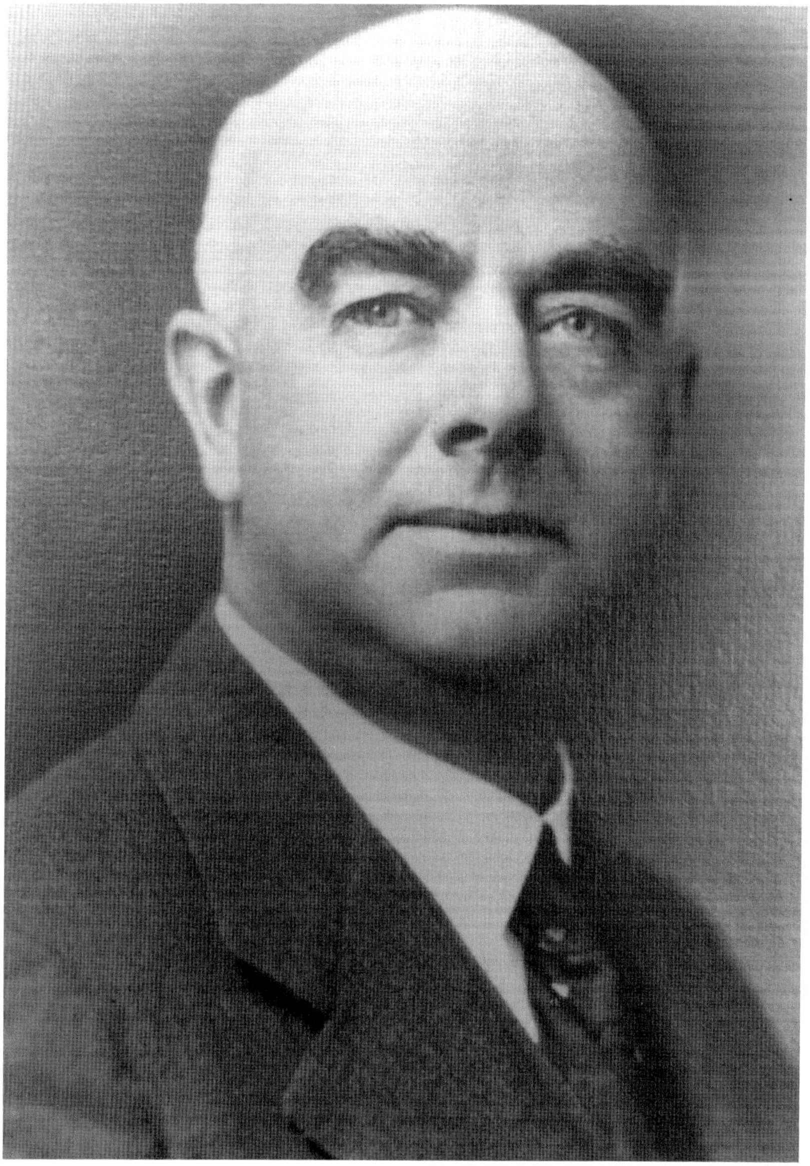

Robert E. Barrett Sr. (1873–1945)

The Holyoke Water Power Company was incorporated by the Massachusetts Legislature on January 31, 1859. The corporators were Francis Bacon, Augustus H. Fiske, George W. Lyman, and William Appleton. Alfred Smith, founder and first president of the company, purchased the Hadley Falls Company for $325,000. The company was successful for 108 years until it became a subsidiary of Northeast Utilities, closing its doors in 1967. In 1920, Robert E. Barrett became the treasurer of the Holyoke Water Power Company and was named president three years later. By 1925, the company had charted rights to generate, transmit, and sell electricity throughout Massachusetts and nearby states. Barrett oversaw a major expansion in electrical supply services; he was also involved in rebuilding damage from a 1936 ice jam that broke over the Holyoke Dam. He was also instrumental in facilitating labor negotiations with the International Brotherhood of Electrical Workers (IBEW) in 1938; it was a relationship that held up for 50 years. (Courtesy of the Holyoke Public Library.)

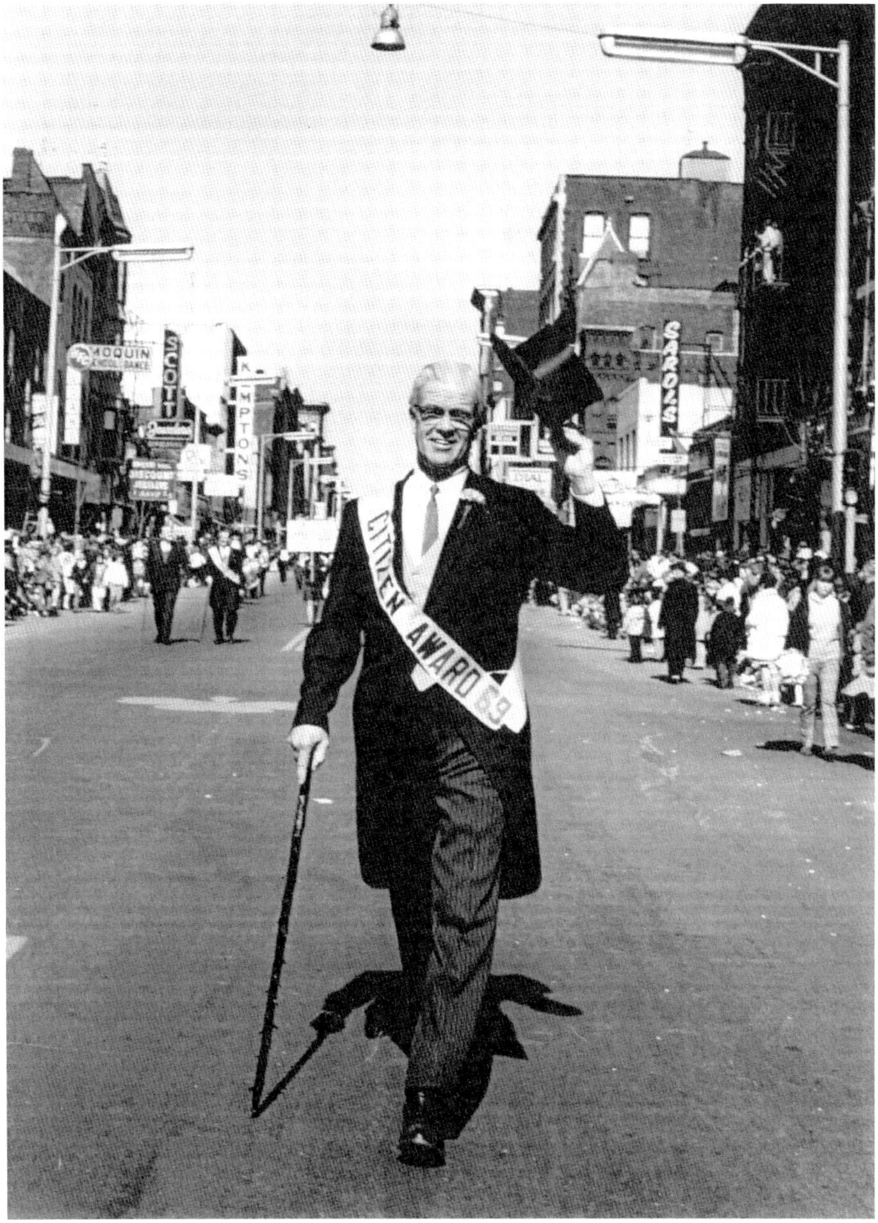

Robert E. Barrett Jr. (1910–2002)
He attended the Holyoke Public School system and graduated from Harvard College in 1930. He worked for the Holyoke Water Power company from 1930 to 1974, becoming its president in 1945. In 1971, he was appointed by Gov. Francis Sargent to the Massachusetts Board of Higher Education. In 1949, he was instrumental in attaining a Federal Power Commission grant that allowed for a 50-year license for the dam, canal system, and hydroelectric properties based on the assurance that the company would construct a fish passage to allow American shad, sea lamprey, and Atlantic salmon to migrate upstream. In the spring, this amazing water-filled fish elevator carries up to 2,000 fish per hour. In 1956, the Holyoke Water Power Company earned the Conservation Service Award because of this effort. Barrett Jr. was awarded the 1969 St. Patrick Citizen Award. (Courtesy of the Holyoke Public Library.)

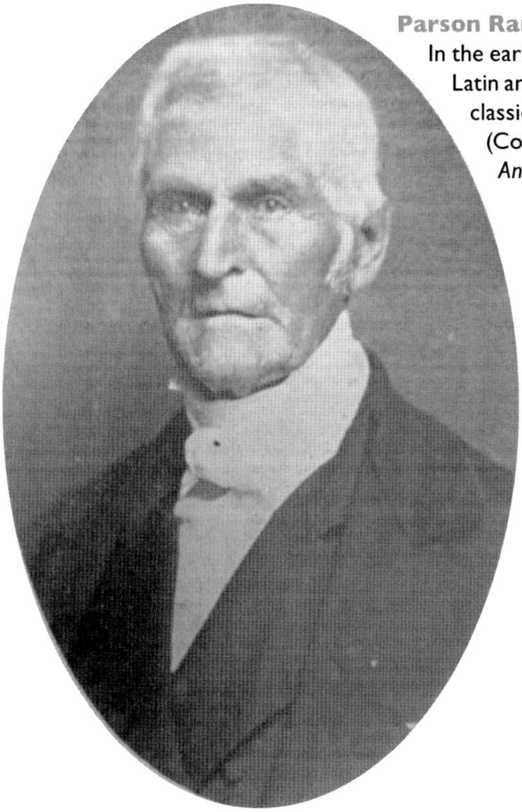

Parson Rand

In the early 1800s, Minister Parson Rand taught clergymen Latin and Greek and tutored boys for a minimal fee in the classics and mathematics at the Parson Rand Academy. (Courtesy of *Honor Holyoke: Old Home Week 75th Anniversary, 1873–1948.*)

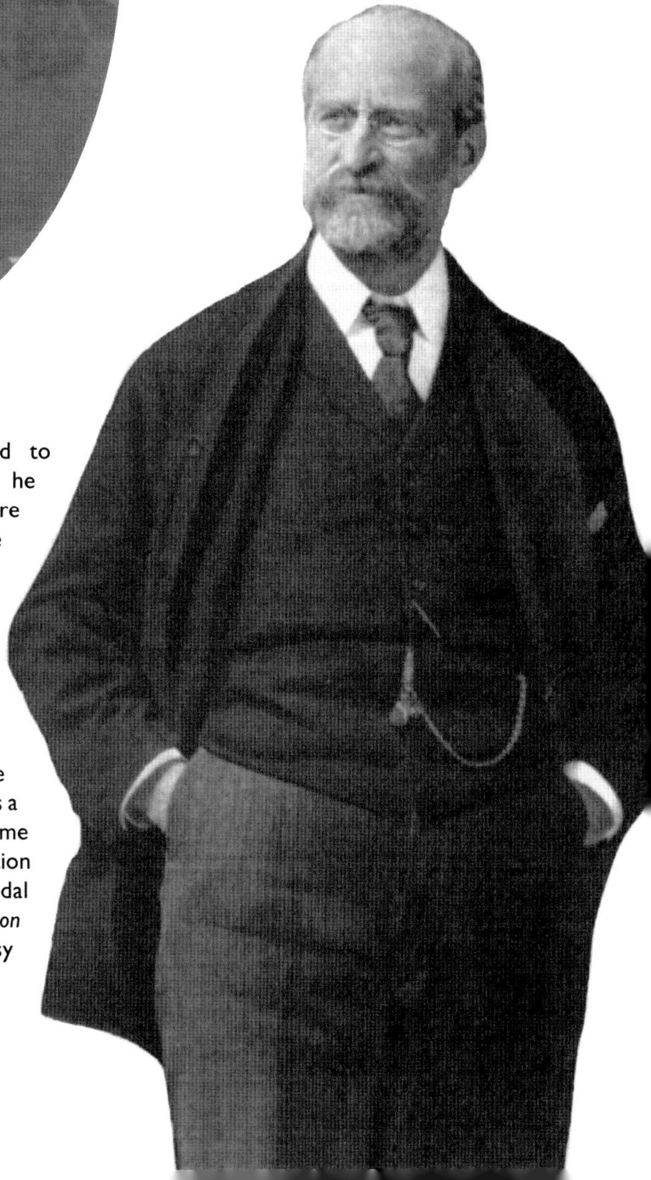

Clemens Herschel (1842–1930)

Born in Vienna, Herschel immigrated to Davenport, Iowa, in 1850. In 1860, he graduated from Harvard University, where he received his bachelor's of science degree from the Lawrence Scientific School. He was a hydraulic engineer from 1879 to 1889 for the Holyoke Water Power Company. He designed a new testing flume called the Venturi meter, which he named after Giovanni Battista Venturi, an Italian scientist of the 18th century who demonstrated the flow of fluids through pipes. Herschel was a member of the Water Industry Hall of Fame and the American Water Works Association and was awarded the Elliott Cresson Medal from the Franklin Institute. (*An Appreciation of Two Great Workers in Hydraulics*, courtesy of the Holyoke Public Library.)

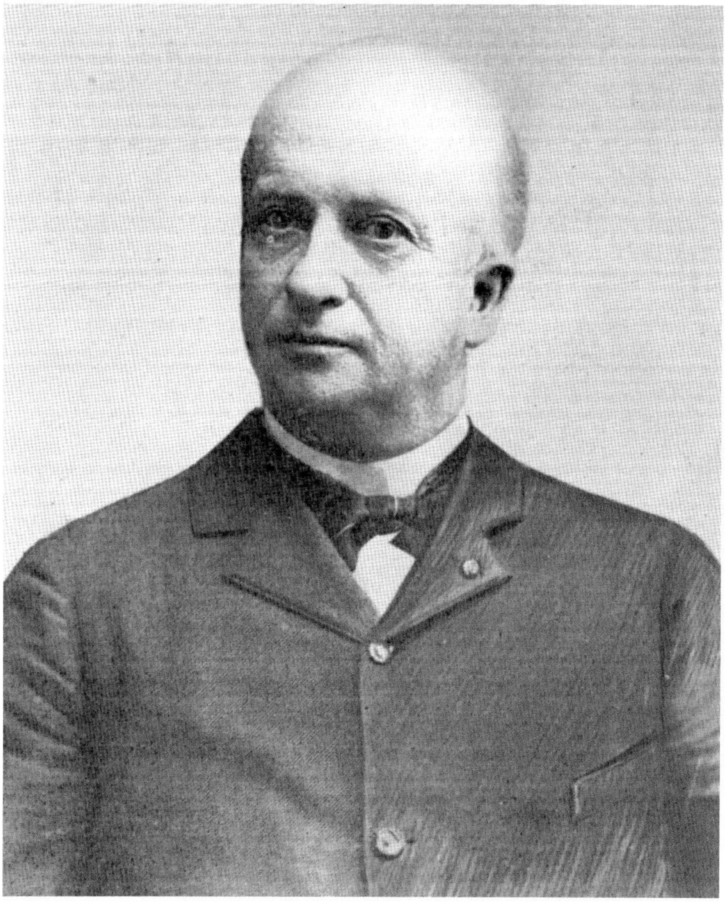

William Loomis (1840–1914)
In 1851, he moved to Holyoke from Monson when his father opened a variety store. In 1862, he fought in the Civil War, and by 1868 he and his brother-in-law E.J. Pomeroy bought his father's store. After several successful years, he bought the *Holyoke Transcript* in 1868 and purchased the controlling interest in the Holyoke Street Railway Company in 1890. Loomis was the director of the Holyoke Street Railway Company, which was incorporated in 1884. The company transported patrons by horse-drawn carriages throughout Holyoke until 1891, when trolley lines were installed. In 1888, he purchased 100 acres on Mount Tom and an additional 500 acres from the Whiting Street Estate in 1894. By this time, he owned property from the Connecticut River to the Mount Tom Summit under the Mount Tom Railway Company. He built an open-air stage and showcased wild animals and created a beautiful floral park in which to stroll. He also offered a section of the park to the Young Women's Christian Association for women and children; the area had picnic tables and a pavilion for entertaining. He sold the Holyoke Street Railway Company and began constructing tracks for a trolley line that went up to what would become known as Mountain Park. In 1898, he donated the land and supported the Holyoke home for the aged on Morgan Street. In 1968, the name was changed to the Loomis House. Mountain Park evolved into a trolley park and, finally, into the Mountain Park Amusement Park on the east side of the range. Loomis's assistant Louis Pellissier managed the park from 1929 until he sold the park in 1953 to John Collins, who owned Lincoln Park in North Dartmouth, Massachusetts. Eventually, his sons Jay and Dennis managed the park until it closed in 1987. Today, the area is home to the Mountain Park Amphitheater, owned by Eric Suher, a local businessman who owns the Iron Horse Entertainment Company in Northampton and ES Sports clothing store in Holyoke. (Courtesy of the Holyoke Public Library.)

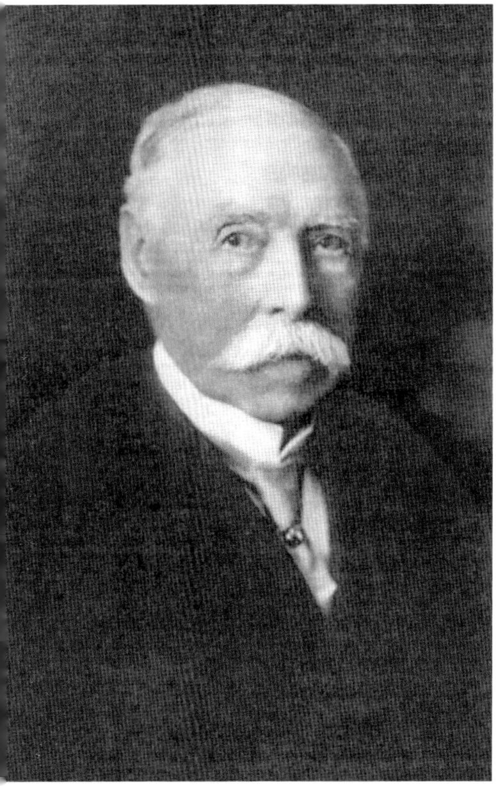

George W. Prentiss (1829–1915

Born and raised in Claremont, New Hampshire, he entered the workforce as a clerk in Fairhaven, Massachusetts, and soon after worked for Henry S. Washburn Wire Works in Worcester, Massachusetts, for three years. He continued to work for the Washburns' Norway Iron Works Company in South Boston for another three years until he partnered in 1857 with another gentleman working with wire in the Prentiss & Gray Company. He acquired his partner's interests and ran the company independently until 1871, when his cousin Marden W. Prentiss became his partner. The company was incorporated as George W. Prentiss & Company when his son William Albert came into the business. Prentiss was active in many important institutions in Holyoke, including Deane Steam Pump Company, Holyoke & Westfield Railroad Company, and many local banks, including the Holyoke Savings Bank, Holyoke National Bank, and the Third National Bank of Springfield. He was a director of the Holyoke Public Library, friend of the Holyoke City Hospital, and affiliated with the Mount Tom Lodge, Free and Accepted Masons. (Courtesy of the Holyoke Public Library.)

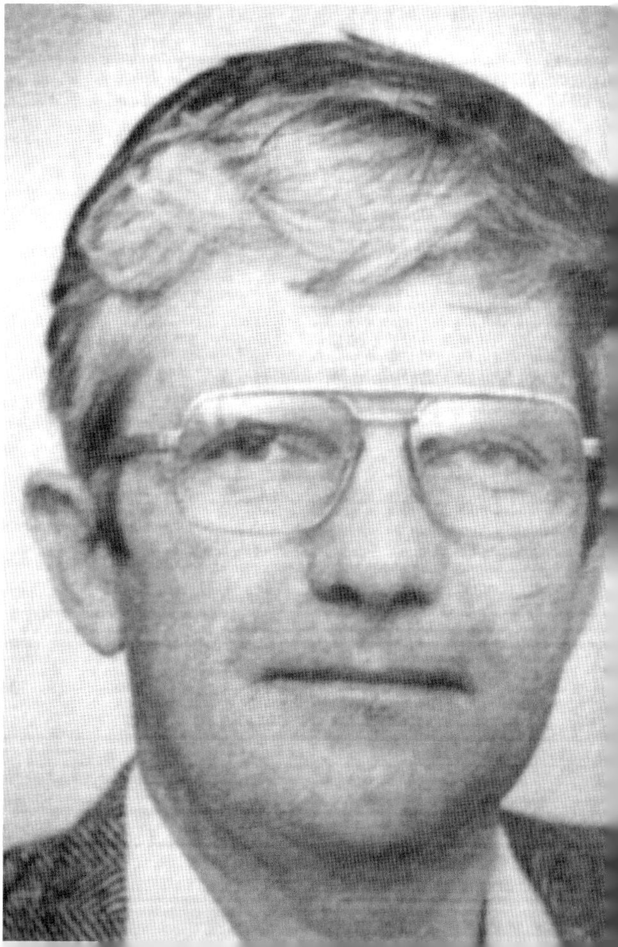

John T. Hickey (1929–2008)

Hickey successfully ran the Holyoke Water Power Company until he retired in 1991. In 1987, Hickey and Angela Wright established a nonprofit group, Friends of the Holyoke Merry-Go-Round. Together, they raised $865,000 to save the Holyoke merry-go-round. Holyoke residents rallied together to raise the needed funds, and donations came in from all over the country. Today, this magnificent merry-go-round is located in Holyoke's Heritage State Park in downtown Holyoke. Hickey not only saved a beloved piece of Holyoke's history, but he also left a legacy of joy and delight for future generations. (Courtesy of the Holyoke Public Library.)

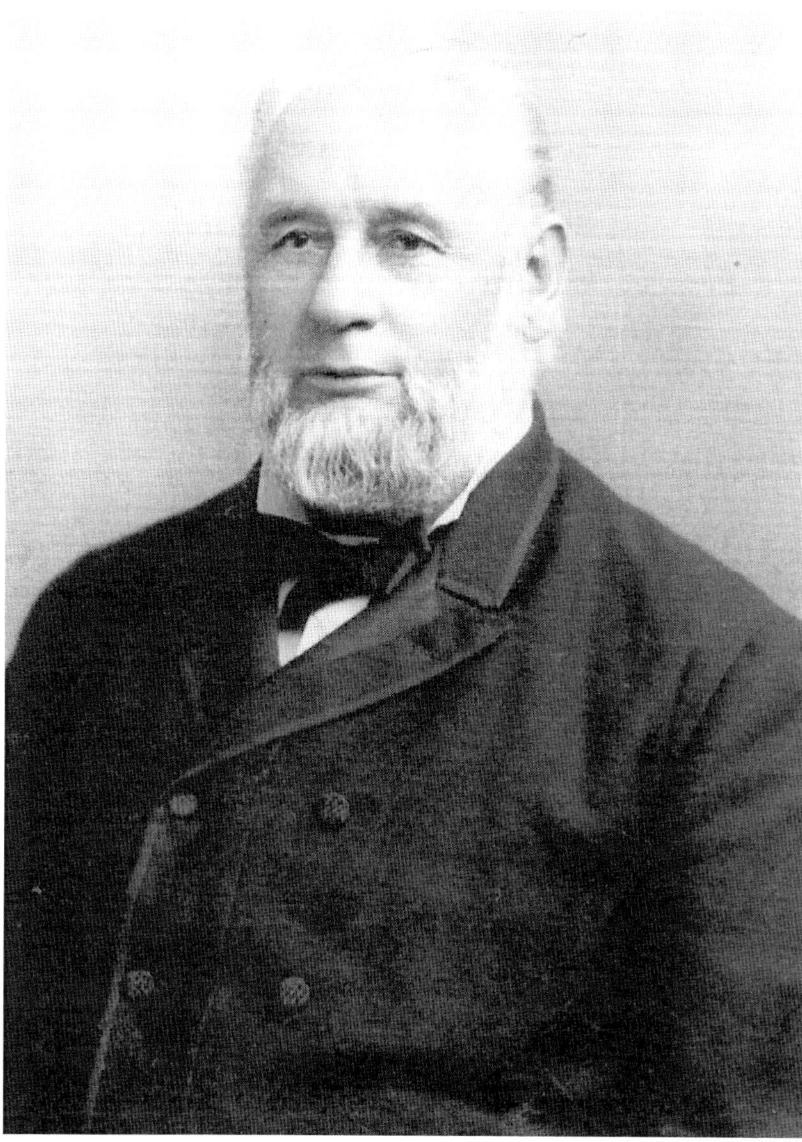

William Skinner (1824–1902)
Skinner immigrated to America from London, England, when he was 19. He established the Uquomonk Silk Mill in Williamsburg, Massachusetts. A major flood destroyed it in 1874. The Holyoke Water Power Company extended a canal site free of rent for five years that offered ample waterpower and space for his mill and a one-block portion of land for his family home for $1. Within a month in 1874, he began manufacturing his goods again in Holyoke. The company was located on Appleton Street and, eventually, became known as the Skinner's Silks and Satin Mill. Skinner manufactured organzine, thread, and raw silk. He also made sewing silk and twists for buttonholes that encouraged garment-makers worldwide. Two of Skinner's sons incorporated the business as William Skinner and Son Manufacturing Company in 1889. In 1891, Skinner and William Whiting, the founder of Whiting Coal Company, donated needed capital to establish the Holyoke Hospital, known today as the Holyoke Medical Center. Skinner was known as the "Old Roman" to his family and friends due to his rugged personality, stoic stature, and honesty; the man even made it home for lunch every day. (Courtesy of the Holyoke Public Library.)

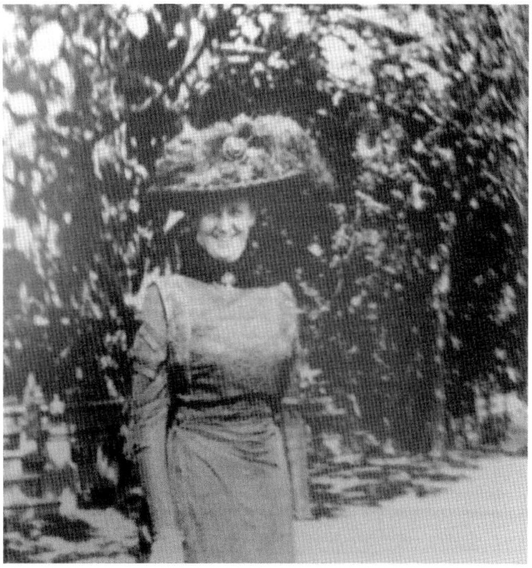

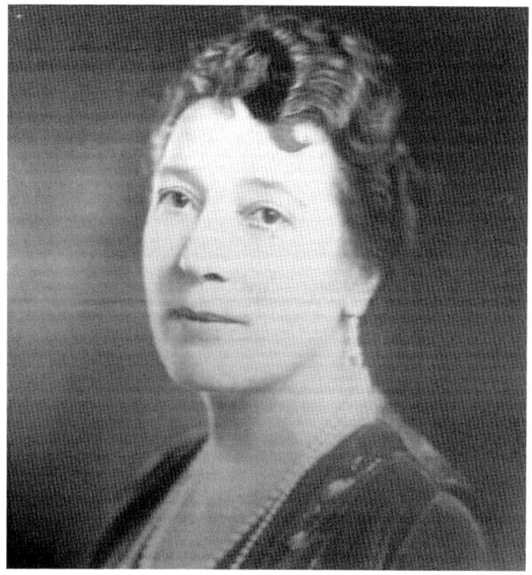

Katherine Skinner (1873–1968) and Ruth Isabel "Belle" Skinner (1866–1928)
Katherine and Ruth Isabel "Belle" were daughters of William Skinner, owner of Skinner's Silks and Satin Mill. After their father passed away, in November 1902, the sisters founded the Skinner Coffee House, a settlement house that helped female workers in downtown Holyoke. Wistariahurst was the original home of the Skinner family since 1874. Katherine Skinner Kilborne, Sarah Skinner, and their heirs donated their home to the City of Holyoke in 1959. Today, it is called the Wistariahurst Museum, a historic house museum with original wall coverings and woodwork and family and local papers, among many other must-see artifacts. The museum offers a plethora of interesting programs, such as lectures, workshops, and demonstrations. (Courtesy of Wistariahurst Museum.)

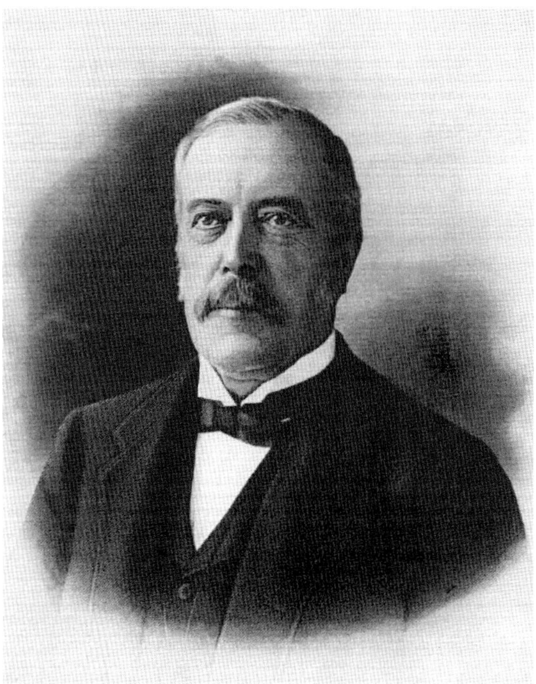

William Whiting (1841–1911)
In 1865, Whiting, with L.L. Brown and E.F. Jenks, organized Whiting Paper Company with funds he earned when he sold the Hampden Company, a paper company. Whiting Paper Company was on Dwight Street and, eventually, employed over 500 people. William Whiting served on the school committee and was city treasurer and mayor of Holyoke. He was also the president of the Holyoke Public Library and the Holyoke Hospital, among many other prominent boards and committees. He was a member of the US House of Representatives from the Massachusetts 11th District from 1883 to 1889. (Courtesy of the Holyoke Public Library.)

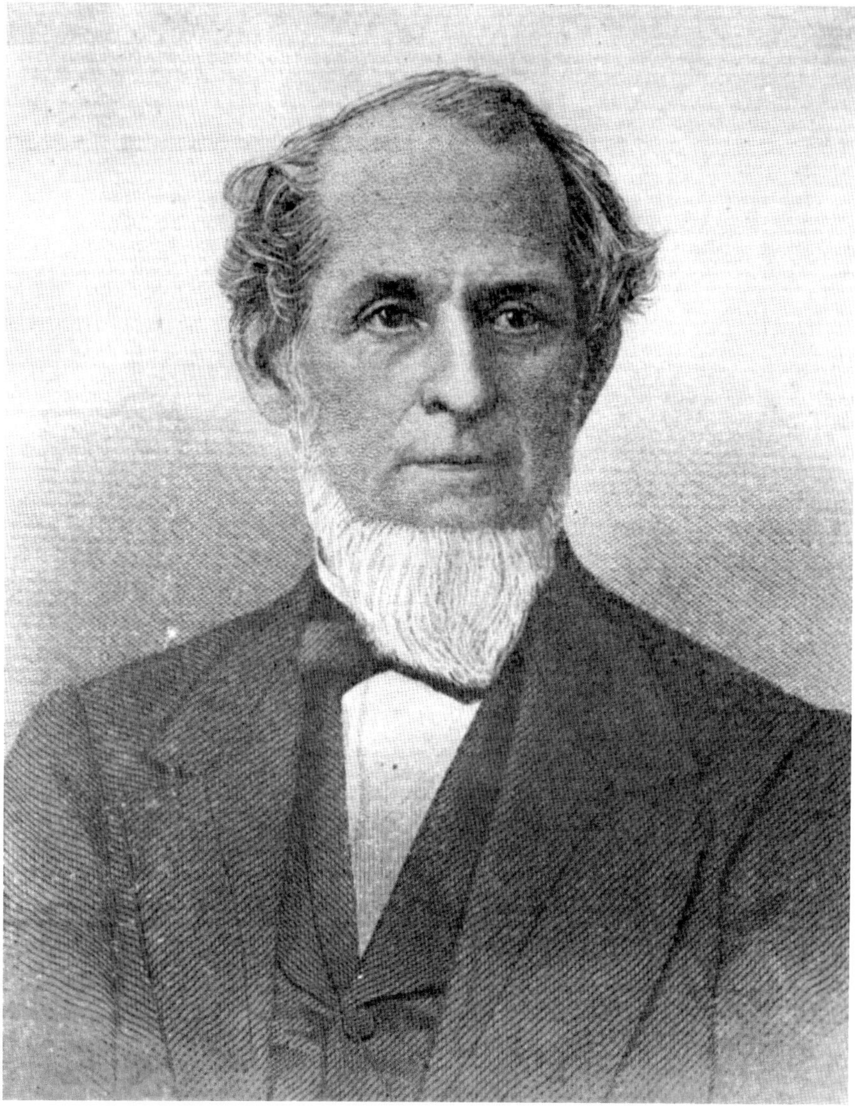

Joseph Clark "J.C." Parsons (1814-1886)
Joseph Clark "J.C." Parsons worked in the pharmaceuticals trade at the age of 14. When he was 25 years old, he had a partner with whom he farmed mulberry trees in Agawam. The business never progressed, but, undeterred, Parsons ventured into the paper business. He worked until he was the general manager of the Ames Mills in Northampton and South Hadley, Massachusetts, and Suffield, Connecticut. In 1852, he wanted to start his own paper company in Holyoke and purchase land along the Connecticut River but was denied by the Boston capitalists who established the Hadley Falls Power Company. They wanted to use the canal system to manufacture textiles. They were doubtful that Parsons's plan to build a brick building to manufacture paper would be successful, but in 1853, the Parsons Paper Company opened its doors and did not shut those golden doors until 2005. Within a decade, Parsons turned his company into the largest writing and envelope paper manufacturer in the country. In 1869, Holyoke had 11 paper mills and was known as the Paper City. Parson was known to be a hardworking man with a penchant for producing high-quality paper and treating his employees with respect—hence the longevity of the company. (Courtesy of the Holyoke Public Library.)

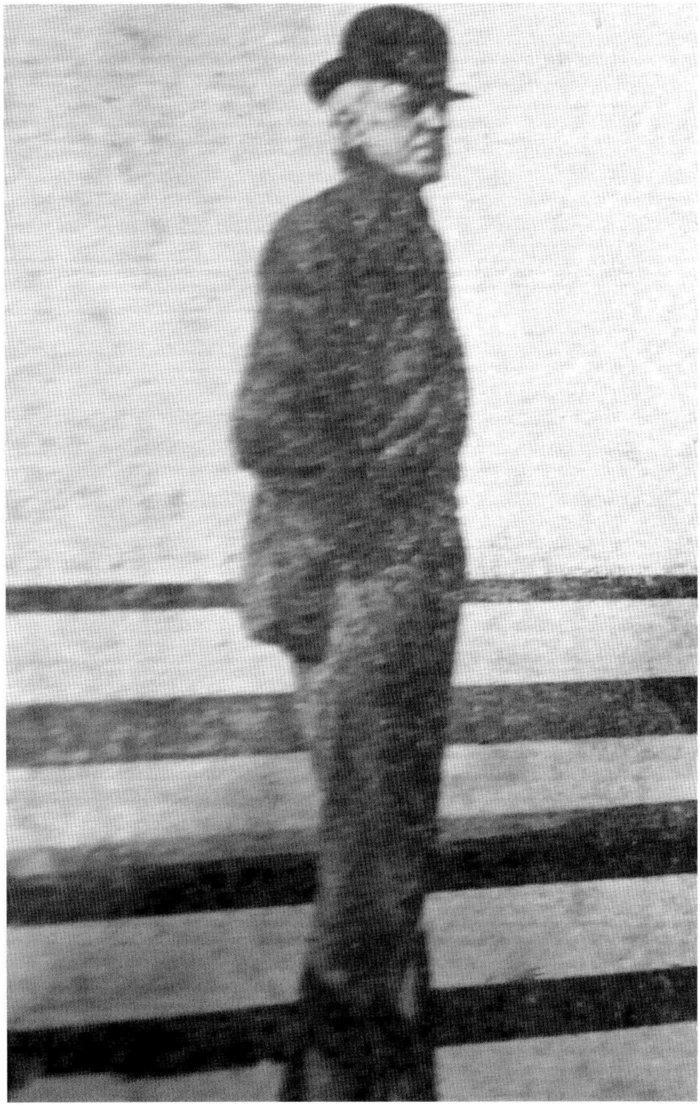

William Street

Heading toward Mount Tom Reservation, entering via East Mountain Road in Holyoke, one travels on Christopher Clarke Road, which leads to a road that goes to the ruins of Eyrie House at the top of the hill. This was the second hotel that William Street built on the Mount Nonotuck peak. Farther up the Mount Nonotuck peak from the stone ruins, Sweet built a five-room hotel in 1861; he added five more rooms in 1870 and, finally, enlarged the hotel to 30 rooms by 1880. The hotel had a long promenade that wrapped around the parameter for his guests to take leisurely walks. There was even a swing that children could play on. In 1877, he built a pavilion for concerts and picnics for his patrons to enjoy. By 1895, he had dug a road that would transport his guest to the hotel by a trolley. Unfortunately, his customers never used the road. In 1901, after a fire was lit to cremate some deceased working horses, which were used to pull guest-filled wagons from the Mount Tom junction, strong winds carried the fire to Street's hotel. He lost everything. Due to the escalating costs of insurance, he was forced to rebuild the wooden hotel with stone, but he was unable to afford the new hotel's construction costs. (Courtesy of the Holyoke Public Library.)

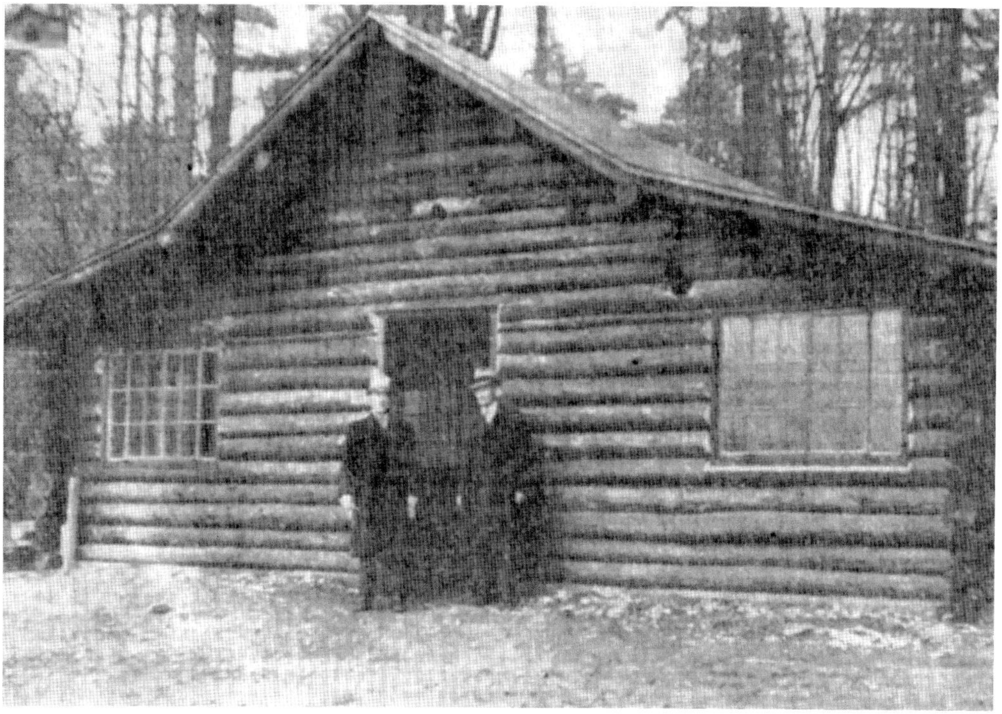

Charles Bray

Commissioner Charles Bray of Chicopee and warden Luther Howes of Holyoke stand in front of the new warming shelter on Bray Lake in 1938. Bray was the first commissioner of Hampshire County and was a chairman of the Mount Tom Reservation Committee. (Courtesy of Mount Tom State Reservation.)

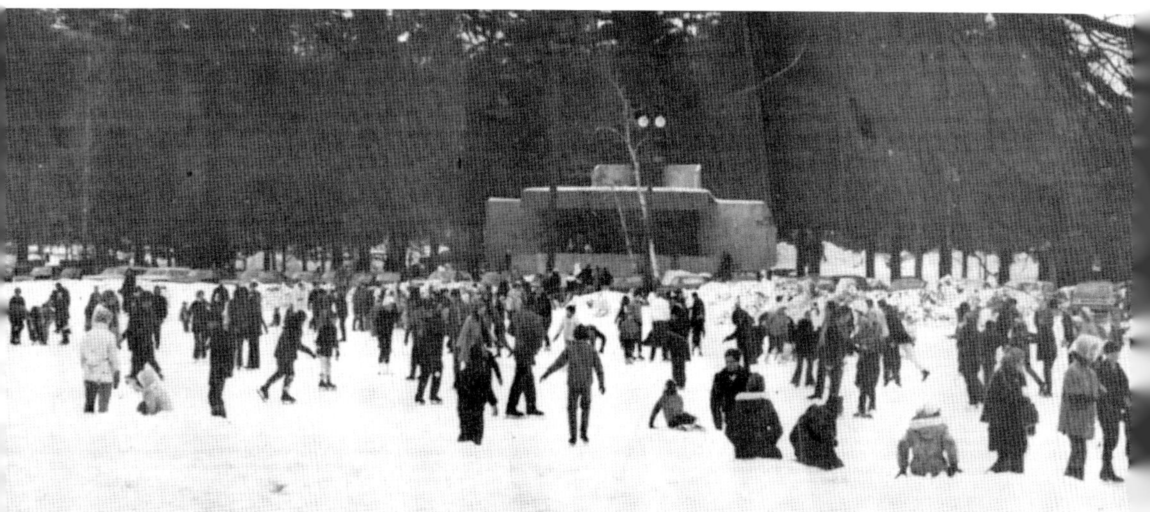

Bray Lake

A new concrete warming shelter was opened in 1970 on Bray Lake on the Mount Tom State Reservation. The old log-cabin warming shelter was demolished in 1980. (Courtesy of Mount Tom State Reservation.)

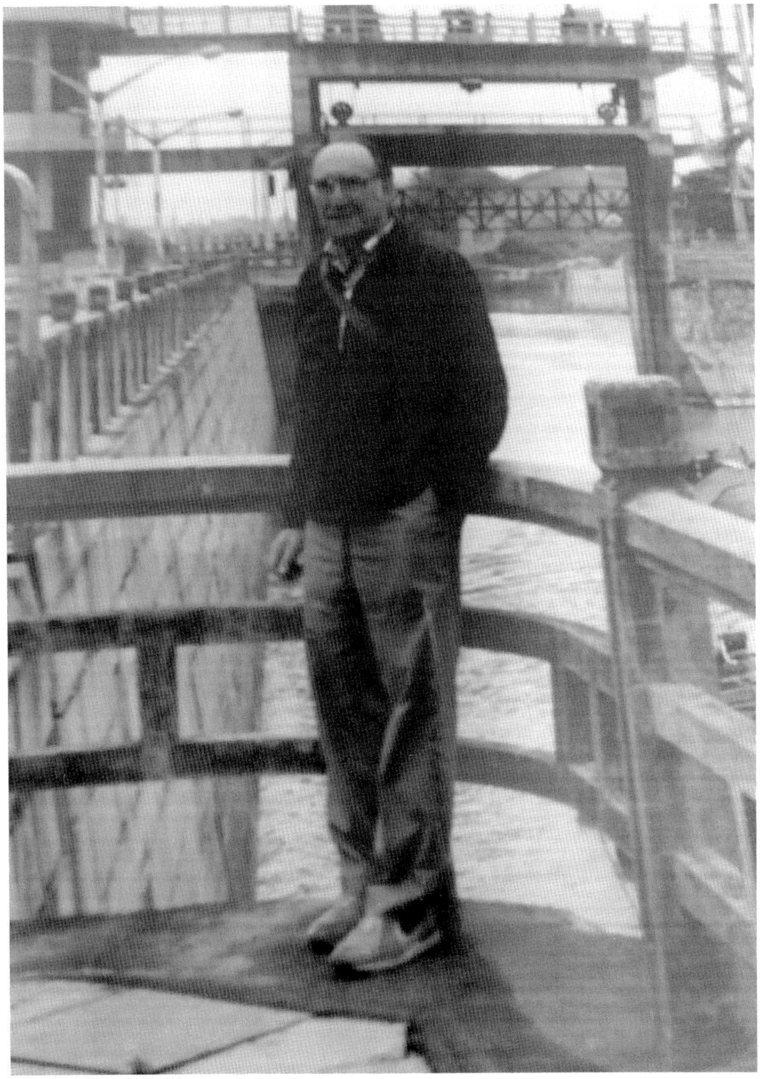

Theodore Belsky (1926–2014)
Theodore Belsky was the son of Charles and Esther (Cohen) Belsky of Holyoke. He attended the Holyoke Public School System, graduating from Holyoke High School in 1944. He attended Bates College in Lewiston, Maine, until the US Army needed his service in Germany from 1946 to 1947. He returned home to help run the family business, Charles Belsky & Sons, when his oldest brother and father died in a car accident in 1949. When it was possible, his love of history inspired him to go back to school and earn his bachelor's degree in 1965, his master's in 1966, and his doctorate of education in 1971 at the University of Massachusetts. In 1969, he worked at American International College in Springfield in the history department until his retirement in 1992; he became an associate dean of the School of Continuing Education and Graduate Studies. He was the founder of the Oral History Center and was recognized as a professor emeritus. He was also a member of the historical commission and the Democratic Town Committee and chairman of the bicentennial committee. He was also a member of the Canal Park Committee, which raises awareness of South Hadley's historic river passage, which is known as the first navigational canal in the United States. He was named the Citizen of the Year by the Lions Club in 2002. (Courtesy of the Holyoke Public Library.)

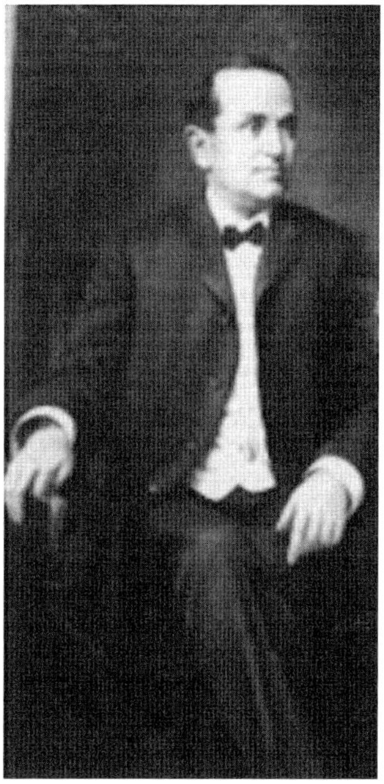

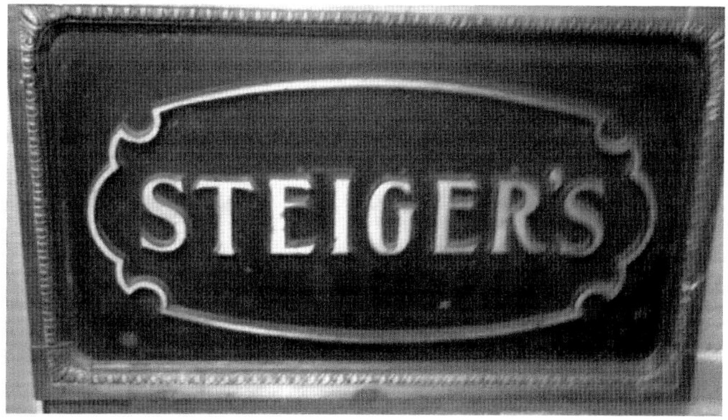

Albert Steiger
Steiger owned Steiger's department stores in New York, New Bedford, Springfield, and Holyoke in the 1800s. He was a successful businessman in New England who was known to be detail oriented with a strong sense of organization and innovative marketing techniques. His sons Ralph, Phillip, and Chauncy all contributed their unique talents to selecting goods, merchandising, and cleverly displaying goods. (Left image courtesy of the Steiger family; right image courtesy of Jimmy Curran.)

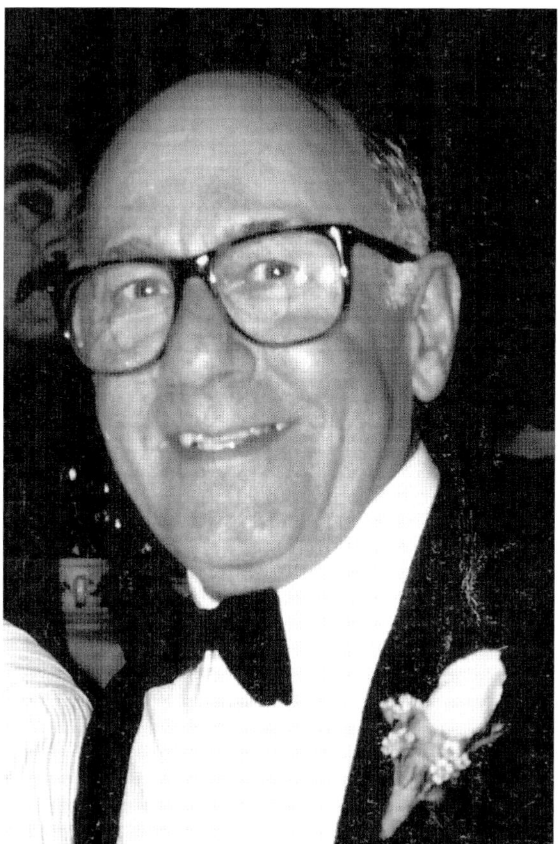

John J. Zwisler (1929–)
In 1999, Zwisler published a book, *Ireland Parish*, which details Holyoke's history. A Holyoke library volunteer of 14 years, Zwisler took on the arduous task of documenting the lineage of Elizur Holyoke dating back to 1490 and has written an article that describes the Holyoke Water Power Company's establishment in 1859, among many other interesting articles highlighting some of Holyoke's innovative manufacturers. (Courtesy of the Holyoke Public Library.)

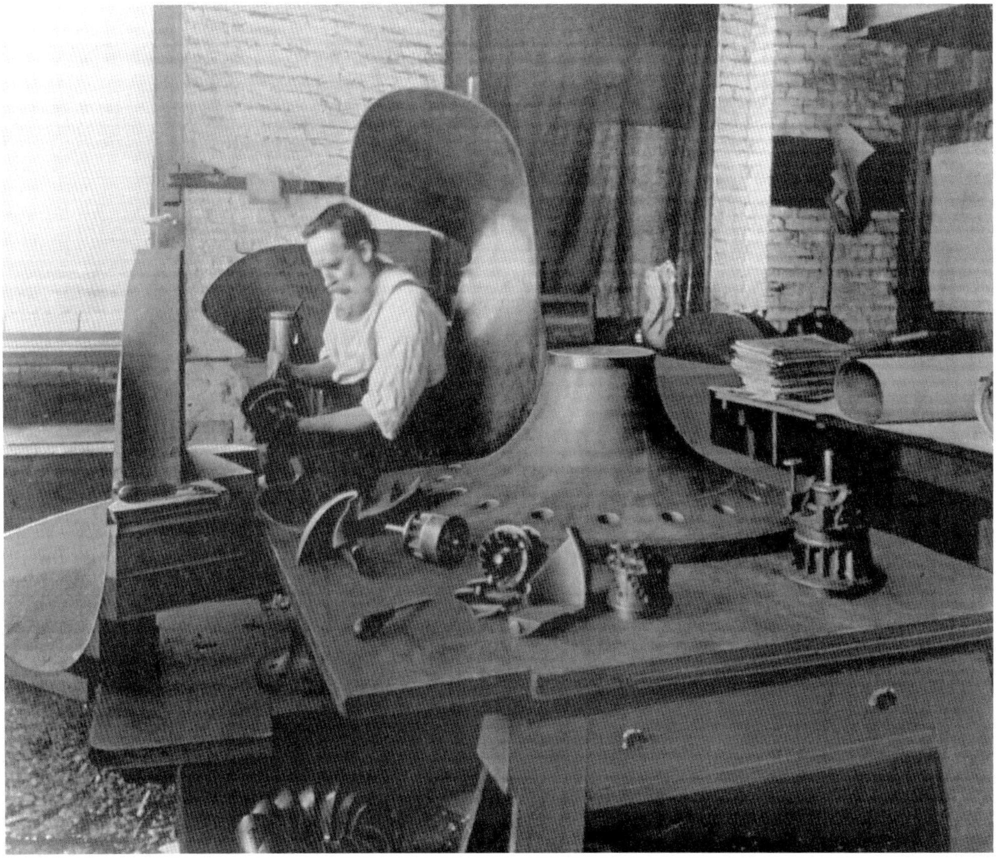

John B. McCormick (1834–1924)

McCormick was born in Blair County, Pennsylvania, to a farming family. As a young man, he was mechanically inclined and found carpentry fulfilling; he made cabinets and chairs in a workshop. He also had an ear for music—so much so that for five months out of the year, for 22 years, he taught music in churches and country schools throughout Indiana. In 1877, after traveling 42,000 miles, he arrived in Holyoke, seeking work at the Holyoke Machine Company. For years, he had been visualizing the creation of a turbine wheel. To finance his vision, he had the Bigelow & Main Company of New York publish his music books. He stayed at the Holyoke Machine Company for 11 years, perfecting this game-changing turbine for the mills in Holyoke. At the time, McCormick's Holyoke turbine was considered one of the most important laborsaving devices, making manufacturing less expensive for mill owners to produce their products, which in turn lowered costs for consumers. The sheer tenacity and skill of this great inventor can never be measured except by the output of his miraculous turbine. (Courtesy of the Holyoke Public Library.)

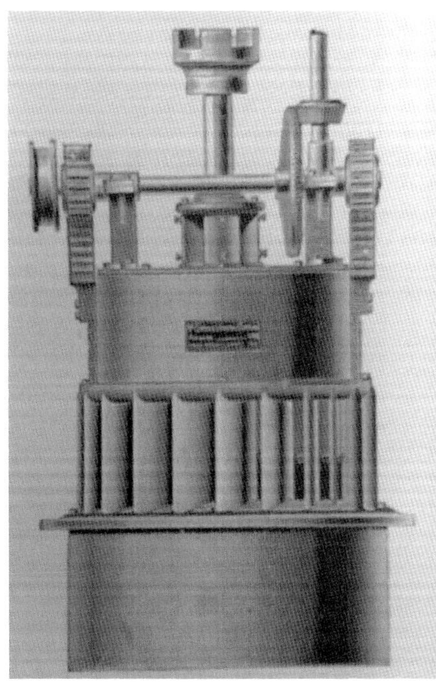

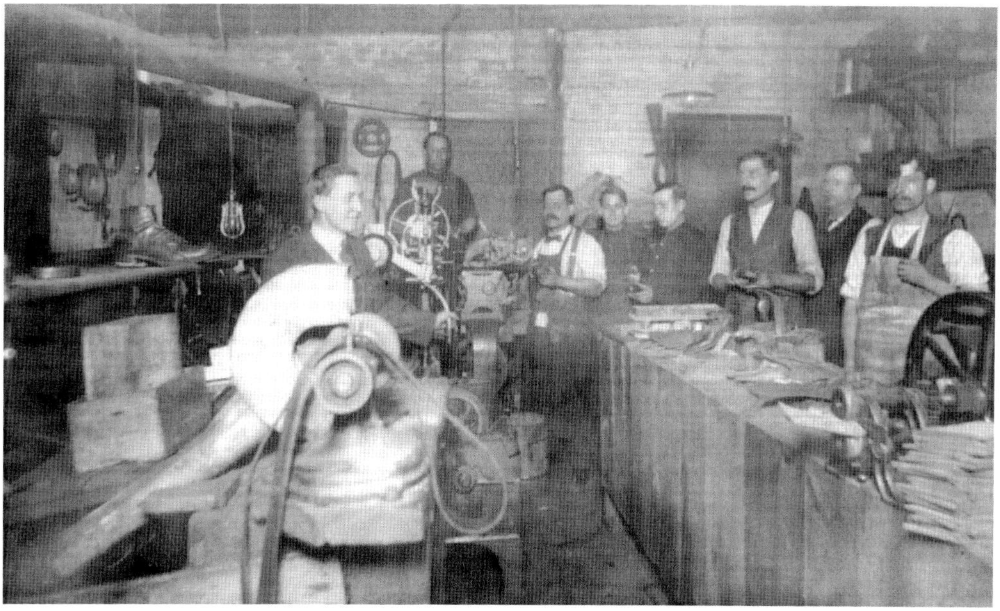

Oscar J. Bail (1927–2011)
Oscar J. Bail is a third-generation owner of the Bail family shoe business. He earned a bachelor's degree in economics from Tufts University and a master's in marketing from the University of Michigan in 1951. His grandfather Napoleon Bail opened a store named after himself in 1890 on Hampden Street. His son Oscar A. (1891–1970) worked in the retail side of the business starting in 1923, and in 1924 the company relocated to 168 High Street. In 1953, Oscar A.'s son Oscar J. started working in the family-owned business. Later, Oscar J.'s son Christopher started working in the store when he was 14 years old. Oscar J., Chris, and Chris's daughter Laura are all board-certified podiatrists, and the store has been renamed Bail's Custom Footcare, located in South Hadley. (Courtesy of the Holyoke Public Library.)

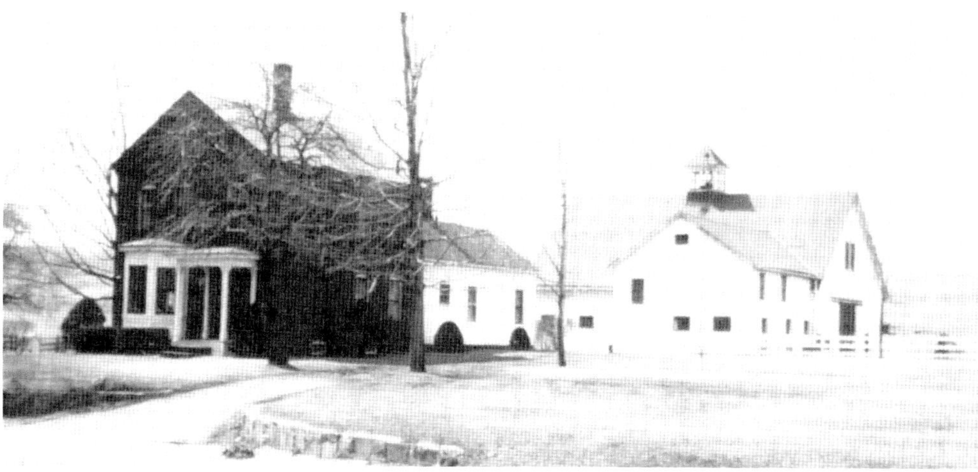

Whiting Street
Whiting Street was a successful farmer that lived in a big unpainted farmhouse with his two sisters and a brother. He was known as an enthusiastic man who enjoyed saving his money and working hard. He saved 58¢ per week and loved to play checkers with a friend from time to time. When he died, he left his fortune in trust to underprivileged people in Holyoke. (Courtesy of the Holyoke Public Library.)

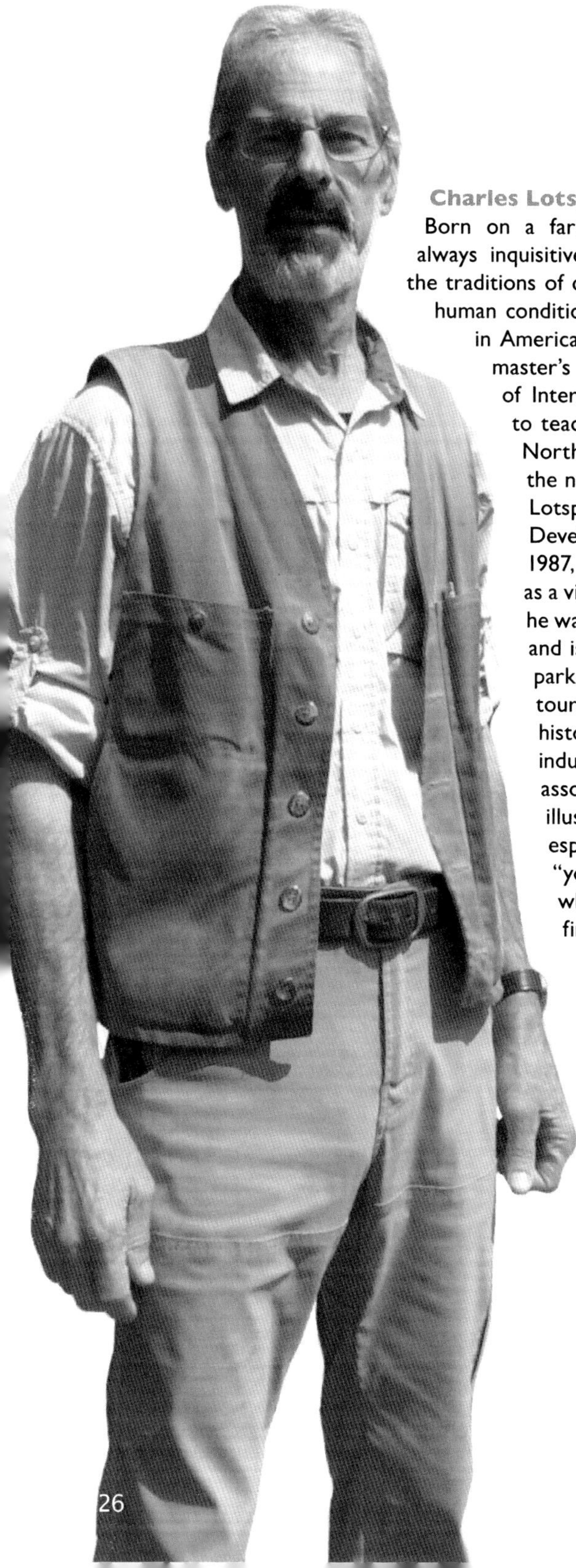

Charles Lotspeich (1947–)

Born on a farm in Cincinnati, Ohio, Charles Lotspeich was always inquisitive and affable; he studied American history and the traditions of countries abroad so that he could understand the human condition. After earning a master's with a concentration in American history from Harvard University in 1968 and a master's in international relations at the Fletcher School of International Relations at Tufts in 1969, he went on to teach in the Berkshire school system for 10 years in North Adams, Massachusetts. In 1977, he worked for the nonprofit Hoosac Institute Guild Program. In 1983, Lotspeich worked for the Northern Berkshire Industrial Development Commission, managing skilled artisans. By 1987, he was an interpreter of history at Walden Pond as a visitor services supervisor. Fortunately for Holyoke, he was hired at the Holyoke Heritage State Park in 2003 and is currently the forest and parks supervisor of the park. He not only supervises the park, but he also gives tours at the visitor's center, where he teaches the history of Holyoke's waterpower, paper manufacturing, industrial past, and its social history. Lotspeich's uses an assortment of tools, including interactive displays and illustrations, to make a tangible impact on his visitors, especially his youngest students. He believes that "young people who are encouraged to think about where they fit into their community are more apt to find a useful role." (Courtesy of Charles Lotspeich.)

CHAPTER TWO

Intriguing Writers

The writer is an explorer. Every step is an advance into a new land.

—Ralph Waldo Emerson

Holyoke is home to some gifted and prolific writers. Constance McLaughlin Green certainly fits this description. She wrote the well-respected book *Holyoke, Massachusetts: A Case History of the Industrial Revolution* for her doctorate, among many other important books. Mike Burke, a former city editor for the now defunct *Holyoke Transcript* and a current columnist for the *Republican* newspaper, has written important news stories and interesting commentary on local events in Holyoke and the surrounding area. Local biology teacher Robert T. McMaster authored a historical nonfiction novel called *Trolley Days*, which takes place in a fictional industrial city based off of Holyoke and its industrial heyday.

Jay Ducharme, a professor of electronic media at Holyoke Community College, wrote Images of America: *Mountain Park* and *The Happiness Machine*, which is about the Holyoke merry-go-round, and another well-respected educator Harper E. Wyatt wrote a vital reference tool about the history of Holyoke, *The Story of Holyoke*. Holyoke Public Library volunteer John J. Zwisler wrote the book *Ireland Parish* in 1999. Writer Kate Navarra Thibodeau, a former curator at the Wistariahurst Museum, wrote two important historical books: *Holyoke: The Skinner Family and Wistariahurst* and *Destination: Holyoke: Immigration and Migration.* Mitch Epstein is not only a world-renowned photographer but also the author of nine books. Esteemed writer Mary Adele Allen wrote *Around the Village Green: Sketches of Life in Amherst.* If one is looking for an honest and objective story, look to Dennis Hohenberger, a local seasoned freelance writer and photographer.

Another interesting writer from Holyoke is Mark McGarrity, who wrote 22 mystery novels starring detective Peter McGarr under the pen name Bartholomew Gill. Also included in this prestigious list of writers is the retired Massachusetts probate and family court judge Gerald McClelland, who writes exciting legal thrillers. Raymond Kennedy wrote a book, titled *My Father's Orchard and Good Night, Jupiter*, among many other interesting short stories. Dr. William A. Nolen's writing career happened by accident, inspiring him to write a syndicated medical advice column and publish nine books. And finally, Alan Eisenstock has successfully written 12 books in addition to writing for popular television shows and national magazines.

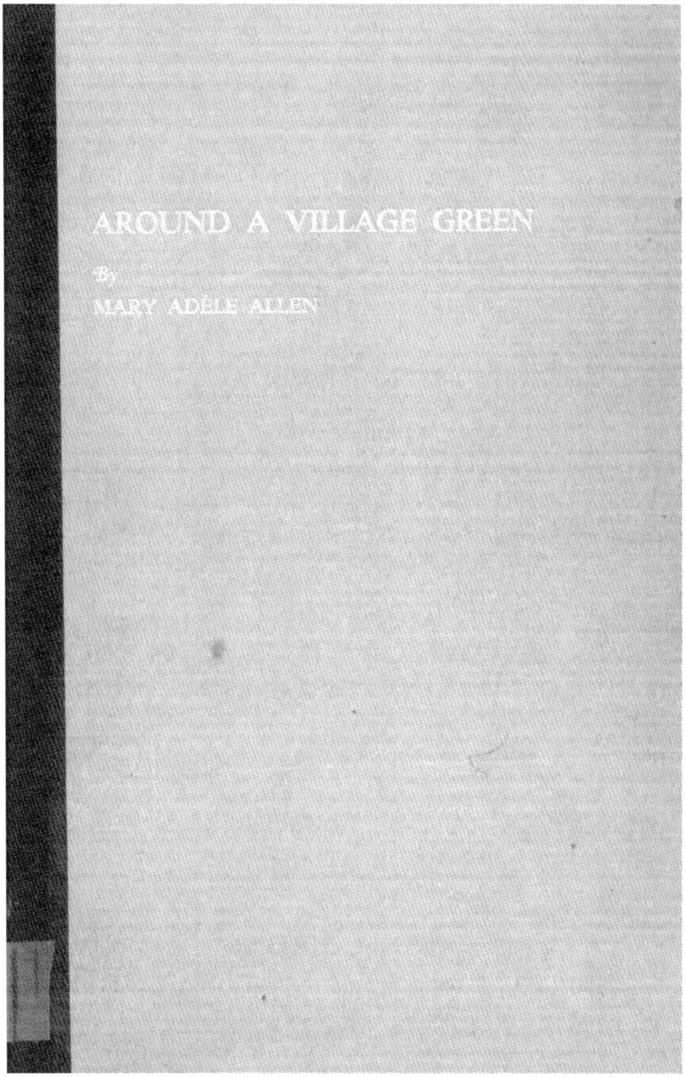

Mary Adele Allen (1864–1944)

Allen was born in the home of the first president of Amherst College in Amherst, Massachusetts, and was a descendant of Pres. John Adams. When she was a child, she knew Emily Dickinson and her father. Allen's family relocated to Holyoke in 1880 when her father established Allen's china store. She graduated from Holyoke High School in 1882 as salutatorian of her class and attended Smith College in 1886. She was a teacher at Holyoke High School and head of the classical department in 1911. She was a member of the New England Association of Colleges and Secondary Schools and the New England Classical Association. She was also a member of Daughters of the American Revolution (DAR), Holyoke Women's Club, Holyoke Teachers Club, Holyoke Business and Professional Women's Club, and founded the Women's Thursday Club. She was a renowned researcher in the first Classical Investigation Committee appointed by the New England Classical Association of 1916. Allen was a sought-after speaker throughout the country due to her unique method of presenting the classics. She was instrumental in revising the Latin curriculum for high school seniors in 1929 throughout Massachusetts. Retiring after 33 years, she wrote the well-received book *Around the Village Green: Sketches of Life in Amherst*. The book highlighted the post–Civil War period in Amherst. (Courtesy of the Holyoke Public Library.)

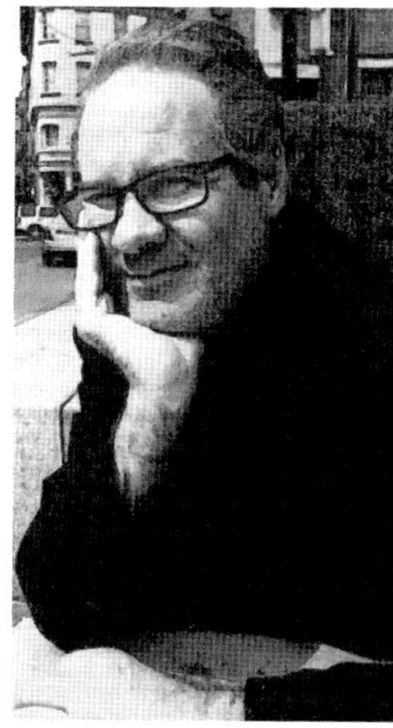

Dennis Hohenberger (1964–)
Born and raised in the city of Holyoke, Dennis Hohenberger graduated from Holyoke High School in 1982 and then earned a bachelor of arts degree in journalism at the University of Massachusetts, Amherst, in 1985. He has traveled extensively throughout the country, at times residing in Los Angeles, Boston, and Washington, DC. Today, he is a freelance reporter-writer and a discerning photographer in Western Massachusetts who highlights his subjects' struggles and triumphs in an authentic and impartial manner. (Courtesy of Dennis Hohenberger.)

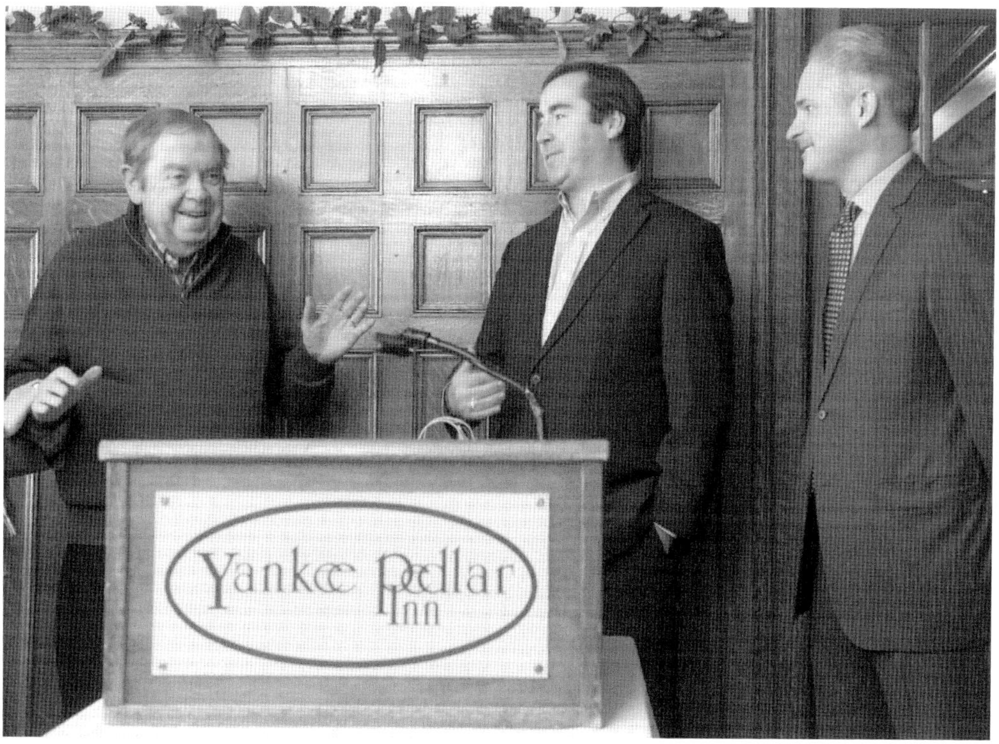

Mike Burke
Burke was the city editor of the former *Holyoke Transcript* newspaper before it was closed in 1993. He went on to work for the *Springfield Republican*, known today as the *Republican* newspaper, as a city editor for Holyoke. He has astutely written about politics and many other serious topics, including fire and police departments, for many years. He is also a knowledgeable, spunky announcer and a chief officer of Western New England Amateur Boxing and was instrumental in reviving the Golden Gloves League in Holyoke. In his retirement, he writes a column called "More Mike Burke" for the *Republican* newspaper. In the column, he has a warm, humorous writing style that the community looks forward to reading. He is the recipient of the Outstanding Citizen Award by the St. Patrick's Parade Committee and countless awards and accolades throughout his career. (Courtesy of the *Republican* newspaper.)

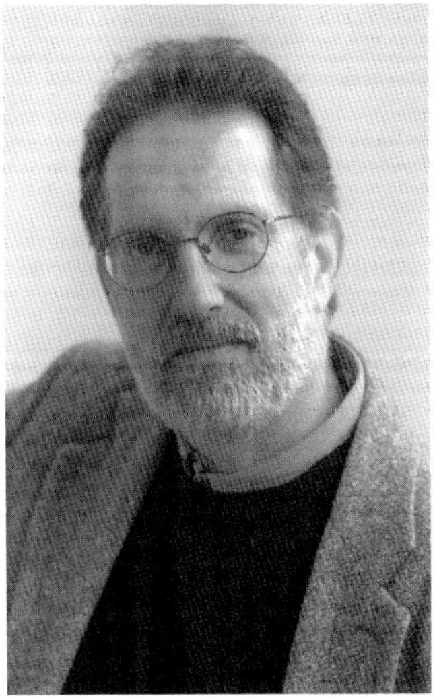

Alan Eisenstock

Alan Eisenstock was born in Holyoke, graduated from Holyoke High School, and earned his bachelor's degree from the University of Michigan. After submitting an American Express advertisement that was a spoof on one of "Detroit's Finest Restaurants," it was published in a newspaper to his surprise and joy. From there, he went on to write for sitcoms *Mork and Mindy, Family Matters, Step by Step*, and *Married with Children*; television movies; and many national magazines. Eisenstock retired from being a screenwriter to become a full-time print writer; since his career change-up, he has written and cowritten 12 books, including his latest, *The Handoff: A Memoir of Two Guys, Sports, and Friendship*, written with John "JT the Brick" Tournour, published by Center Street/Hachette Book Group, in August 2013. (Courtesy of Alan Eisenstock.)

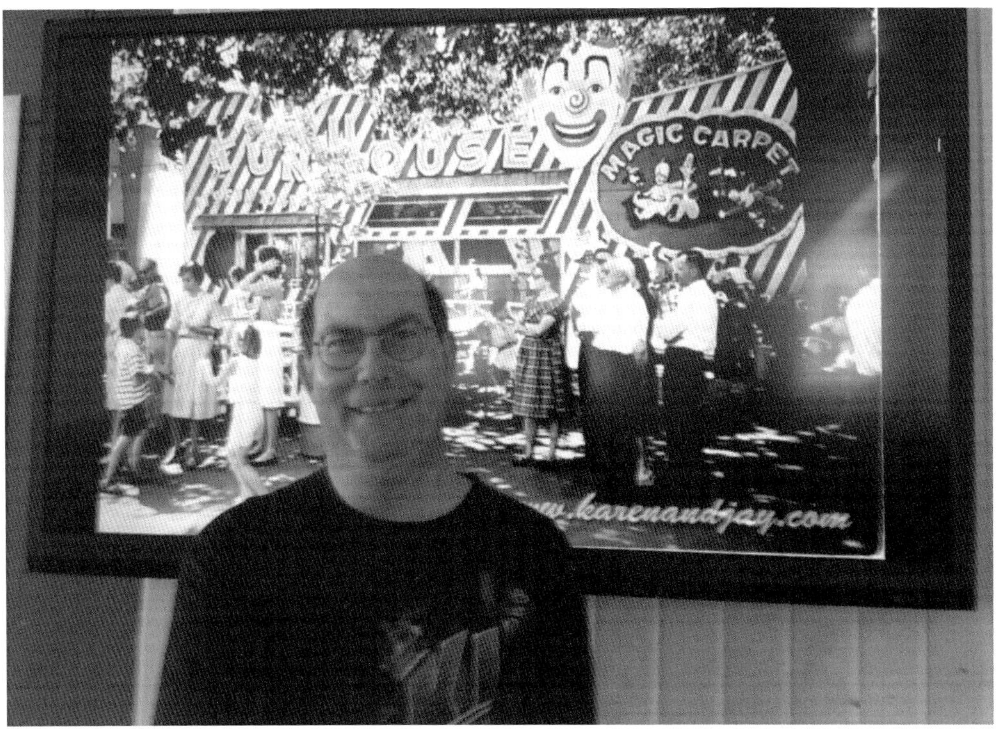

Jay Ducharme (1958–)

Ducharme grew up in Easthampton and graduated from Easthampton High School in 1976. He earned an associate's degree from Holyoke Community College in 1978, a bachelor's of arts in playwriting in 1982 at the University of Massachusetts, and a master's in theater directing at the University of Mississippi in 1983. He moved to Holyoke in 1977. Ducharme is a professor of electronic media at Holyoke Community College, a musician, and a composer. He has released six albums as a solo artist and was in a band called The Dots. He is author of the ever-popular Images of America: *Mountain Park; The Destination We All Loved in Holyoke*; and *The Happiness Machine,* in which he beckons people to visit their childhoods once again on the Holyoke merry-go-round. (Courtesy of Jay Ducharme.)

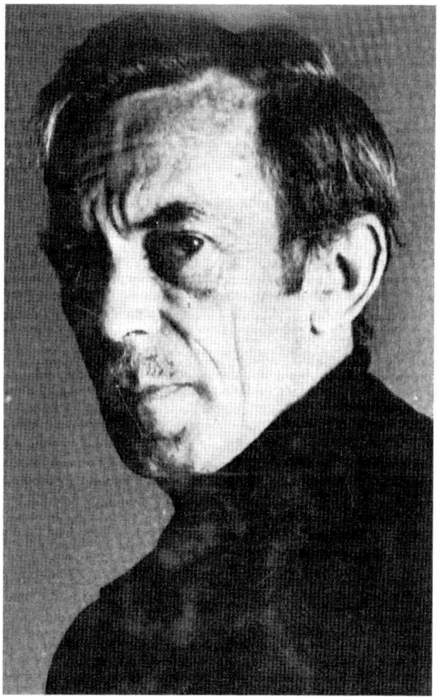

Raymond Kennedy (1934–2008)
Kennedy is a nonfiction author of *My Father's Orchard* and *Good Night, Jupiter*, and some short stories that were published in national magazines, including *Esquire*. His 1981 book *Columbine* is set in the Holyoke area in the 1940s after World War II. He calls his fictitious community Ireland Parish and uses the names of Holyoke's existing streets and familiar landmarks in the book. He served in the Army and then graduated from the University of Massachusetts in the class of 1960. While there, he studied writing under Denis Johnston, Robert Tucker, and the poets Ted Hughes and Joseph Langland. (Courtesy of Raymond Kennedy.)

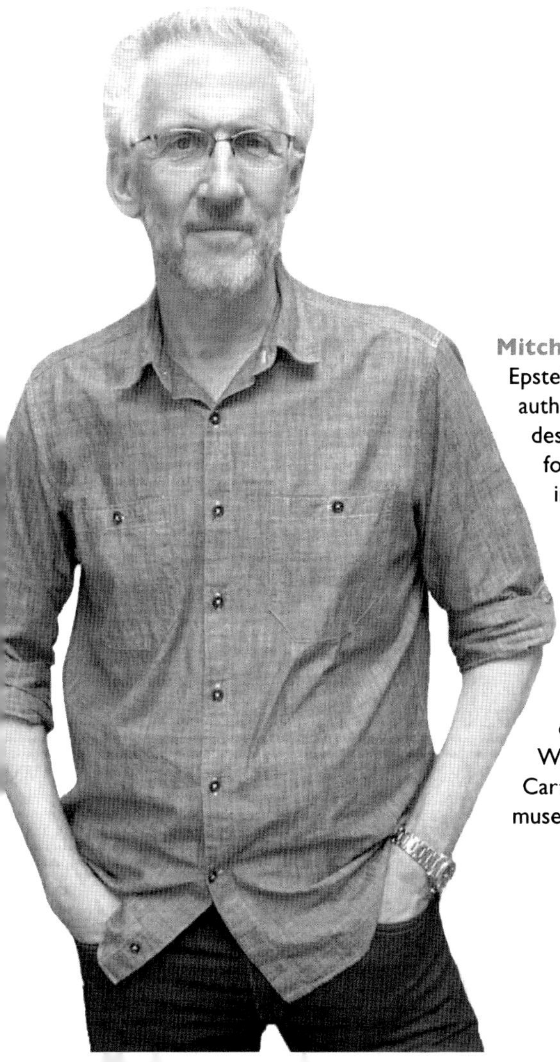

Mitch Epstein
Epstein is a world-renowned professional photographer, author, director, cinematographer and production designer. He has been awarded the 2011 Prix Pictet for his American Power series, the 2008 Berlin Prize in Arts and Letters by the American Academy in Berlin, and a 2003 Guggenheim Fellowship. He is the author of nine books, including *Family Business*, which is about his father's furniture business in Holyoke, which won the 2004 Kraszna-Krausz Photography Book Award. Epstein's exquisite photographs are in museums around the world including New York's Museum of Modern Art, Metropolitan Museum of Art, the Whitney Museum of American Art, and the Henri Cartier-Bresson, Paris, among many other prestigious museums. (Courtesy of Mitch Epstein.)

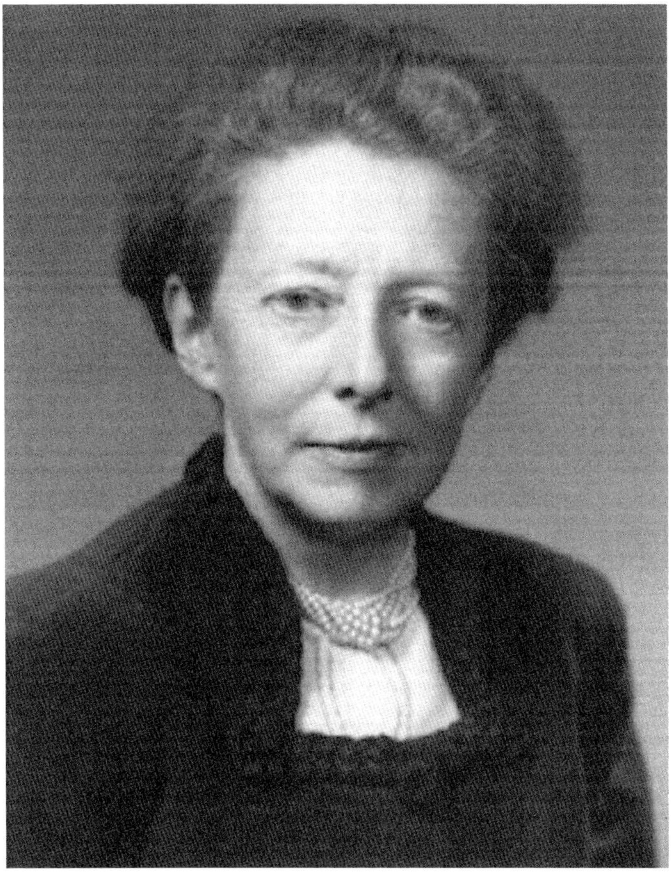

Constance McLaughlin Green (1897–1975)
Green was born in Ann Harbor, Michigan, and her parents are Andrew Cunningham McLaughlin and Lois Angell Mclaughlin. Her father was on the faculty of the University of Michigan, taught at the University of Chicago, and earned a Pulitzer Prize. Green graduated from Smith College in 1919 and earned her master's degree from Mount Holyoke College in 1925 and a doctoral degree from Yale University in 1937. She married Donald Ross Green, the principal officer of the Farr Alpaca Company in Holyoke. She wrote *Holyoke, Massachusetts: A Case History of the Industrial Revolution* for her doctorate. From 1925 to 1932, she taught history at Mount Holyoke College and Smith College. In 1963, she won a Pulitzer Prize for her book *Washington: Village and Capital, 1800–1878*, the first half of a two-volume series. First Lady Jacqueline Kennedy placed her work in the White House Library. Green also attended a term in Fräulein von Heydenaber Höhere Töchter Schule in Munich to study history. She majored in history for two years at the University of Chicago and transferred to Smith College to teach history and was named head of the Smith College Council of Industrial Relations. In 1942, she was the Army's ordnance department historian at the armory in Springfield. After her husband's death, she became a consulting historian for the American National Red Cross. In 1948, as a chief historian for the ordnance department, she headed a team of researchers who wrote the technical service volume *The United States Army in World War II*. In 1952, she became a historian at the Research and Development Board of the Office of the Secretary of Defense in Washington. In 1954, she was the director of the Washington History Project, administrated by American University. Her books concentrated on the urbanization of the United States and other relevant community themes. Green was certainly one of Holyoke's treasures and a true legend. Green was dedicated to researching the intricacies and travails of her subjects. (Courtesy of the US Army.)

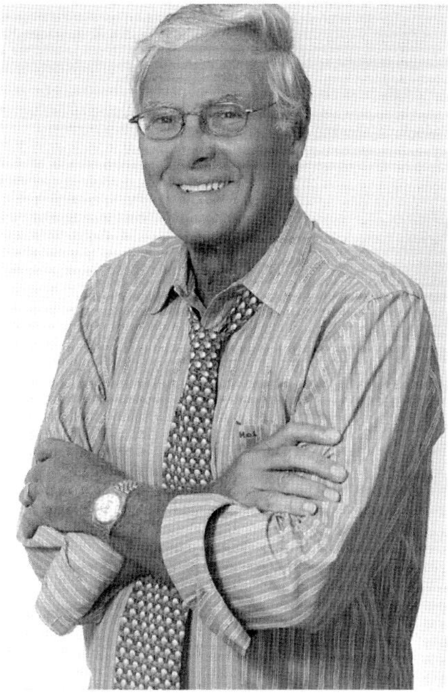

Gerald D. McLellan
He graduated from Holyoke High School and earned a bachelor's of arts in economics at the University of Massachusetts, Amherst. He attended the St. John's University School of Law and passed the bar in 1960. McLellan was a Massachusetts probate and family court judge for eight years and practiced family law for over 26 years in Boston. He garnered some of his reference material for his exciting legal thrillers, including *Old City Hall, A Permanent Bond, A Silent Cry*, and his 2014 book *The Bully*, from some of the cases that he presided over. (Courtesy of Gerald D. McLellan.)

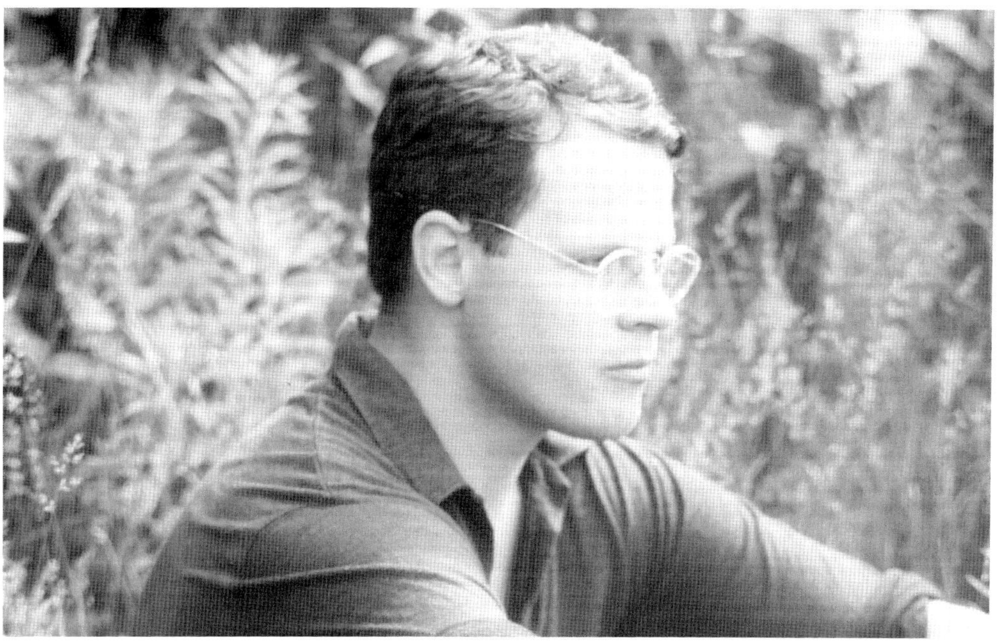

Mark McGarrity (1943–2002)
Holyoke-born McGarrity earned a degree from Brown University in Providence, Rhode Island, and a master's degree from Trinity College in Dublin, Ireland. He lived in Morristown, New Jersey, where he worked for the *Star-Ledger of Newark* newspaper. He wrote feature articles and was a nature and recreation columnist. In 1973, he started writing the mystery novel series of Peter McGarr. Written under the pen name Bartholomew Gill, which was McGarrity's grandfather's name, this popular 22-book series is about a clever and resourceful Irish detective named Peter McGarr. McGarrity also wrote five novels. (Courtesy of Bill Finn.)

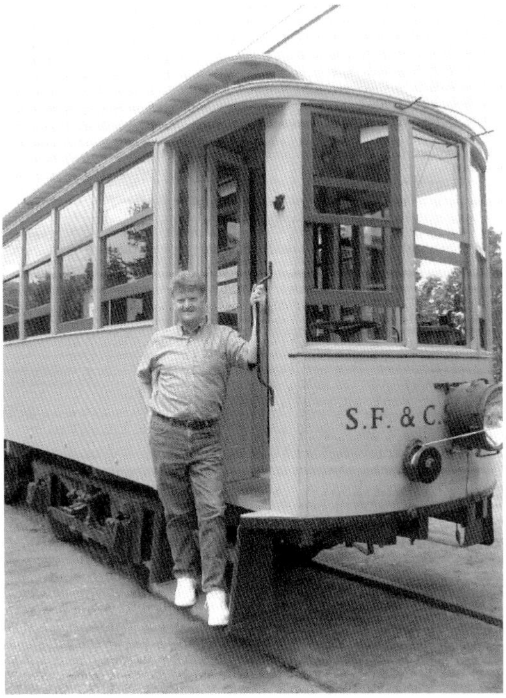

Robert T. McMaster

McMaster is a well-respected and beloved retired biology teacher at Holyoke Community College and is the author of the historical nonfiction novel *Trolley Days* and its sequel *The Dyeing Room*. The story takes place during World War I in the fictional city of Southbridge. To his amazement and joy, McMaster learned that he taught biology to his students on paths behind Holyoke Community College that at one time were trolley lines. (Courtesy of Robert T. McMaster.)

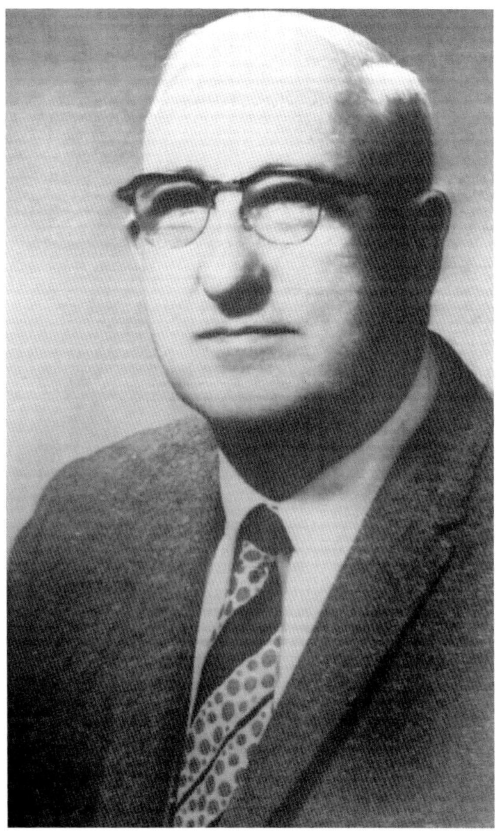

Wyatt E. Harper

Born in 1924, he was the prolific author of the book titled *The Story of Holyoke*, a comprehensive reference tool about the history of Holyoke and its people. He was a well-versed historian, a history teacher at Holyoke High School, and an adviser to the writing club. He also contributed his editorial and historical expertise in Ella Merkel DiCarlo's book *Holyoke-Chicopee: A Perspective 1892–1982*. There is a beautiful park off of Cherry Street named in his honor. (Courtesy of the Holyoke Public Library.)

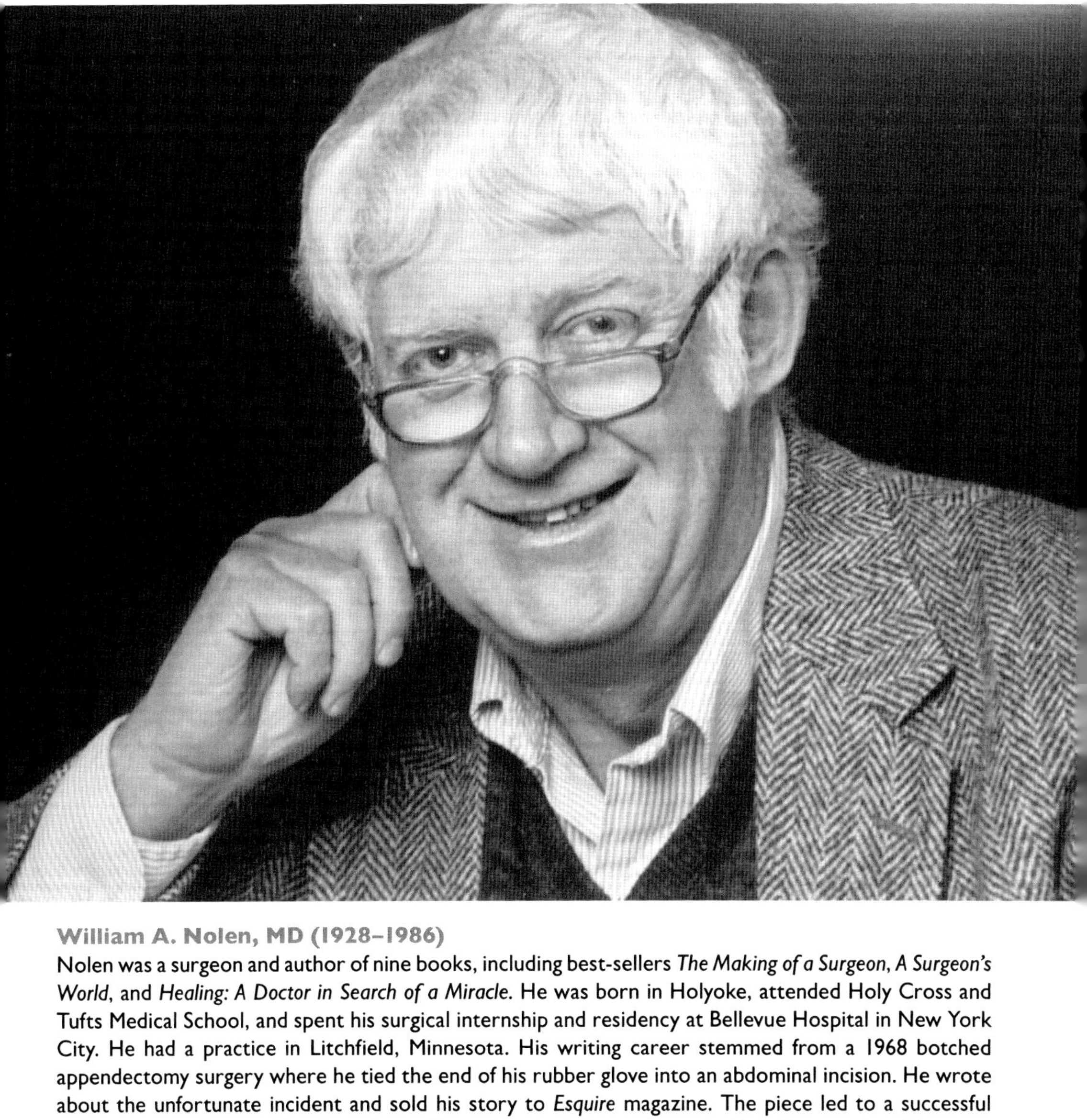

William A. Nolen, MD (1928–1986)
Nolen was a surgeon and author of nine books, including best-sellers *The Making of a Surgeon, A Surgeon's World*, and *Healing: A Doctor in Search of a Miracle.* He was born in Holyoke, attended Holy Cross and Tufts Medical School, and spent his surgical internship and residency at Bellevue Hospital in New York City. He had a practice in Litchfield, Minnesota. His writing career stemmed from a 1968 botched appendectomy surgery where he tied the end of his rubber glove into an abdominal incision. He wrote about the unfortunate incident and sold his story to *Esquire* magazine. The piece led to a successful writing career of medical books and a syndicated medical advice column in *McCall's* magazine. (Courtesy of Judy Crimmins.)

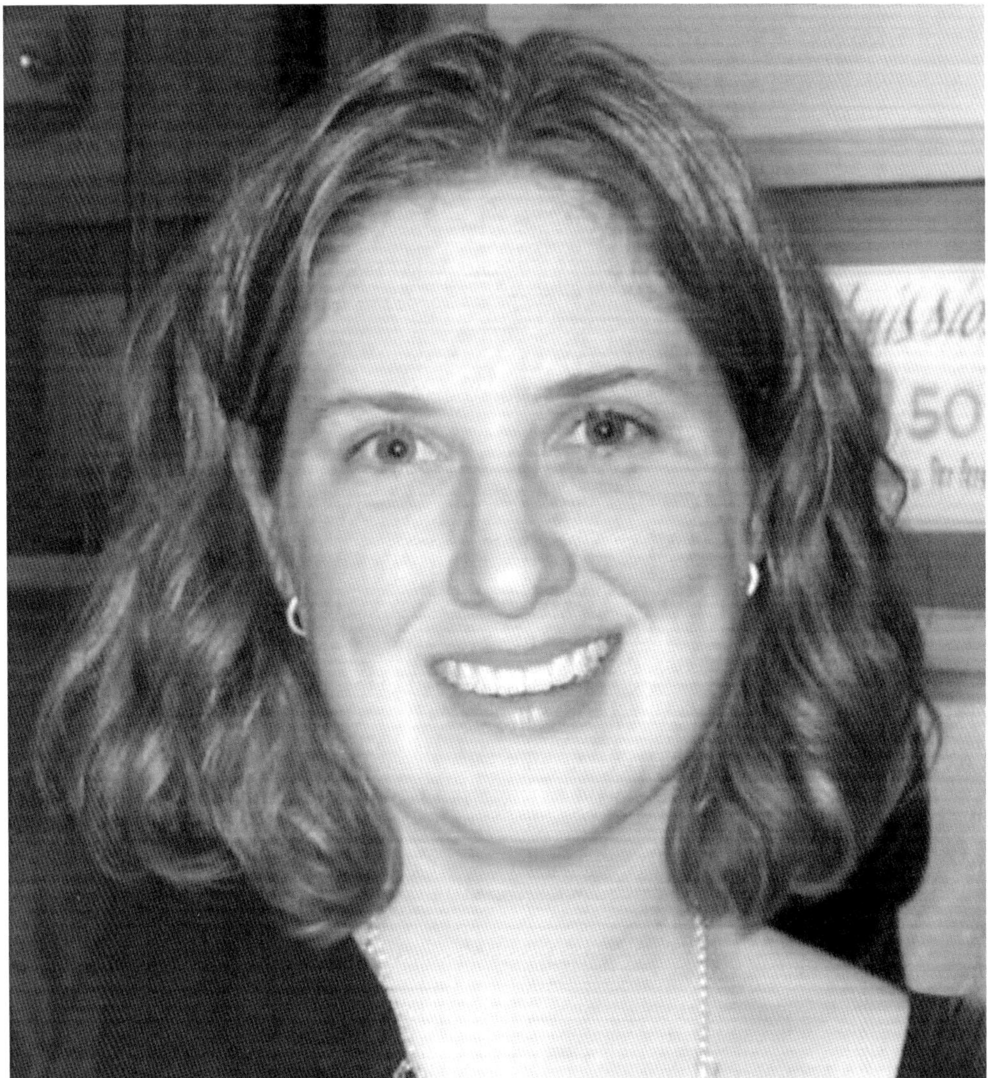

Kate Navarra Thibodeau (1979–)
An interpretative public historian and curator, Thibodeau was born in Torrance, California, and raised in Los Gatos, California. She attended the University of Rochester, graduating *cum laude* with a bachelor's degree in anthropology in 2001. Practicing archeology in Alaska, she yearned for deeper understanding of man's past and innovative ways to illustrate these important and interesting stories to the public. After extensive research, she attended the University of Massachusetts, Amherst, due to its program in public history. She went on to earn her master's in history with a public history concentration in 2005. She interned at the beautiful Wistariahurst Museum in Holyoke for an Introduction to Public History Class and, eventually, became the curator as her fascination blossomed from reading the historical journals, letters, and oral histories of the distinguished Skinner family. As a public historian, she showcased the treasures of Wistariahurst through a collaborative approach with stakeholders, community members, and professional colleagues. She is the author of Arcadia Publishing's Images of America: *Holyoke: The Skinner Family and Wistariahurst* as well as *Destination Holyoke: Immigration and Migration.* (Courtesy of Kate Navarra Thibodeau.)

CHAPTER THREE

Veterans of Distinction

Patriotism is not a short and frenzied outburst of emotion but the tranquil and steady dedication of a lifetime.

—Adlai Stevenson

The Holyoke War Memorial Building and the Soldiers' Home in Holyoke honor and provide ample space for veterans to be recognized and cared for. Veteran Henry Jennings served in the Army and the Air Force and has worked hard to maintain the Holyoke War Memorial Building. FIC (Fireman First Class) Dennis J. Buckley Jr. sacrificed his life for his shipmates in 1943, and Maj. William J. Crosier served honorably in World War I and for the City of Holyoke in its Parks and Recreation Department. John A. Lucey served in the US Army during World War II as a first sergeant of Company A, 263rd Engineer Combat Battalion, in Europe. Brian Willette gallantly gives credence to his fellow veterans and has faithfully served the US Army. Rear Admiral Theodore J. Wojnar of the US Navy traveled around the world protecting the freedom of citizens of the United States. Edwin Parsons served in the Air Force in World War I as he flew for the elite Lafayette Escadrilles Squadron. James "B.J." Hoar served in the Army in Germany and returned home to continue serving veterans. George E. Hogan was a proud Marine who continued to honor his community until the day he died. Cesar Lopez, another respectable Marine, volunteers for the Holyoke School Committee and founded an important nonprofit organization. Raymond O. Beaudoin was awarded the Badge of Valor from the Congressional Medal of Honor Society of the United States for his brave service. Another courageous veteran, Joseph E. Muller, was given many awards for his bravery and dedication to country and fellow servicemen. Receiving a Medal of Honor, John S. MacKenzie was recognized by Franklin D. Roosevelt. Martin (Maurcheen) Reilly received the Medal of Good Conduct, and Henry J. Flynn bravely fought for his country in 1944. Frank English was awarded a Purple Heart for his valor and commitment. A woman of courage, Charlotte Peltier served her country when most women stayed home. Landing on D-Day on Omaha Beach, John J. "Jinx" O'Connor extended medical aid to his crew and came home to lead Holyoke High School athletes to victory. Three young men, Sgt. Pettis Amos Jr., George M. Williston, and Cpl. Paul B. Osmyn, bravely served in the Civil War, while George M. Williston was only 18 years old and Cpl. Paul B. Osmyn was not any older. Ronald Lamadeliane also served, as did the tenacious Elmer McMahon. Pearl Harbor changed Nello Rota's time in the service, and Glenn R. Baker was a proud member of the US Army who landed with the Normandy invasion on D-Day.

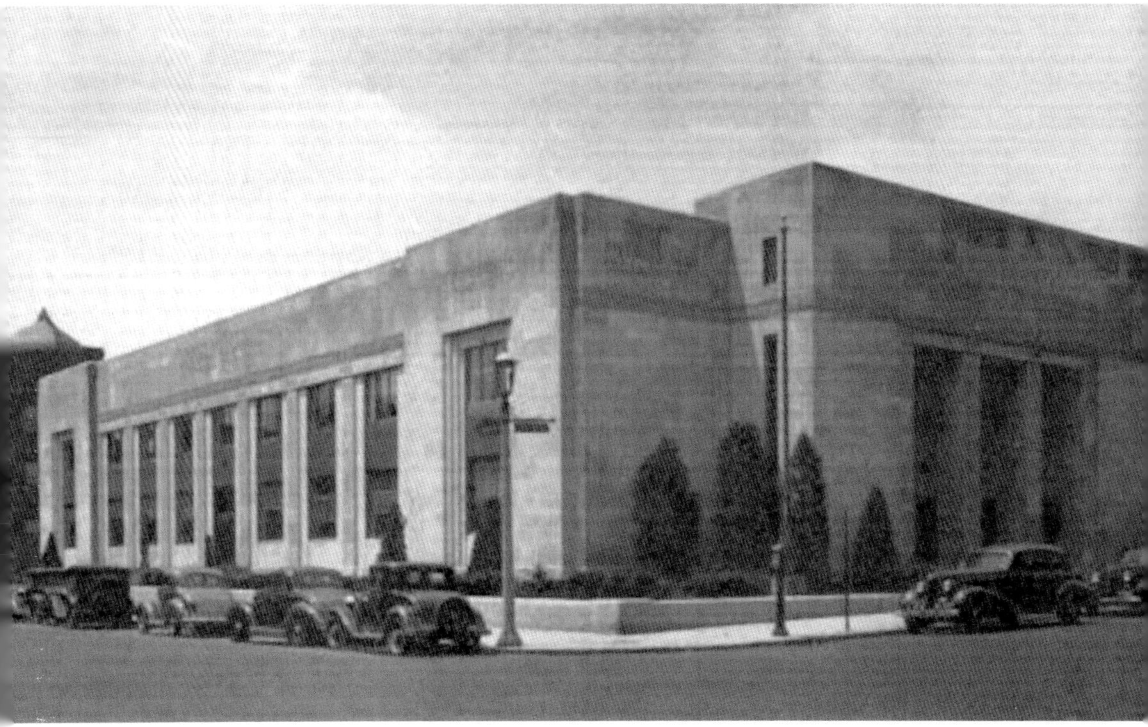

Holyoke War Memorial Building

This stately building was erected in September 1937 with the assistance of the New Deal agencies of the Public Works Administration. It serves as a community center for the city of Holyoke. "The Veterans of the World War share this memorial tribute with American Veterans of all times" is inscribed on the Appleton Street facade of the building. The interior has a fantastic auditorium, three meeting rooms, and additional smaller meeting rooms. There are several rooms for the veterans' memorials, plaques, and wreaths, among many other portraits of honorable veterans in the building. It is an important site for veterans and the city of Holyoke. (Courtesy of Harry Craven Jr.)

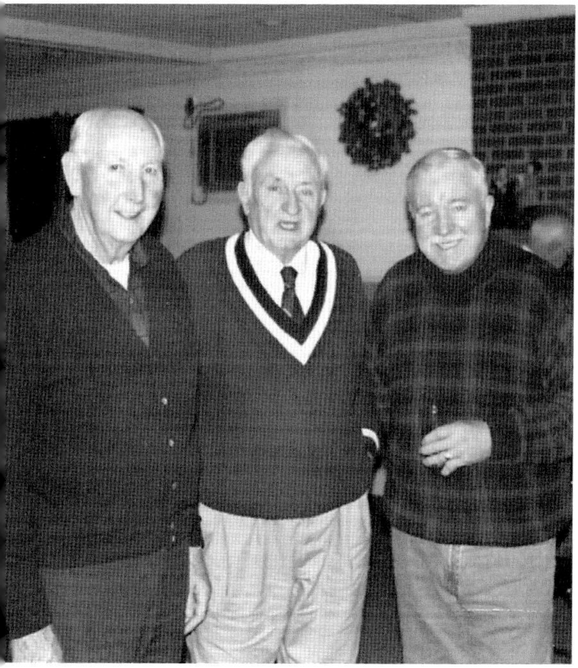

Martin "Maurcheen" Reilly (1940–2014)
Pictured third from left, Martin "Maurcheen" Reilly immigrated to Holyoke in 1960 from Ireland and attended Springfield College. He was a member of the John Boyle O'Reilly Club and a Gaelic football coach for the Springfield Wolftones. He worked for Nonotuck Wire and the Holyoke Housing Authority. He served in the Army in Vietnam and was stationed in Alaska. He was a private first class in the Army and received a Good Conduct Medal from Headquarters, 33D, Single Battalion in Fort Richardson for exemplary behavior, efficiency, and fidelity in the Federal Military Service. He was also a member of the American Legion Post No. 325 in Holyoke. (Courtesy of Deirdre Reilly.)

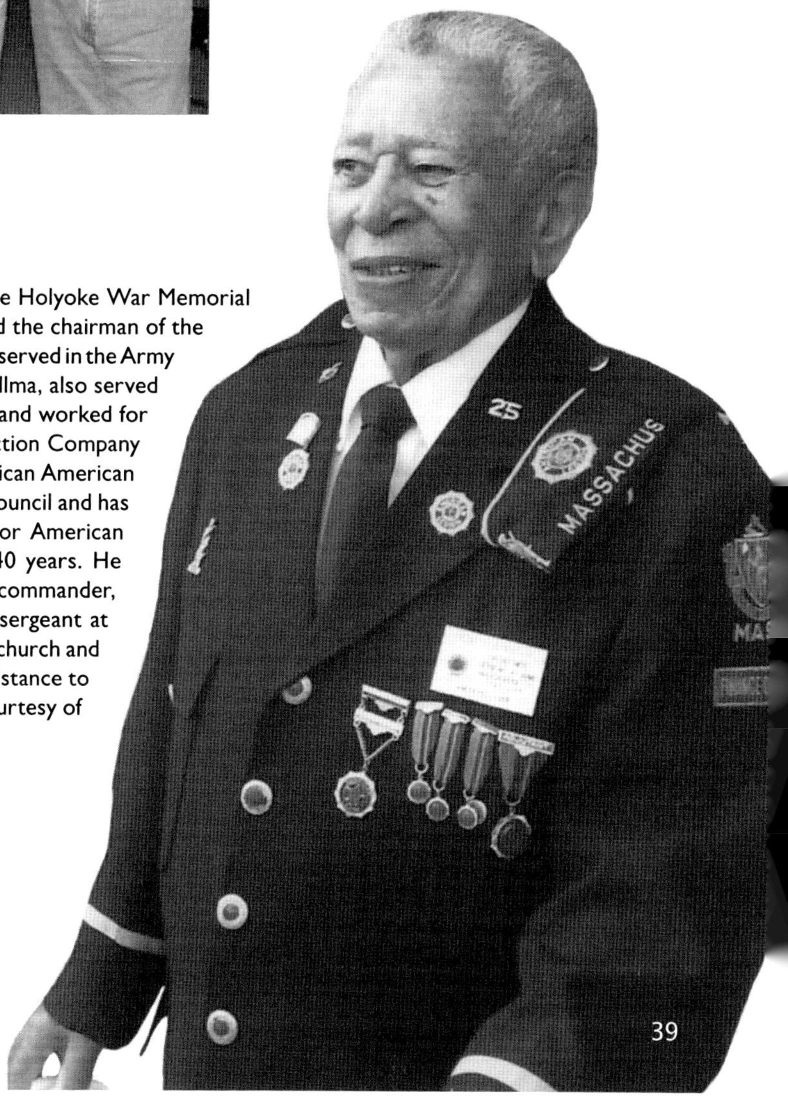

Henry Jennings, (1923–)
Jennings was the manager of the Holyoke War Memorial Building on Appleton Street and the chairman of the War Memorial Commission. He served in the Army and the Air Force. His wife, Willma, also served in the Army. He was a teacher and worked for the Daniel O'Connell Construction Company in Holyoke. He was the first African American to serve on the Holyoke City Council and has served as a post commander for American Legion Post No. 25 for over 40 years. He has held the titles of county commander, sergeant at arms, and national sergeant at arms. He has volunteered in his church and provided countless hours of assistance to his community and beyond. (Courtesy of Henry Jennings.)

Dennis J. Buckley Jr. (1920–1943)
Fireman First Class Buckley enlisted in the US Navy on September 30, 1940. On March 10, 1943, he boarded and salvaged a blockade-runner intercepted by his ship, the destroyer USS *Eberle* (DD-430). Planted by the blockade-runner's crew, demolition charges exploded and ended his life. He was awarded the Silver Star for displaying exceptional courage and fortitude. On December 20, 1944, his mother, Mrs. D.J. Buckley, sponsored the USS *Dennis J. Buckley* (DD/DDR-808). On March 2, 1945, the ship was commissioned and officially named in his honor. It faithfully served the US Navy from 1945 to 1973. (Courtesy of George Estey: djbuckley.com.)

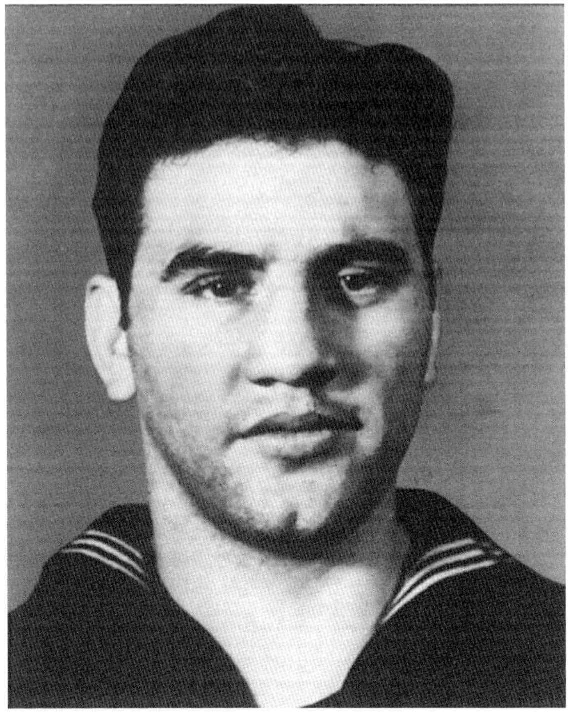

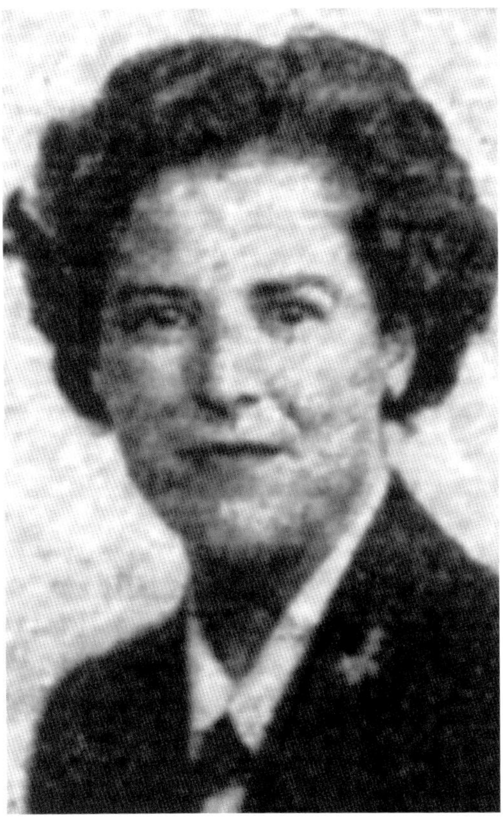

Charlotte Peltier
The daughter of Leon Peltier of Beacon Avenue, Charlotte Peltier graduated from Holyoke High School and from Rivier College in Nashua, New Hampshire. In 1942, Peltier was the first woman to enlist in the Women Accepted for Volunteer Emergency Service (WAVES) in Holyoke during World War II. When she returned home from her service, she taught alien education at Holyoke Evening High School for two years and was a substitute teacher in local schools. (Courtesy of Newspapers of Massachusetts, Inc.)

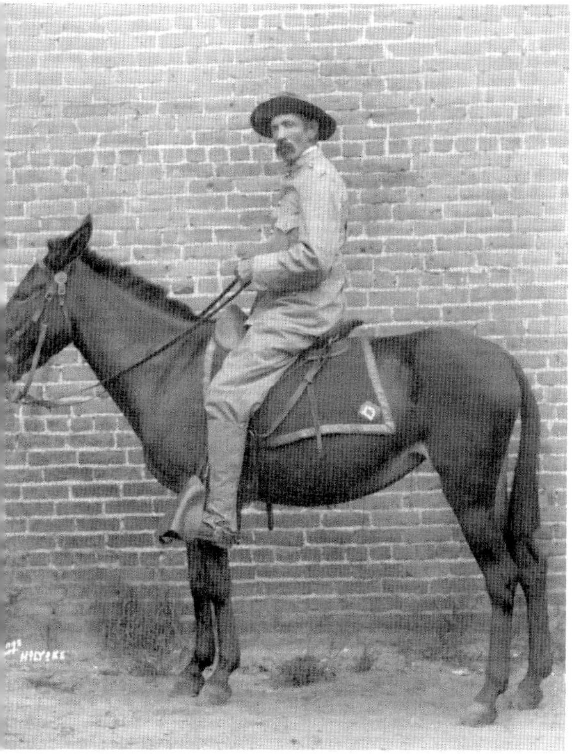

Maj. William J. Crosier

This sturdy man served in World War I. He was the superintendent of Holyoke's parks and playgrounds for 15 years. Crosier Field was originally known as Soldier's Field until Armistice Day (Veteran's Day) in 1939, in memory of Maj. William J. Crosier, a year after his death. It is one of Holyoke's most popular parks due to the many activities it offers, including 60-foot, 75-foot, and 90-foot baseball fields, five tennis courts, and two soccer fields, and one field hockey field. (Courtesy of the Holyoke Public Library.)

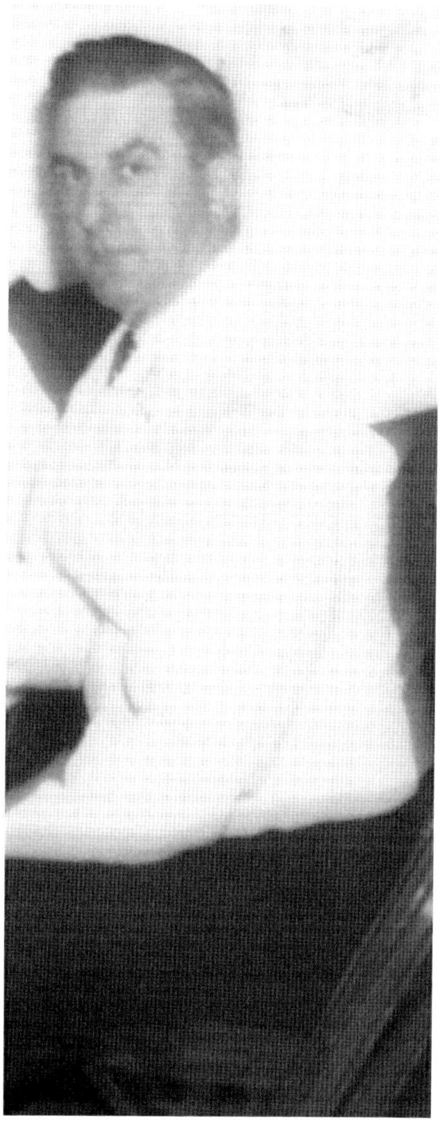

John A. Lucey (1917–2012)

He served in the US Army during World War II as a first sergeant of Company A, 263rd Engineer Combat Battalion, in Europe. Lucey served as city assessor, as well as an assistant tax collector and the chairman of the board of assessors for 30 years. When he retired, he received a citywide proclamation, declaring his retirement date the "John A. Lucey Day." He was a well-liked dedicated family man who volunteered to be the first clerk for the Holyoke St. Patrick's Parade Committee among many other good deeds he bestowed upon the citizens of Holyoke. (Courtesy of Harry Craven Jr.)

Brian Willette

This courageous man has paid homage to his comrades on the battlefield as well as to his fellow Veterans at home. Army staff sergeant Willette of Company F, 1st Battalion, 102nd Infantry Regiment, 1st Brigade Combat Team, deployed to Afghanistan, and on September 13, 2010, the 33,000-pound gun truck that he was commanding was struck by a large improvised explosive device (IED). He and his squad members sustained various injuries. Despite his own injuries, he refused medical evacuation to remain in battle to assist other injured soldiers. Brian was awarded the Combat Action Badge and had the honor of having his Purple Heart Medal pinned on by his son, Specialist Kevin Willette, who was just beginning his own tour in Afghanistan. Brian is the commander of the Military Order of the Purple Heart of Western Massachusetts; commander of the Veterans of Foreign Wars Hampden, District 7; a member of the American Legion; and an active member of the Agawam Veterans Memorial Cemetery Firing Detail and Honor Guard. (Courtesy of Brian Willette.)

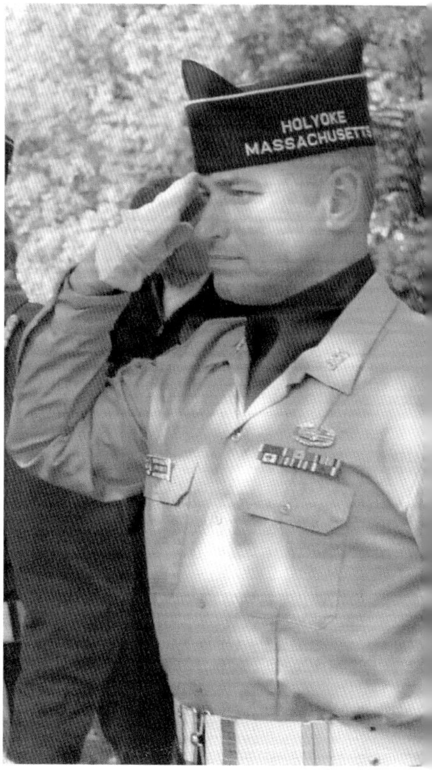

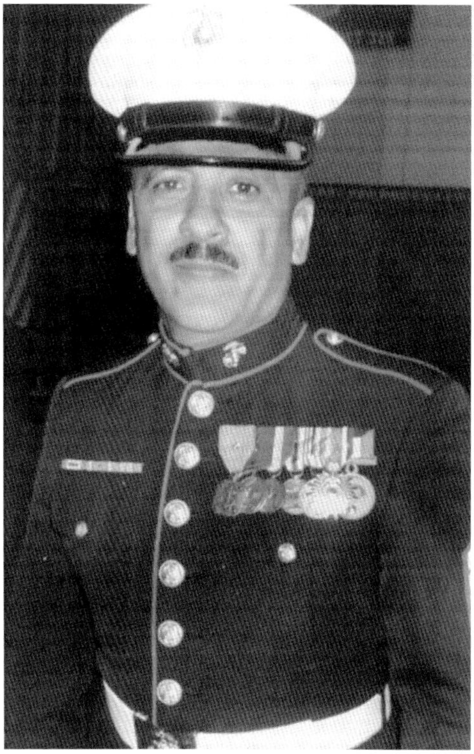

Cesar Lopez

He moved to the United States in 1977 from the Dominican Republic. He lived in New York City and attended George Washington High School before moving to Holyoke in 1988. He is proud of being an immigrant, serving his country in the US Marine Corps, and of being the master of arms at the Holyoke War Memorial Building on Memorial Day ceremonies. He is a program analyst on the C-5 air transport planes at Westover Air Base in Chicopee. Lopez is the father of five children and a member of the Holyoke School Committee. He is the founder of the Fundacion de La Famitia Nuevos Horizontes in Santo Domingo in the Dominican Republic. The foundation helps children in the Dominican Republic go to school by asking people to donate their gently used shoes. In 2010, this kind and resourceful man and his friend Manuel Colon volunteered their time and muscle to preserve the Holyoke Soldier's Monument in Veterans Park. (Courtesy of Cesar Lopez.)

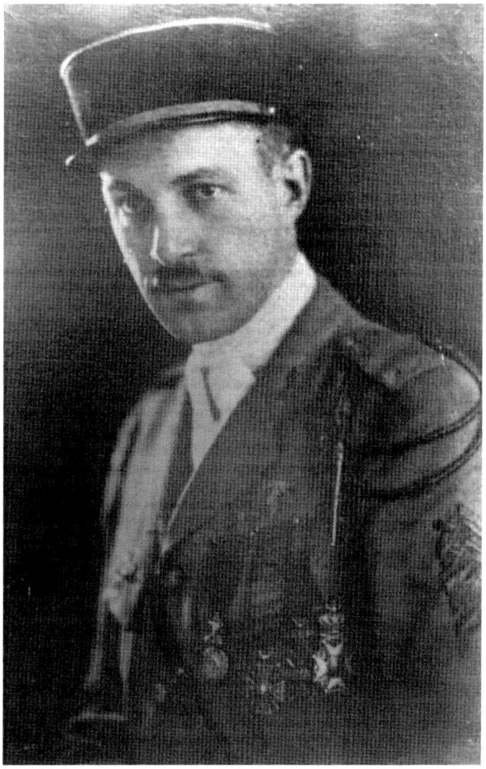

Edwin Parsons
The Lafayette Escadrille was an American volunteer pilot flying fighters squadron in World War I. Parsons joined these brave pilots on January 24, 1917, several months before America was involved in the World War I. He was one of 38 American pilots who volunteered before the war started. He was a member of the Federal Bureau Investigation after the war and learned the technical aspects of filming moving pictures. He served in the Navy during World War II as a rear admiral. (Courtesy of the Holyoke Public Library.)

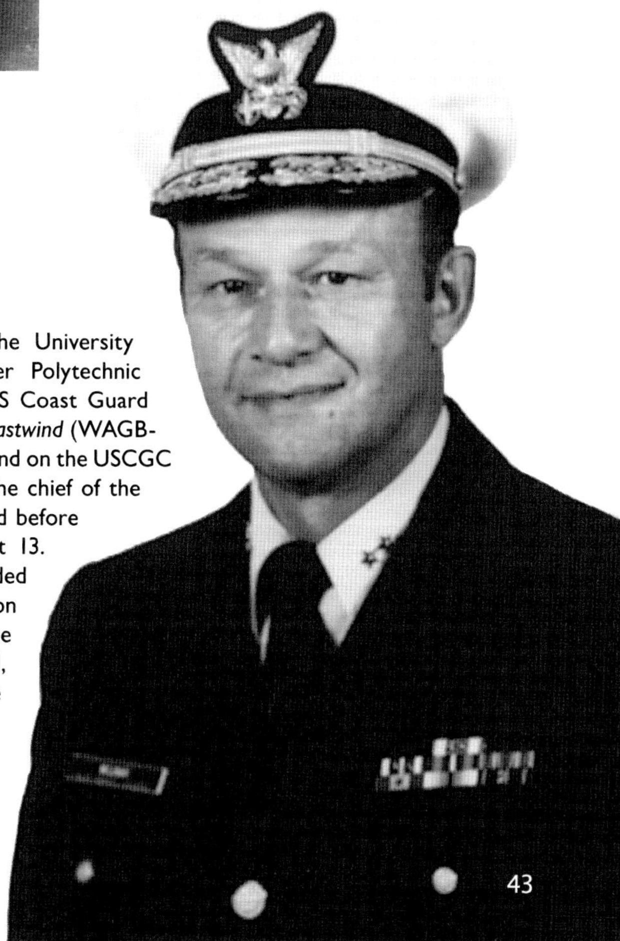

Theodore J. Wojnar (1930–)
Wojnar was born in Holyoke, went to the University of Massachusetts, Amherst, and Rensselaer Polytechnic Institute. In 1953, he graduated from the US Coast Guard Academy. He was stationed on the USCGC *Eastwind* (WAGB-279) serving with the International Ice Patrol and on the USCGC *Chincoteague* (WAVP-365). In 1986, he was the chief of the Civil Engineering Division of the Coast Guard before assuming command of Coast Guard District 13. During his illustrious career, he was awarded the Commandant's Letter of Commendation Ribbon, Legion of Merit, the Meritorious Service Medal, the Coast Guard Commendation Medal, the Coast Guard Achievement Medal, and the Arctic Service Medal. (Courtesy of Theodore J. Wojnar.)

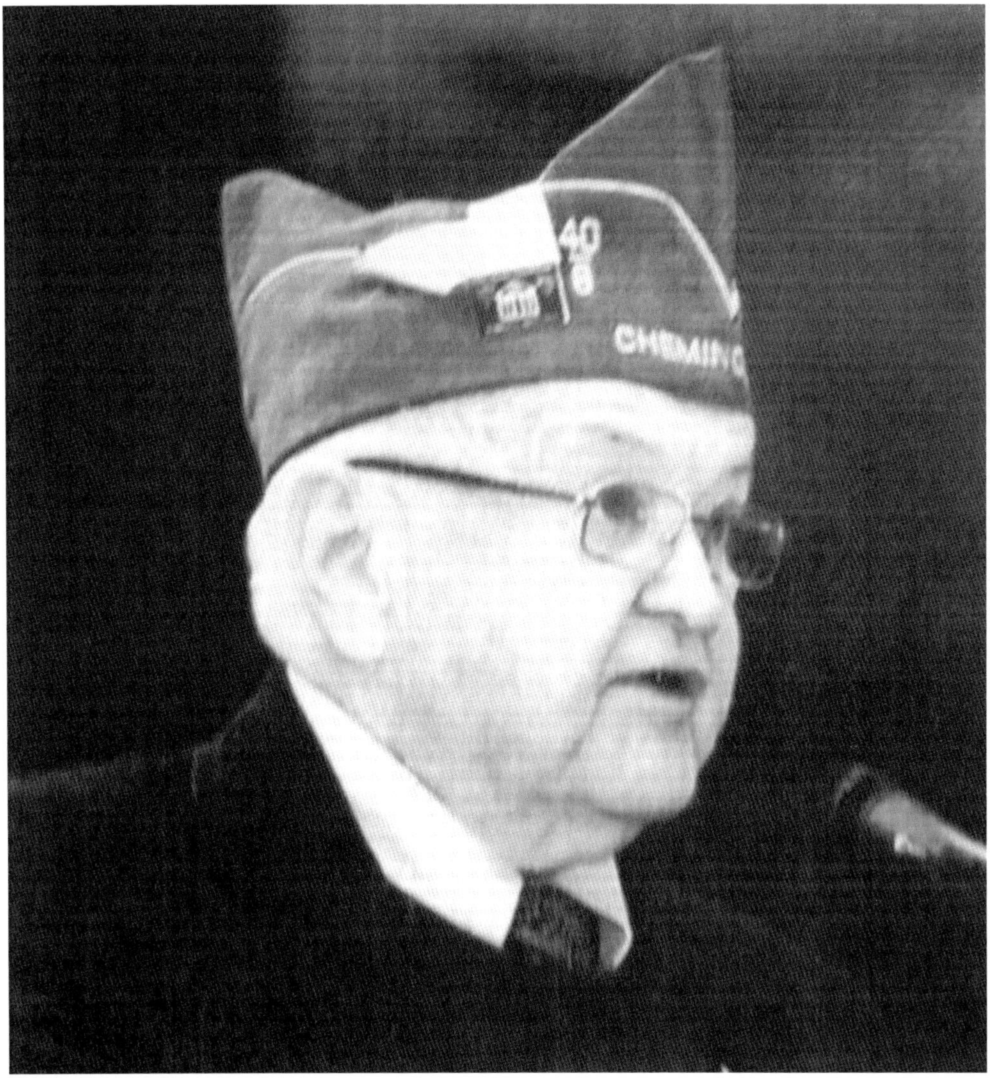

James "B.J." Hoar (1935–)
He was born in Holyoke and attended St. Jerome High School, graduating in 1953. He volunteered for the US Army from 1954 to 1956. He served in Germany. He returned to Holyoke and enrolled in Holyoke Junior College in 1959 and earned an associate's degree in business. He also took classes at American International College and Elms College. He worked construction jobs and at the Mount Tom Power Station. In 1971, he became a Holyoke Park policeman. He worked for Holyoke for 18 years while he worked at Hamilton Standard on the space program in the evenings and worked as a supervisor for Piels Brewery on the weekends in Chicopee. In 1999, he worked for the Holyoke Gas & Electric Company as a credit investigator and retired in 1999. Hoar was active in countless organizations, including the United Veterans of Holyoke, the Holyoke War Memorial Commission, and the American Legion. Hoar was district commander for Hampden County and is the master of ceremonies for the Memorial Day observance at the Holyoke War Memorial Building. He has dedicated his life to serving the community. He was named Holyoke's Veteran of the Year in 2004. This patriotic and dedicated man believes in "a sense of obligation to his country, God, and his Irish Heritage." (Courtesy of James "B.J." Hoar.)

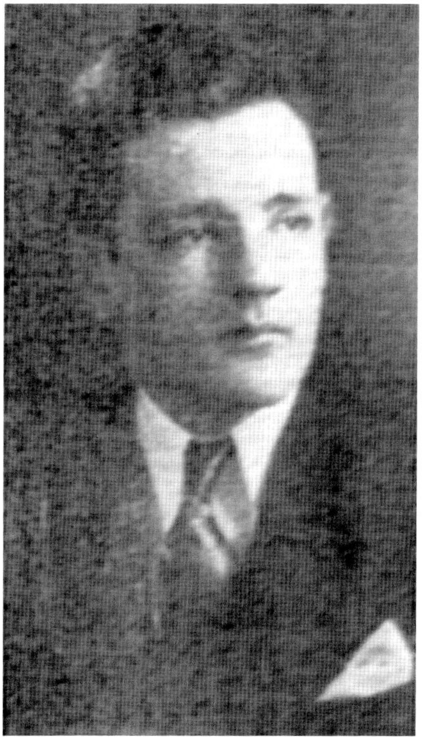

Henry J. Flynn
Flynn played basketball and baseball at Holyoke High School and Dean Academy. He coached the Highland team that won the 1940–1941 championship. While serving in the Army, he fought many battles and took part in the invasion of France. He was killed in action on August 11, 1944. (Courtesy of the Holyoke Public Library.)

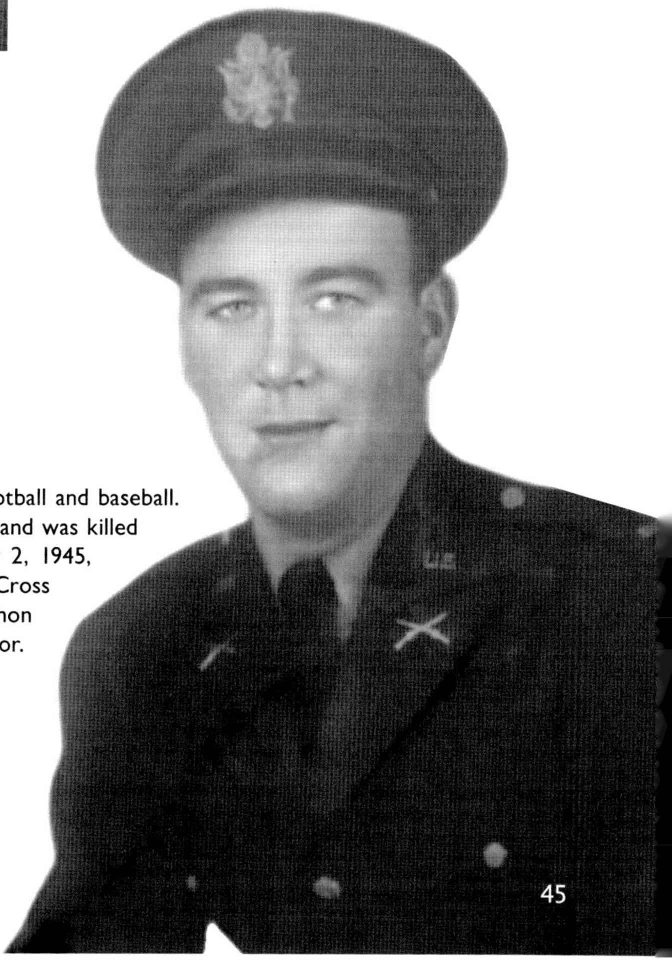

Elmer J. "Pubba" McMahon
Holyoke-born McMahon loved to play football and baseball. He served in the Army in the Philippines and was killed in action in World War II. On February 2, 1945, he received the Distinguished Service Cross for courage and heroism in battle. McMahon School on Kane Road was named in his honor. (Courtesy of the Holyoke Public Schools.)

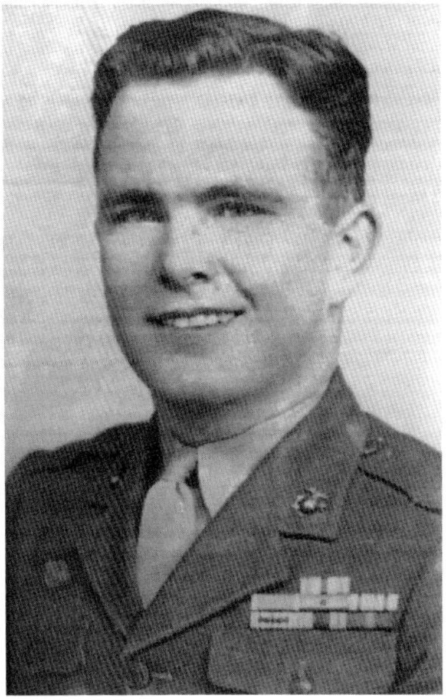

George E. Hogan (1924–2012)

He was born in Holyoke and attended the Holyoke Public School System. His mother, Mary Hogan, emigrated from Dingle, County Kerry, Ireland, and his father's people were from Castle Gregory. George E. Hogan enlisted in the US Marine Corps the day after Pearl Harbor was attacked—though he was only 17. He served with A Company, 1st Marine Division, in the Pacific theater. He fought in all of the 1st Division campaigns, from Guadalcanal, Cape Gloucester, and Pavuvu to Northern Solomons Peleliu and Teneru River. The fighting was so intense at Peleliu that he had to take over his platoon due to all of the officers and noncommissioned officers who were severely wounded. After a long and tedious battle surviving raging fires and intense gunfire, he led his platoon to victory. He was awarded the Silver Star, three Purple Hearts, and two Presidential Unit Citations. Upon his return home, he started working for Holyoke Post Office and continued for the next 25 years. He was a sought after carpenter. George married Barbara O'Neil in 1957, and they had three children. Fellow Holyoke veterans honored him with a Veteran of the Year Award in 1999. He was an active member of the American Legion Post No. 325 and the United Veterans. He developed heartwarming friendships with the veterans and staff members at the Soldier's Home and War Memorial in Holyoke. He was an avid reader of military tributes as well as Holyoke history books, and he loved to talk about the history of Ireland. He supported Northern Irish Aid. He loved to go for hikes and travel. This brave and well-respected man lived his life in a complete and honest manner, one that was not riddled in drama, but rather with an unassuming and unpretentious charm. (Courtesy of the Hogan family.)

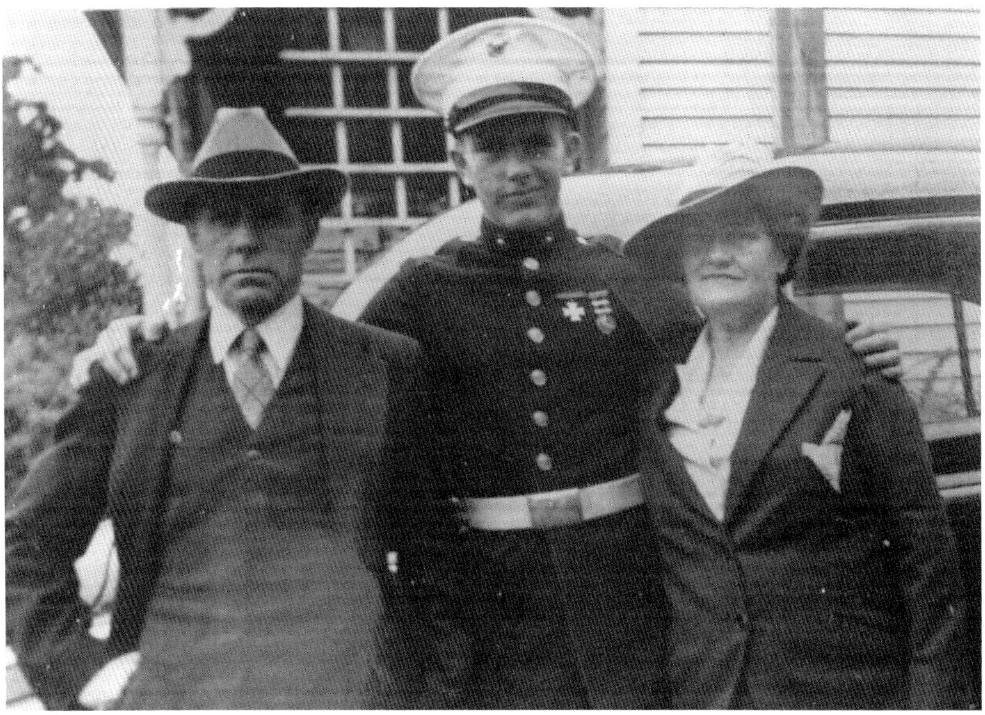

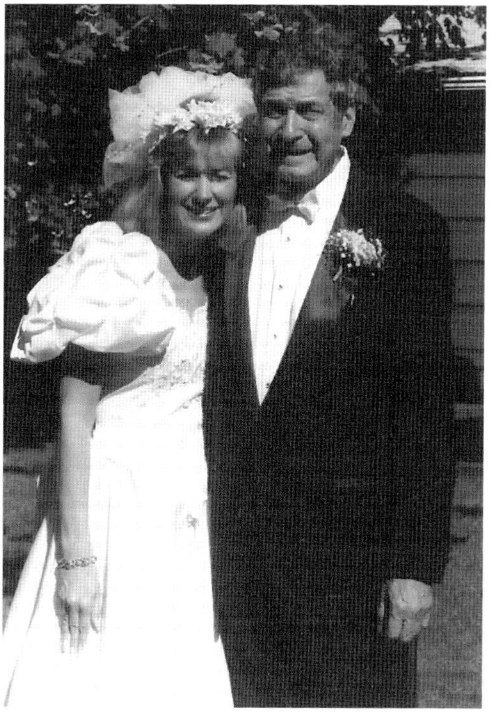

Frank English (1921–2013)
While serving as a Marine in World War II from 1941 to 1945, Frank English was wounded in battle and was awarded the Purple Heart for his brave service. He continued to keep citizens safe by working as a safety inspector for BF Perkins and at Springfield Armory in retirement. (Courtesy of the English family.)

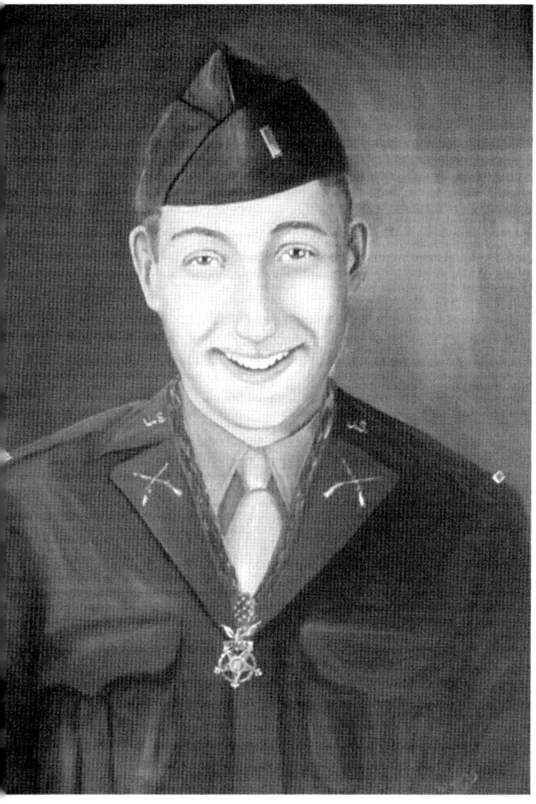

Raymond O. Beaudoin (1918–1945)
In World War II on January 25, 1946, First Lieutenant Beaudoin led the 2nd Platoon of Company F, 119th Infantry, 30th Army Infantry Division, out of the line of fire from German soldiers in Hamelin, Germany. In doing so, he lost his own life. He was awarded the Badge of Valor from the Congressional Medal of Honor Society of the United States. He was awarded the Medal of Honor (Posthumous); Bronze Star Medal; Purple Heart for wounds received on August 11, 1944; and Purple Heart (Posthumous). He was also awarded the Good Conduct Medal; Distinguished Unit Emblem; Meritorious Unit Emblem; American Defense Service Medal; American Campaign Medal; World War II Victory Medal; European-African-Middle Eastern Campaign Medal with on Silver Service Star (in lieu of five Bronze Service Stars) for participation in Normandy, Northern France, Rhineland, Ardennes-Alsace and Central Europe campaigns; Combat Infantryman Badge; and Belgian Fourragere. (Courtesy of Holyoke War Memorial.)

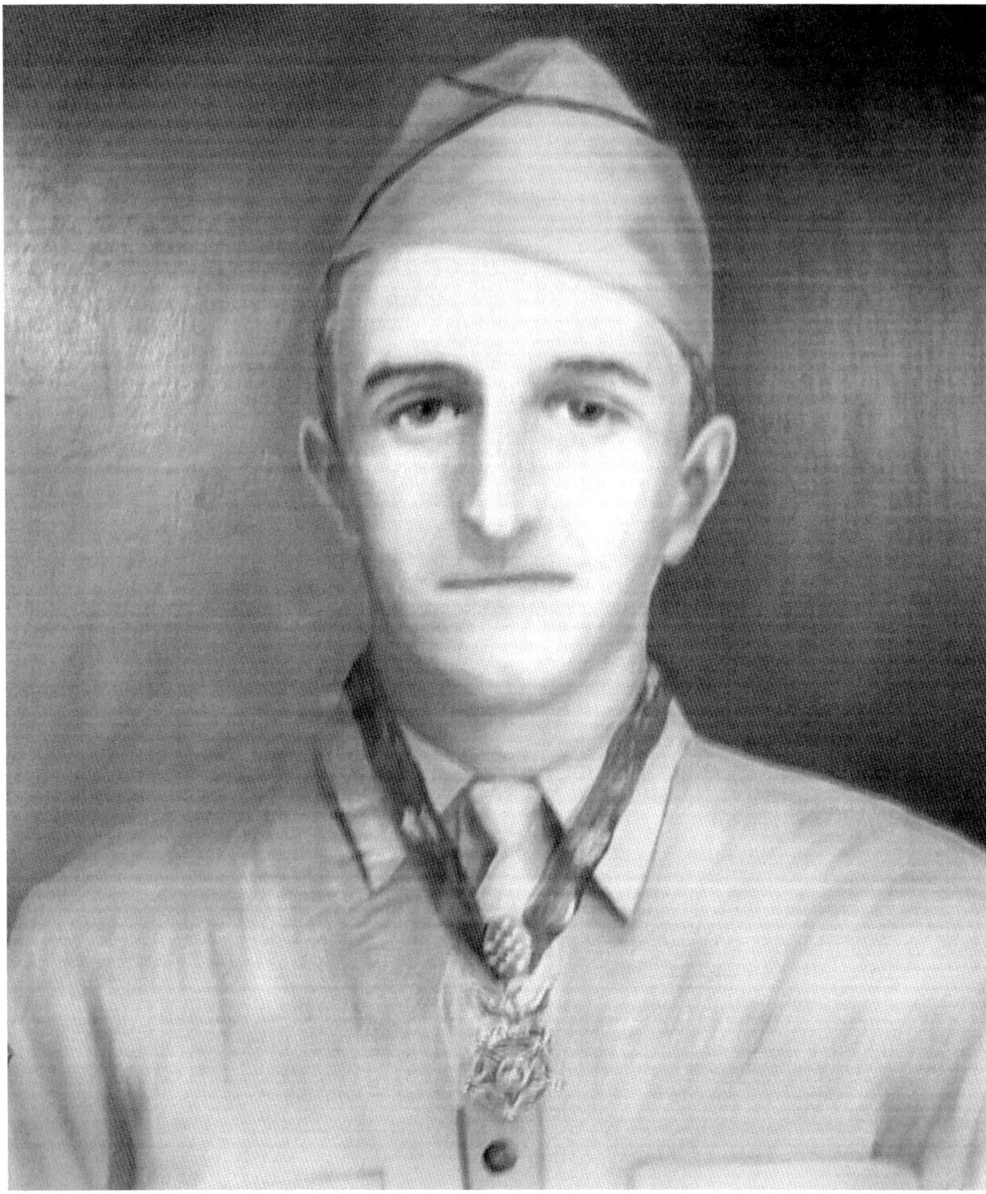

Joseph E. Muller (1908–1945)
Holyoke native Muller served in the Massachusetts National Guard in 1926. He was inducted into the Army in 1942. On May 16, 1945, he was a sergeant in the Army when he was killed in action at Okinawa, Ryukyus Islands. He was awarded the Medal of Honor (Posthumous), Bronze Star Medal with "V" device; and a Purple Heart (Posthumous) for his brave service. He was also given the following awards: the Good Conduct Medal; American Campaign; Asiatic-Pacific Campaign Medal with bronze arrowhead and three bronze service stars for participation in Western Pacific, Ryukyus and Leyte campaign; World War II Victory Medal; Expert Infantryman Badge; Combat Infantryman Badge; Philippine Liberation Ribbon with one Bronze Service Star; and Philippine Presidential Unit Citation Badge. A bridge between Holyoke and South Hadley is named in his honor. Muller was a good friend of Raymond Beaudoin, who lived next door to him. (Courtesy of Holyoke War Memorial.)

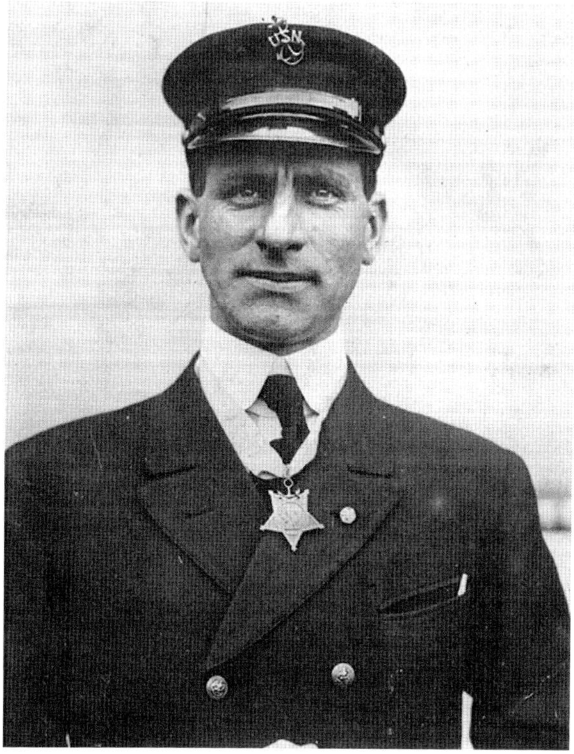

John S. MacKenzie (1886–1933)
In 1918, during World War I, MacKenzie received a Medal of Honor for saving the lives of his shipmates by safely securing a depth charge (a can filled with explosives and a fuse that detonates at a preset depth based on hydrostatic pressure). Franklin D. Roosevelt was the acting secretary of the Navy at the time. MacKenzie Field in Holyoke was named after him. (Courtesy of the Holyoke War Memorial.)

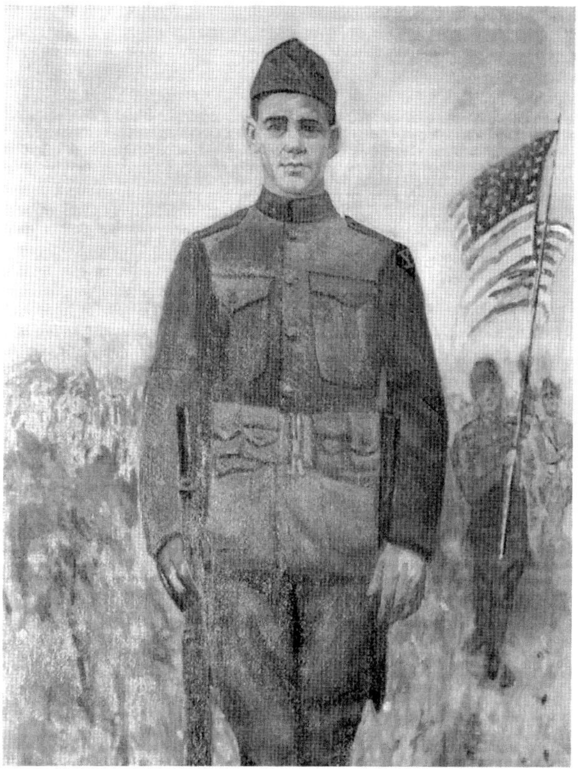

George G. Clarke (1889–1918)
This brave man lived on 244 Sargeant Street. Clarke was a US Army private assigned to Company F, 104th Infantry Regiment, 26th Infantry Division. He was killed in a battle against the German army in Chemin des Dames in Northern France in World War I.

His cause of death was listed as "accidental gunshot wounds." The Veterans of Foreign Wars (VFW) is investigating his death. He is one of the 4,500 Americans still missing in action from World War I. His remains were never recovered. Private Clarke was the first casualty of the 104th Infantry Regiment. VFW Post No. 801, located in the Holyoke War Memorial Building, was named after him. (Courtesy of the Holyoke War Memorial.)

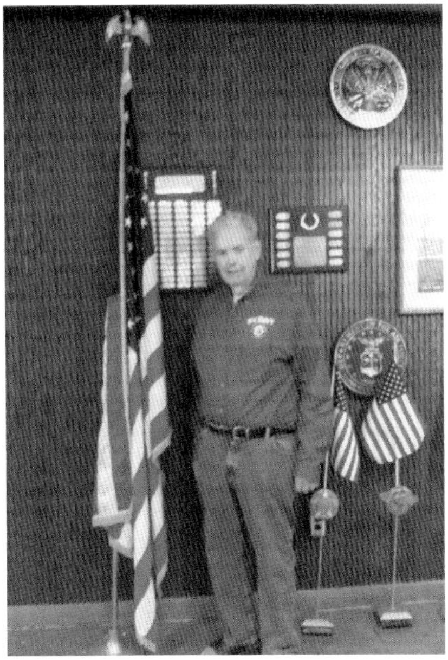

Robert Murphy (1941–)
He grew up in Westfield and then faithfully served in the Navy from 1960 to 1964 on the USS *Lake Champlain*, which blocked military supplies from Russia to Cuba during the Cuban Missile Crisis. He returned home to earn his bachelor's in foreign affairs from Assumption College. In 1968, he was a bilingual social worker for the Massachusetts Department of Public Welfare until he worked as a mental health clinician for the Holyoke Hospital in the 1970s. When asked about his favorite part of the job, he said, "I liked working with people, I like to help people." (Courtesy of Robert Murphy.)

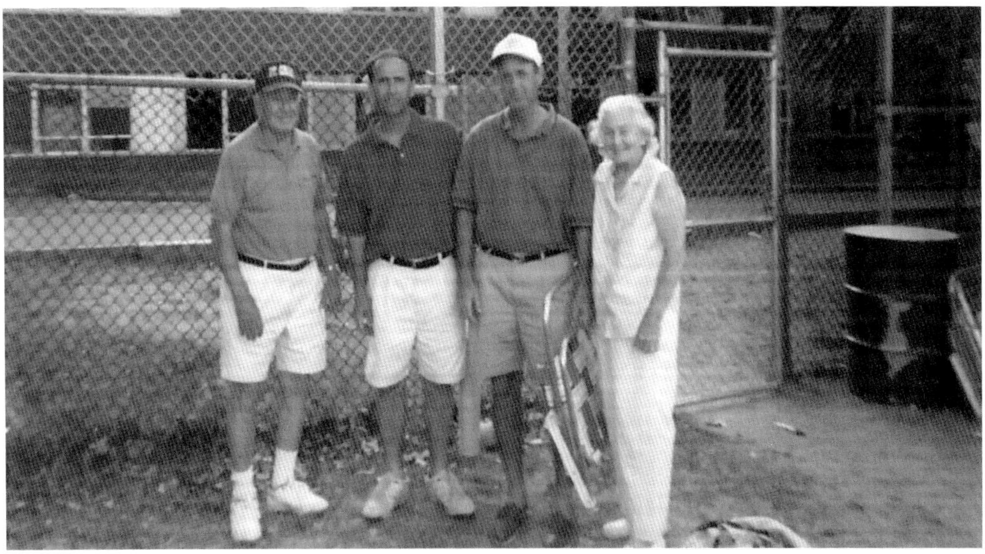

John J. "Jinx" O'Connor (1915–2005)
Born in Holyoke and brought up in the "old" Ward 4 section of the city, John J. "Jinx" O'Connor (far left) was a staff sergeant in the medical section of the commando-trained Rangers of the Army that landed on D-Day on Omaha Beach in World War II. After serving in the Army, he applied to New York University, where he played varsity basketball and baseball for a year and was an assistant coach. In 1954, he started coaching the Holyoke High School basketball and baseball teams. The basketball team had a record of 341-195 wins and nine Valley League championships and three Western Massachusetts tittles and the Purple Knights baseball team won the state championship in 1978. He received many awards, including the Edward J. Hickox Award from the Basketball Hall of Fame Tip-off Classic Committee in 1992. He was also a member of the Massachusetts State Coaches Association Hall of Fame for both basketball and baseball. The City of Holyoke named the Holyoke High School gym after him. (Courtesy of the O'Connor family.)

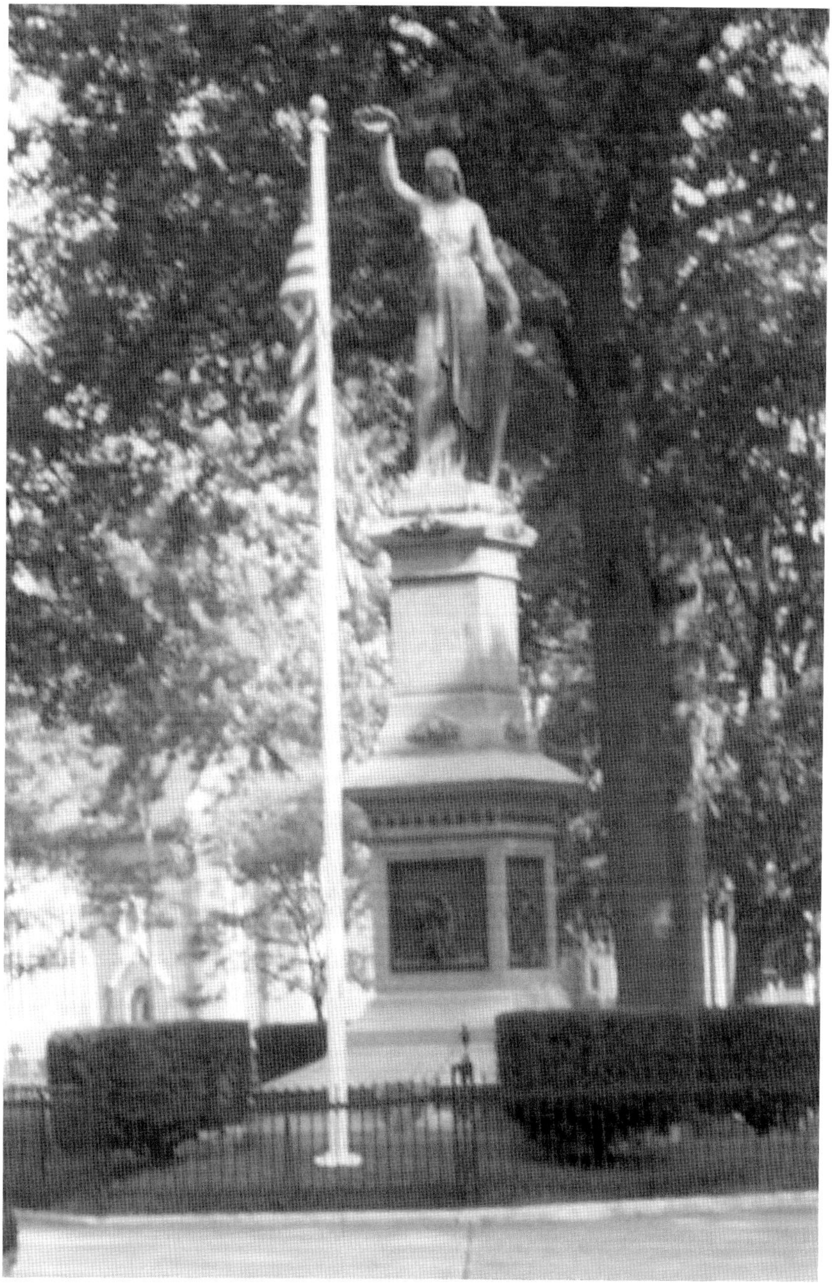

Holyoke Soldier's Monument

This stunning monument stands to honor Civil War soldiers who died from 1861 to 1864. It is a nine-foot-high bronze sculpture that sits atop a 10-foot granite base. Henry Jackson Ellicott sculpted the monument, and the M.H. Power Bronze Foundry cast the monument that was erected on July 4, 1876, in Hampden Park, known as Veterans Park today. Inscribed on the monument are the names of the 55 young men died serving in the Civil War; the following are just a few of those men: Sgt. Pettis Amos Jr. (1845–1863), Cpl. Paul B. Osmyn (1846–1864), and George M. Williston (1845–1863). (Author's collection.)

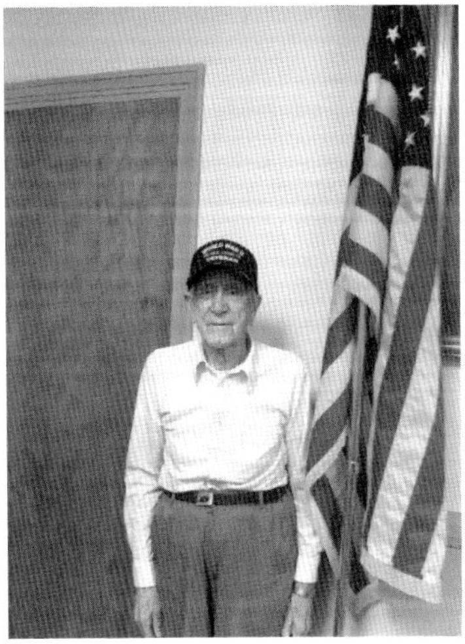

Nello Rota (1914–2015)

Rota grew up in Holyoke, attended Holyoke High School, and served in the US Army. He was going to be discharged from the Army until the attack on Pearl Harbor on December 7, 1941, when he was reassigned to the 3rd Infantry Division until the culmination of the war. He was the commander of the George G. Clarke Veterans of Foreign Wars Post No. 801 in Holyoke, where he was involved with the Honor Flight New England Program that helps veterans visit their memorial in Washington, DC. He passed away on January 22, 2015, at the age of 100. (Courtesy of William Beven.)

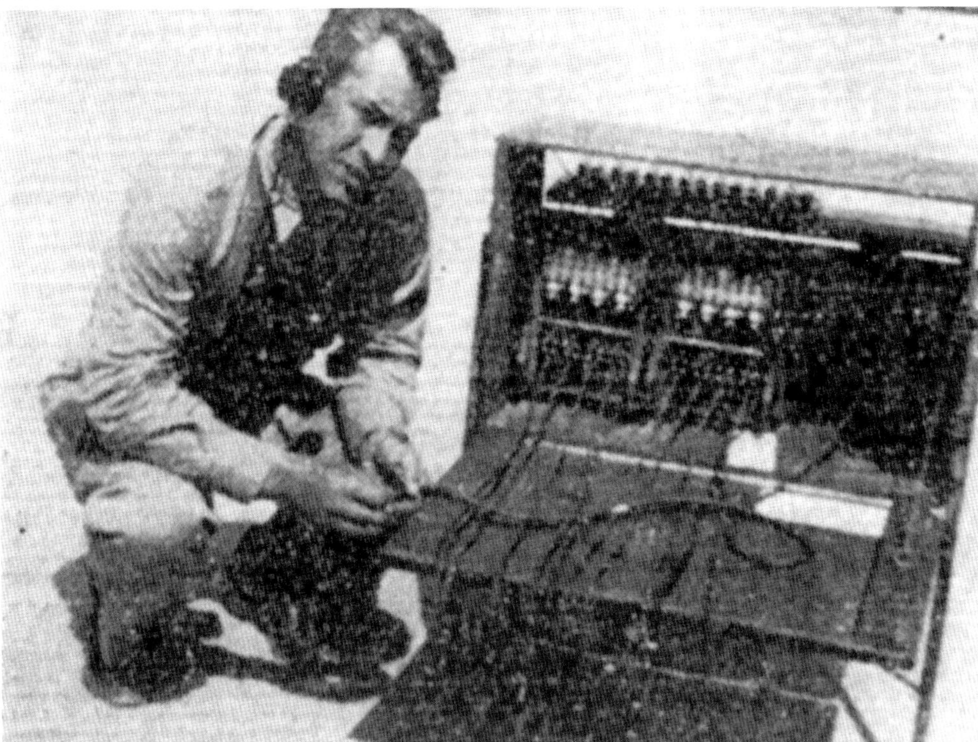

Sgt. Glenn R. Baker

He lived on 11 O'Connor Avenue in Holyoke, graduated from Holyoke High School, and worked for the Crocker-McElwain mill in 1940. He was inducted into the Army in 1941 and served as a field switchboard operator in World War II. He was awarded the Bronze Star, for his heroic action in stringer communications over the Remagen Bridge under heavy German fire. This brave man landed with the Normandy invasion force on D-Day, and he fought battles in the 1st Army in France, Holland, Belgium, and Germany.

Sgt. Glenn Baker had accumulated 119 points under the discharge system following the end of World War II. (Courtesy of Newspapers of Massachusetts, Inc.)

CHAPTER FOUR

Remarkable Athletes

The five S's of sports training are: stamina, speed, strength, skill, and spirit; but the greatest of these is spirit.

—Ken Doherty

One cannot measure a man's full athletic ability only by the length of his stride, but one must also assess his attitude and steadfast resolve. John Francis "Jack" Buck had to deal with his father's death. He never wallowed in his loss; instead, he went on to entertain sports fans with his distinctive broadcasting style for 47 years. Herman G. Steiner was a versatile athlete who played football and baseball and was a track coach at a university. A winner of the Golden Gloves, Danny Buckley was the favorite of the Valley Arena boxers in 1930s before it burned down. A left-handed pitcher and outfielder, Dick Burns was a talented Major League Baseball player with all the right moves. Pierce George "Gerry" Geran never stopped playing hockey even when his team disbanded; he went on to win a silver medal at the 1920 Summer Olympics in Antwerp. Coach Bill "Kaner" Kane's positive affirmation "do your best" has carried his students to the finish line with speed and fortitude. Surely, Joseph "Scootch" Earl Lucey was an honorable athlete, servicemen, and public servant. Billy L. Mitchell's eye-and-hand coordination were legendary. Fran Healy is a gifted pitcher and quick-witted sports announcer that keeps us well informed. Daniel "Rudy" Langieza's calm and reassuring voice elevates young athletes to phenomenal heights. Mark Wohlers was considered one of the best closer in the Major League Baseball at one time. Thomas A. Sears Sr. shares not only his name with his son, but also his vitality and determination to help lead his Irish football team to victory. "Mintonette" was William Morgan's game and the original name of volleyball. George Mulry is the executive director of the Volleyball Hall of Fame and has received myriad of important professional awards as a coach, an official, and a player. "Buttermilk" Tommy could catch a ball with ease and finesse, while pitching sensation Freddy Andujar is the man to keep an eye on.

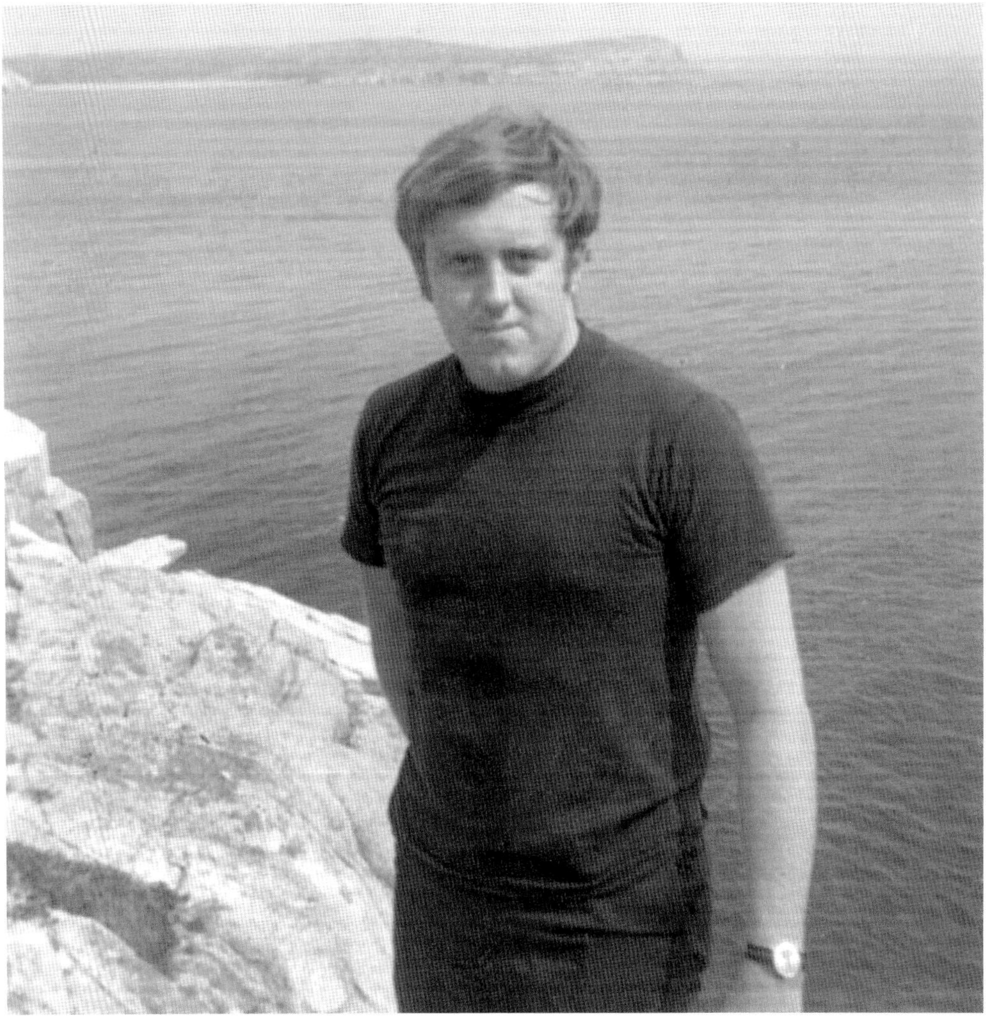

John (Smokey) Keane (1941–2003)
Keane was born in Holyoke and graduated from St. Jerome High School in 1959. While in high school, he was a star athlete on the basketball team where lead his team to victory with his gritty intercepting defense and his famous twisted layups. He continued to play amateur basketball into his fifties at the YMCA. His peers considered him one of "the greatest living Gael," a person who speaks Gaelic. Keane was an awesome pitcher too for the American Legion and was on many Holyoke baseball teams since childhood. He proved to be an asset once again on the football field by receiving the All-Western Massachusetts Quarterback Award in 1961. He earned an associate's degree at Holyoke Community College, a bachelor's degree at St. Anselm College, and a master's degree at Boston College. He served in the Volunteers in Service to America (VISTA) in Harlem from 1966 to 1968. The program was designed by Lyndon Johnson's Economic Opportunity Act of 1964 to help fight poverty in the United States. Keane went on to work at the Lowell Housing Authority as the director of public housing and eventually became the director of operations in the Cambridge Housing Authority. After his death from pulmonary fibrosis, the Cambridge Housing Authority named a community center after him in his honor, and the city of Cambridge had a John "Smokey" Keane Day. He dedicated his life to assuring that all people, especially senior citizens, have the right to live in adequate housing with a pleasant and well-maintained environment. (Courtesy of Meghan Keane.)

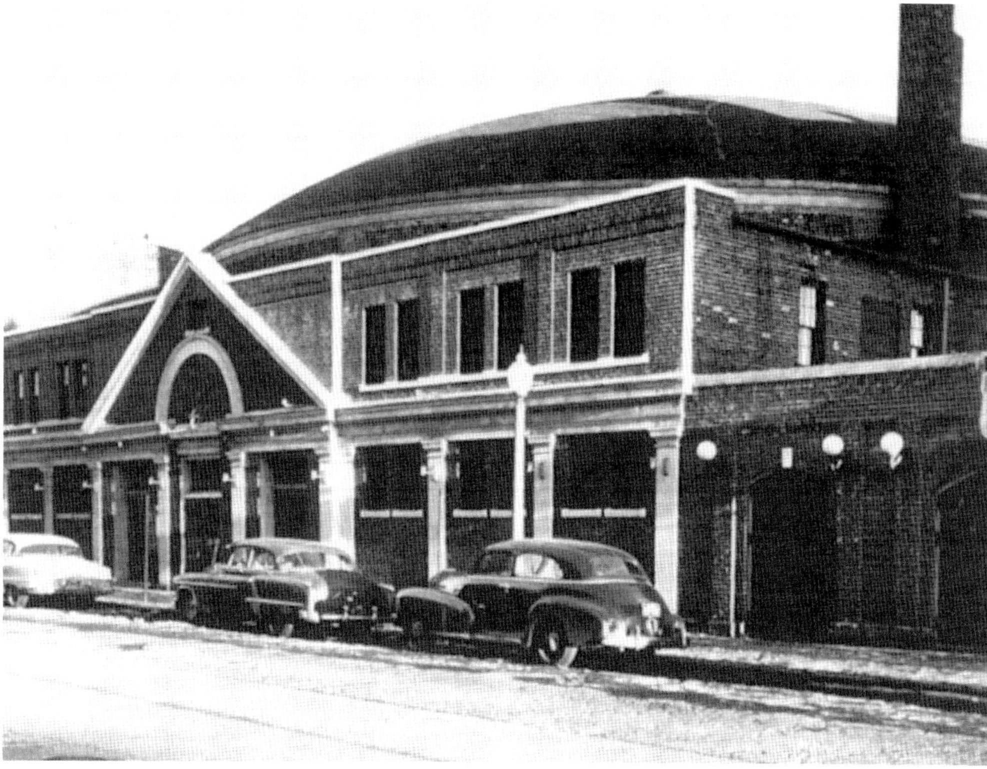

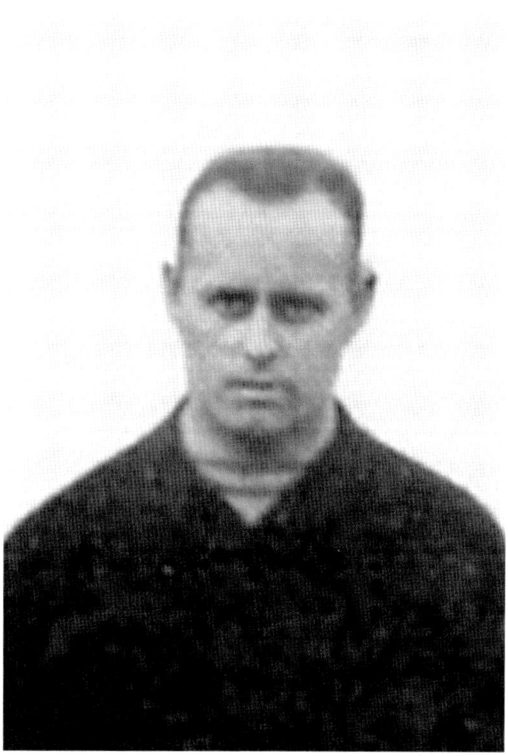

Danny Buckley

Danny Buckley was one of the favorite Valley Arena boxers in 1930s before it burned down. He started boxing as a senior in Holyoke High School and went on to win the Golden Gloves Tournament as a Middleweight. (Courtesy of Harry Craven Jr.)

Herman G. Steiner (1897–1982)

Steiner's father, Albert Steiner, was a German immigrant carpenter living in Brooklyn, Massachusetts in 1910. By 1918, Steiner moved to Holyoke, Massachusetts. He was a captain on the Syracuse University football team and then attended the International Young Men's Christian Association Training School (currently known as Springfield College) in 1918. He served in World War I in the Army and attended the Normal College of Physical Education in Indianapolis. He was a captain of a basketball team and coached track and football at Trinity College (now known as Duke University). He also played minor league baseball. (Courtesy of Harry Craven Jr.)

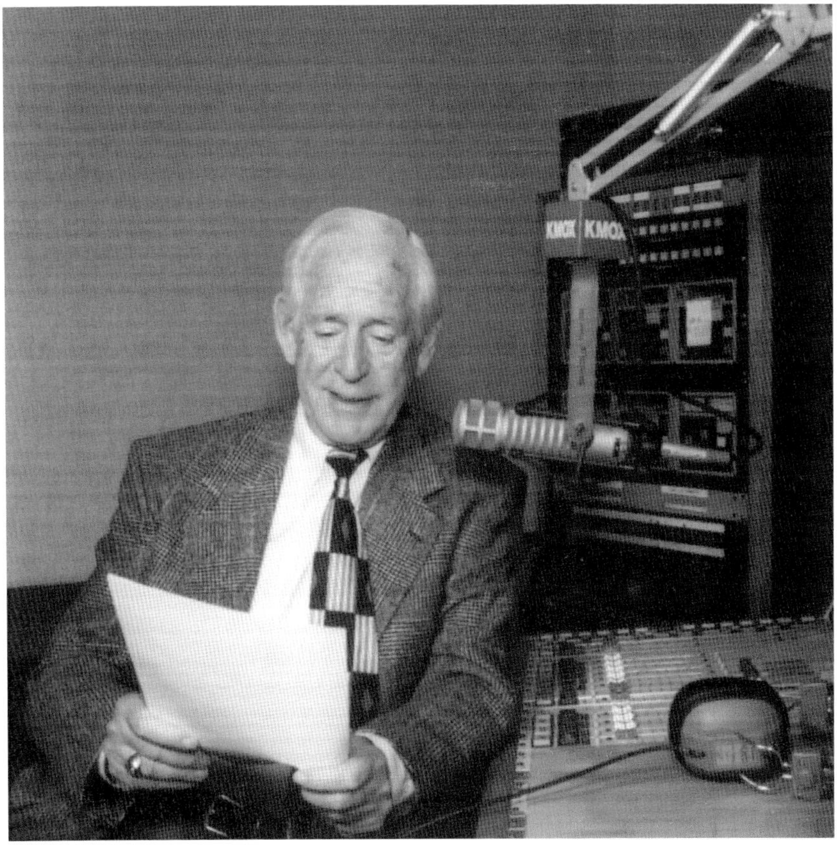

John Francis "Jack" Buck (1924–2002)
Buck was born in Holyoke and had six siblings. His father, Earl Buck, was a railroad accountant in New Jersey. Fred Holey who would broadcast Boston Red Sox games when he was a child inspired Buck. The Buck family moved to Cleveland, Ohio, in 1939 to join their father who had taken a job with the Erie Railroad Company. Sadly, his father developed high blood pressure and succumbed to uremic poisoning, dying at the age of 49. Buck worked on shipping boats on the Great Lakes after graduating from high school. He was drafted into the US Army in 1943; he was awarded the Purple Heart for his service. Upon returning home from war, he graduated from Ohio State University, majoring in radio speech with a minor in Spanish. He originally started broadcasting for Minor League games affiliated with the St. Louis Cardinals. In 1946, he was promoted to radio play-by-play of the Cardinal games on the KMOX radio station. Buck's clever and unique poetic style succinctly informed listeners to the play-by-play calls for baseball, football, and hockey for 47 years. When he called Mark McGwire's single-season record-tying 61st run in 1998, he said, "Mike Morgan is the pitcher. Here's the pitch to McGwire . . . SWING . . . Looky there! LOOKY THERE!!!! Looky there! McGwire's number 61!!! McGwire's flight 61 headed for Planet Mars! History! Bedlam! What a moment! Pardon me while I stand up and applaud!"

He also called wrestling, boxing, and bowling. Buck was a talented national sportscaster who received countless awards, including the Ford C. Frick Award for broadcasting from the National Baseball Hall of Fame in 1987 and the Pete Rozelle Radio-Television Award from the Professional Football Hall of Fame in 1996. He was also named Missouri Sportscaster of the Year 22 times, among many other important accolades. There is a bronze statue of him at the Busch Stadium in St. Louis, a highway section named after him, and a new bridge on the Mississippi River that will also be named in his honor. (Courtesy of John Francis Buck.)

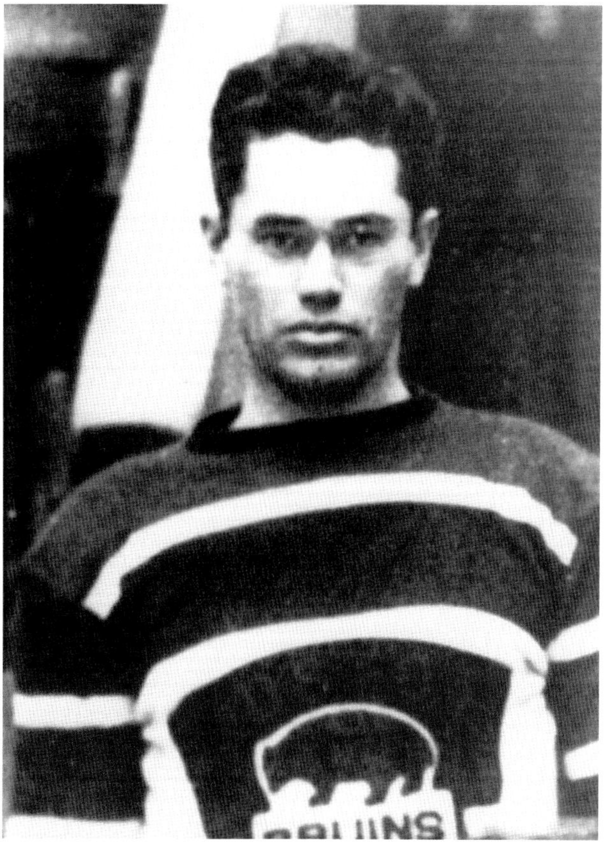

Pierce George "Gerry" Geran (1896–1981)
Geran was the first player from the United States to make the National Hockey League in the 1917–1918 inaugural season with the Montreal Wanderers. After playing in four games with the Montreal Wanderers the arena was destroyed by a fire and the team disbanded. At the 1920 Summer Olympics in Antwerp, he won a silver medal with the (11 member) US hockey team. In 1925, he played in 37 NHL games with the Boston Bruins. He scored 5 goals and six points. (Courtesy of the Hockey Hall of Fame.)

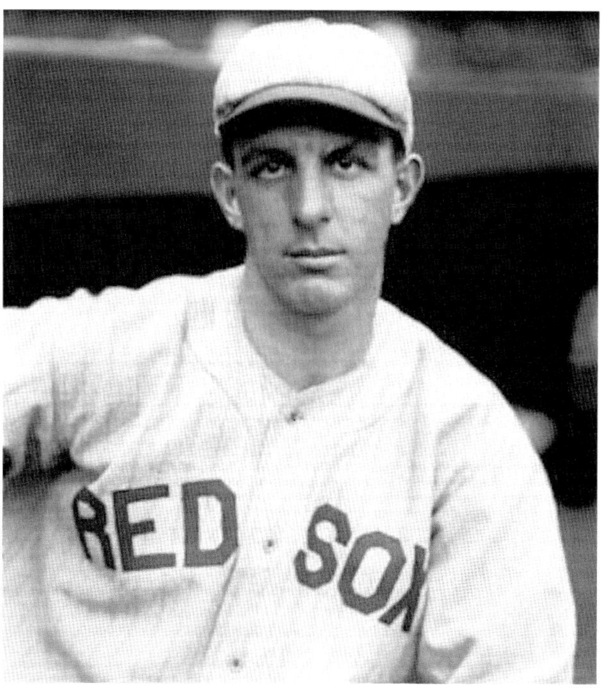

Joseph Earl "Scootch" Lucey (1897–1980)
Lucy played for the New York Yankees in 1920 as a pitcher and a shortstop. He went on to pitch seven games, including two starts for the Boston Red Sox in 1925. He batted and threw right-handed. He was a .111 hitter (2-for-18) in 13 games. As a pitcher, he posted a 0-1 record with a 9.00 earned run average in 11.0 innings of work. He was 6 feet tall and weighted 168 pounds. He also served in the US Army, was a member of the Holyoke School Committee, and ran for mayor in 1939. He was the head of US Internal Revenue Service's Western Massachusetts Regional Office and was a city treasurer for Holyoke from 1944 to 1972. (Courtesy of Harry Craven Jr.)

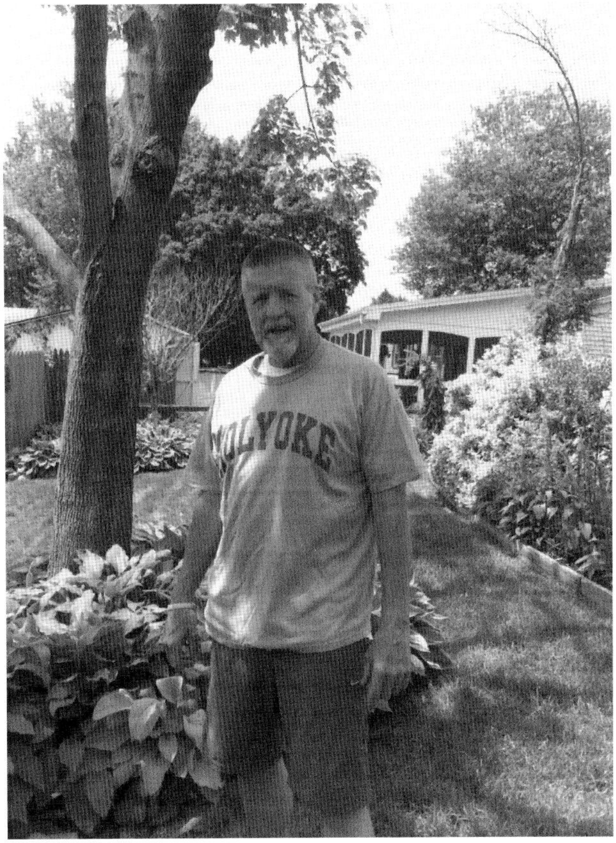

Bill "Kaner" Kane (1949–)
The son of a factory worker and a compassionate nurse, Kane grew up in Holyoke on Brown Avenue, attended Holyoke High School, and graduated from Westfield State College. He was a student teacher at Holyoke High School and taught in Greenfield for a few years. In 1974, he returned to Holyoke High School to teach a popular science class and coach a ski team. Within a year or so, he started coaching cross-country and track with his wife, Eileen, a successful coach in her own right. On April 12, 2007, after coaching the Holyoke Purple Knights for 30 years, he was awarded the Massachusetts Track & Field Coach Hall of Fame Award. Upon receiving the award he said, "I've tried to teach them a little bit about this sport and an awful lot about society's loftiest ideals, like brotherhood and sportsmanship and perseverance. It has been about celebrating the unbridled thrill of life's victories and getting through the crushing pain of life's defeats—about winning with humility and losing with dignity." "Do your best [DYB]" was his coaching motto. One of his students, Rafael Santos, wrote in a card congratulating him on the award and said, "I hope to follow in your footsteps and continue your legacy." He thanked him once again for being a great coach and beloved father figure. Another student, Chris Rigali, wrote, "He was professional, caring, just and forgiving all at once—qualities I believe are necessary for a high school coach to have." The Massachusetts State Track Coaches Association (MSTCA) received 17 reference letters for his candidacy, which is a MSTCA record. He was instrumental in building the indoor and outdoor track programs, and he helped design the Rogers Field Sport Complex at the Holyoke High School. He also officiated two Olympic Trials, the NCAA championships, and the Goodwill Games. In 1996, he proudly officiated the Atlanta Olympic Games and received the respected Joao Rodriguez Award from the Massachusetts Secondary Schools Athletic Directors Association (MSSADA) for his outstanding service to schools in 2005 and 2014. It is obvious that his parents instilled in him the importance of working hard with an even hand and an open heart. (Courtesy of Bill Kane.)

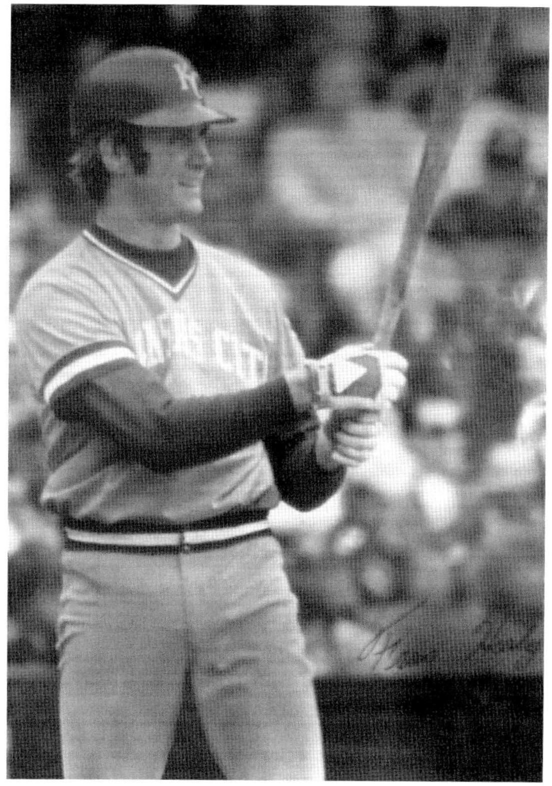

Fran Healy (1946–)

He grew up in Holyoke learning to play baseball from his father, Bernard, who played outfield in the Cardinals' Minor League team in the 1930s. After he graduated from high school, he signed a contract with the Cleveland Indians and earned a history degree from American International College in the off-season. The Kansas City Royals recognized his agility as a talented catcher and signed him in 1969. He was then traded to the San Francisco Giants, where he won the Western Division title in 1971. In 1976, he played for the New York Yankees and won the American League title and a World Series championship. Since 1978, he has been a sports broadcaster for major networks, including the Fox and MSG Network in New York. (Courtesy of the Healy family.)

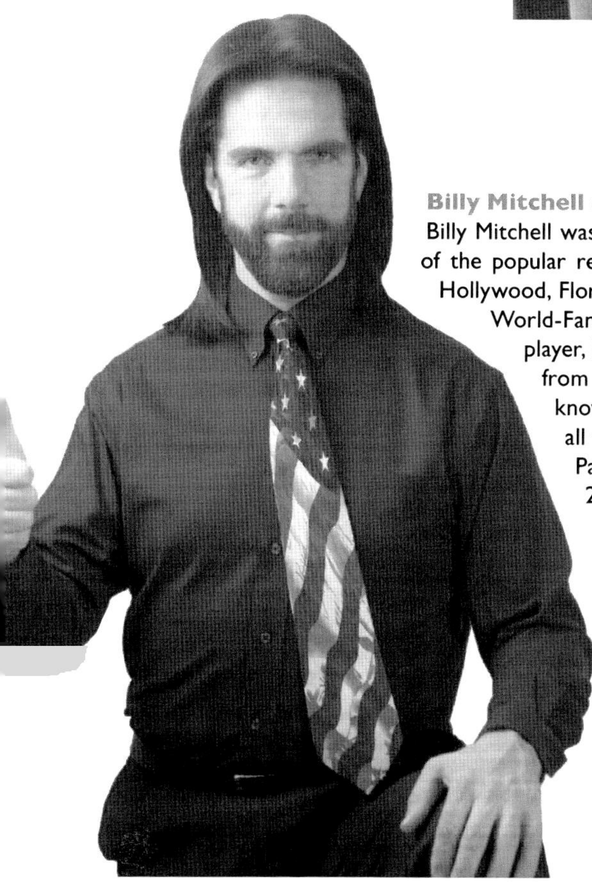

Billy Mitchell (1965–)

Billy Mitchell was born in Holyoke. He is the successful owner of the popular restaurant chain Rickey's Sports Bar & Grill in Hollywood, Florida. He sells a line of hot sauces called Rickey's World-Famous Sauces. He is an extreme video game player, best known for recording high scores in classics from the Golden Age of Arcade Games. He is also known as the greatest arcade video game player of all time. Mitchell played the first perfect score in Pac-Man and is featured with Steve Wiebe in a 2007 documentary, *The King of Kong*. (Courtesy of Billy Mitchell.)

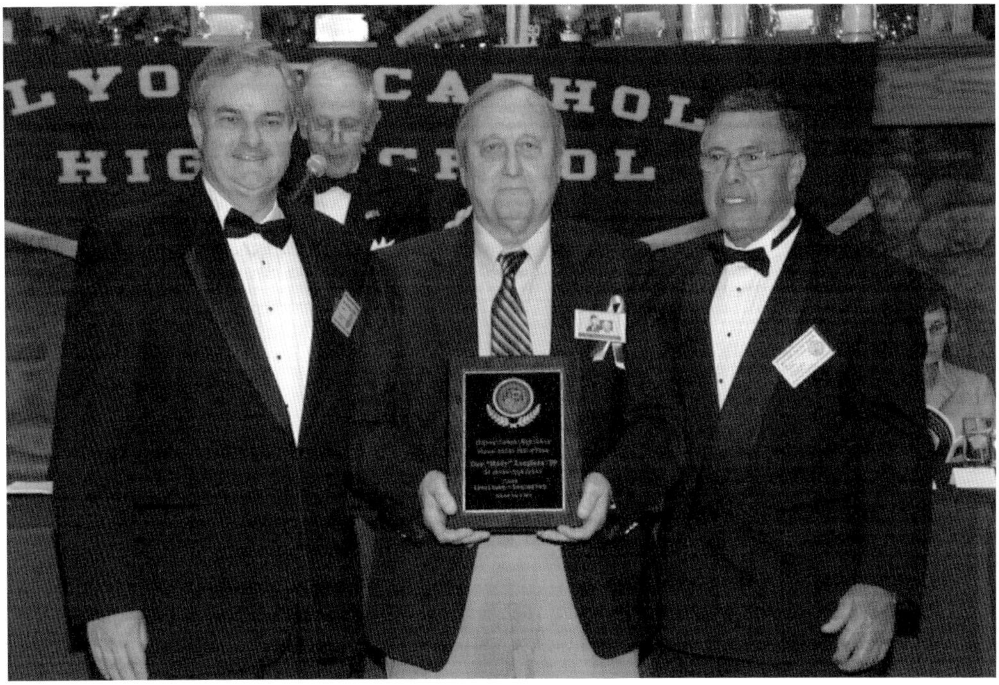

Daniel "Rudy" Langieza (1942–)
He was born and raised in Holyoke and was a member of the US Marines. In 1964, he became a coach of the Holyoke Catholic High School track and field team and continues today, 50 years later, to the delight of the athletes. He currently works for Chagrin Insurance Company in Holyoke. A former student, Dan Laprade believes that he is a remarkable man who has made a positive difference in the lives of athletes. He was inducted into the Massachusetts High School Coaches Hall of Fame in April 2010 in Randolph, Massachusetts. (Courtesy of Daniel "Rudy" Langieza.)

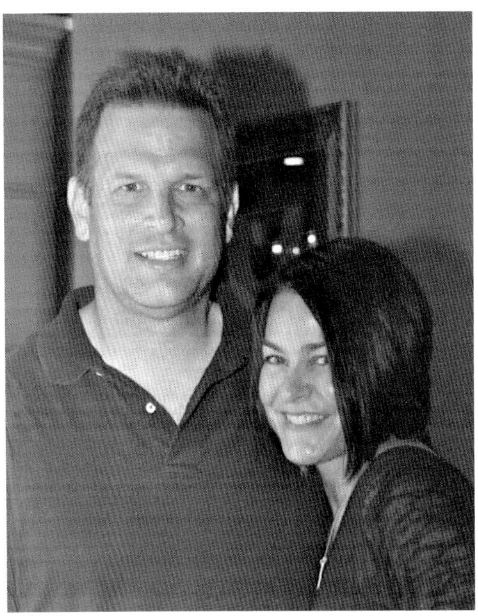

Mark Wohlers (1970–)
This former Major League Baseball player who won the World Series in 1995 with the Atlanta Braves was considered one of the best closers in the majors. He was a right-hander who played 12 seasons as a relief pitcher. Wohlers was known as the third-fastest recorded pitcher in baseball history, having thrown a pitch recorded at 103 miles per hour during a spring training session in 1995. In 2006, pitcher Joel Zumaya of the Detroit Tigers broke this incredible record with a 104-mile-per-hour pitch. (Courtesy of the Wohlers family.)

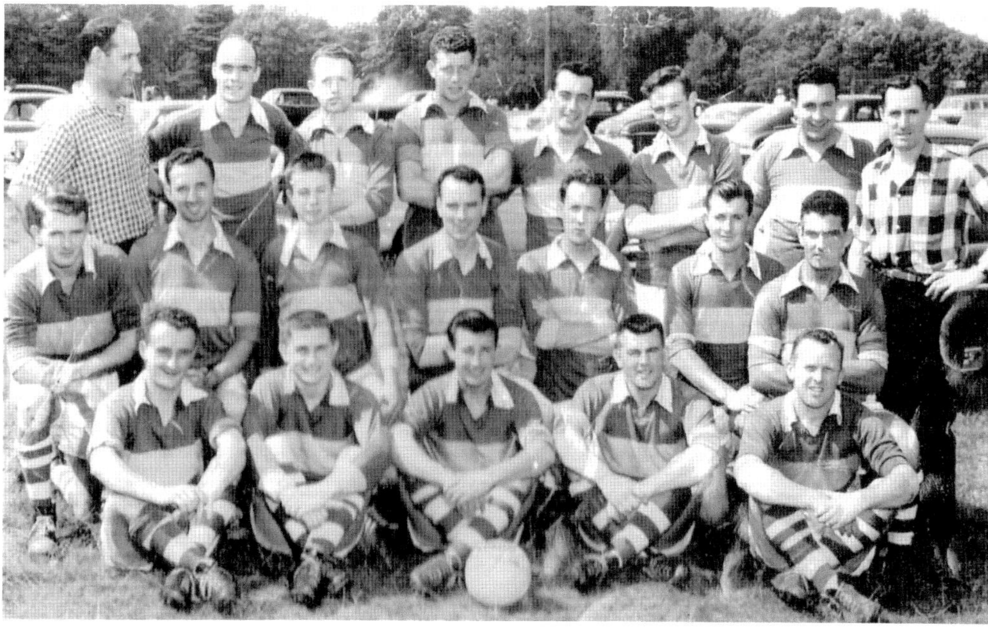

Thomas A. Sears Sr. (1935–) and Thomas A. Sears Jr. (1964–)
In 1960, Thomas A. Sears Sr. was the vice captain of the Gaelic football team in Springfield, Massachusetts, that won the 1960 Southern New England championship. In 1991, his son Thomas A. Sears, who was the captain of the Springfield Wolftones, also won the Southern New England championship 31 years later. (Courtesy of Pat Manghan.)

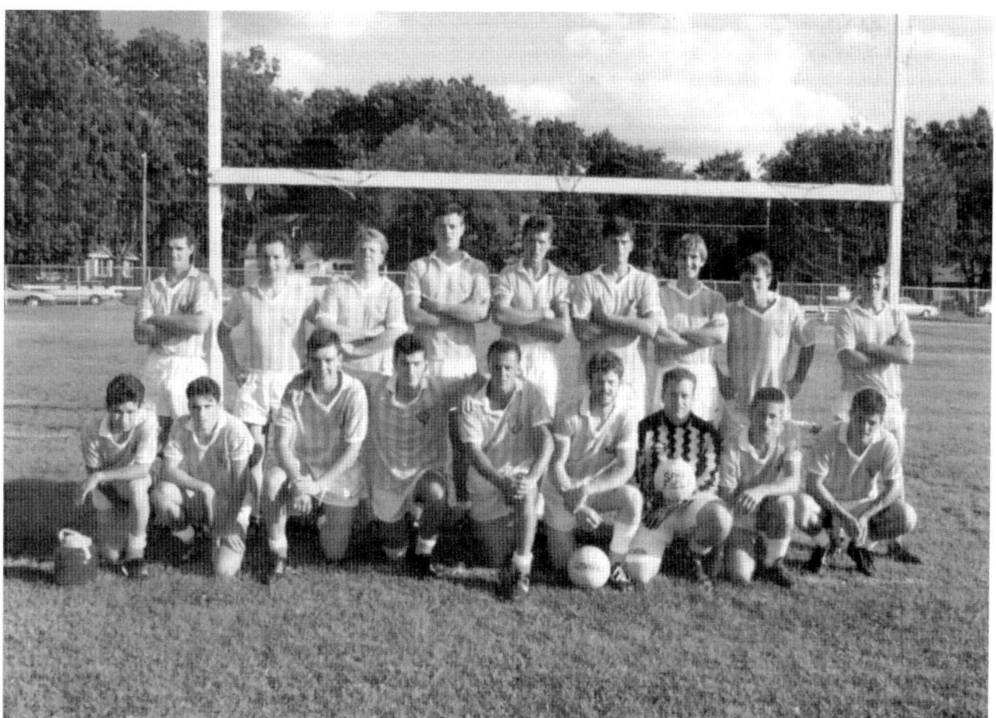

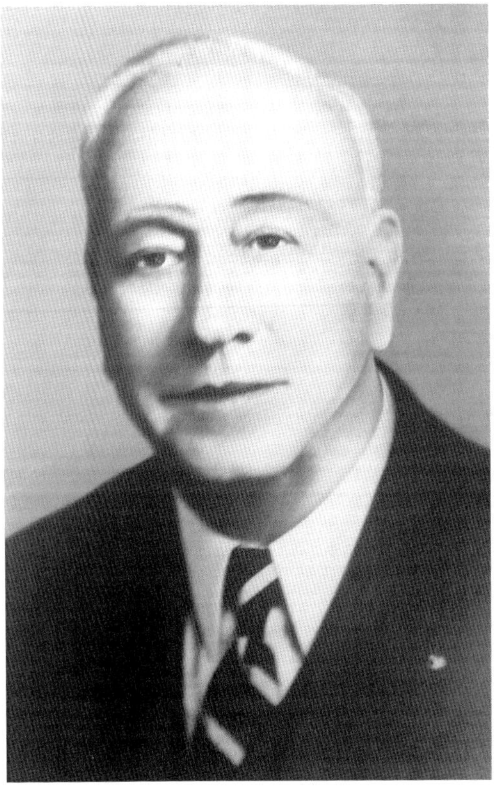

William G. Morgan (1870–1942)

He was born in Lockport, New York; attended public schools; and worked in his father's boatyard on the Erie Canal. In 1891, he entered Mount Hermon Preparatory School in Northfield, Massachusetts, where he befriended James A. Naismith, who would eventually create the game of basketball. He encouraged Morgan to attend the International Young Men's Christian Association Training School in Springfield, Massachusetts (later Springfield College), due to his dexterity in sports. He played football under Alonzo A. Stagg, one of the "Grand Old Men of Football." When he graduated in 1894, he was hired to be a physical director of the Auburn, Maine, YMCA. After a year in Auburn, he took a comparable position in Holyoke. In 1895, he realized that some of the games, including basketball, were too hard for local businessmen to do, so he improvised and came up with a game called "mintonette." He borrowed from established sports at the time including the size of a basketball, nets from tennis, playing off walls and overhangs from handball, and baseball for the innings. It was a success and won an audience at the YMCA Physical Director's Conference in Springfield, Massachusetts, the next year. Dr. Alfred Halstead, a Springfield College professor, suggested he call the game *volleyball* instead of mintonette. The new name was popular, and it became the norm. Today, the game is played throughout the world because of Morgan's tenacity, imagination, and forethought. He realized how important it is to stay healthy and the benefits from exercise. There is an International Volleyball Hall of Fame in Heritage State Park in Holyoke. (Courtesy of the Volleyball Hall of Fame.)

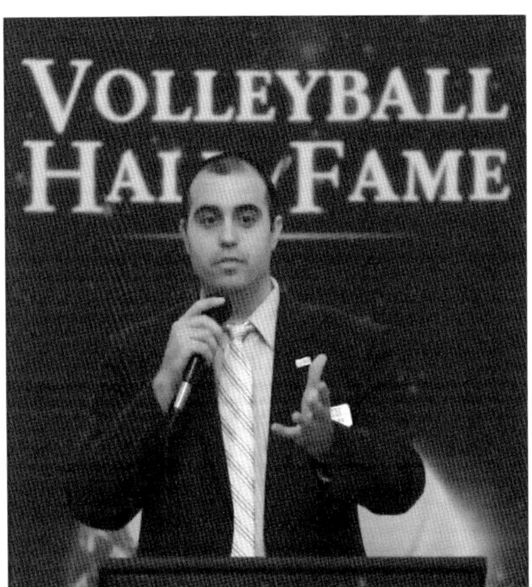

George Mulry

He grew up in Holyoke; earned a bachelor's degree in sports management at University of Massachusetts, Amherst, in 2003; and established the Pioneer Valley Juniors nonprofit volleyball program. They won three New England volleyball championships under his leadership. He is a coach at the Longmeadow High School and has inspired the Lancers to win five league and sectional championships. He also coached Holyoke High School boys' junior varsity volleyball team and the Western Massachusetts Junior Olympic volleyball team, winning medals year after year. He is the current executive director of the Volleyball Hall of Fame and has received myriad of important professional awards as a coach, an official, and a player. (Courtesy of the Volleyball Hall of Fame.)

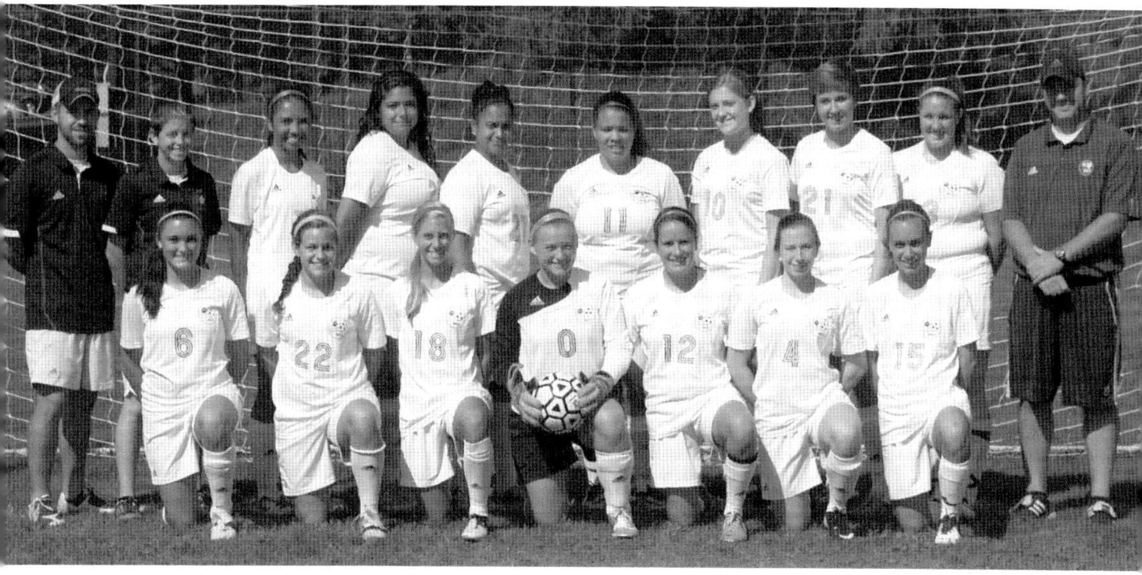

Holyoke Community College Cougars Women's soccer team
These amazing women captured the 2013 women's soccer third-place ranking nationally, the best finish ever in school history. They were also New England and district champions. (Courtesy of Holyoke Community College.)

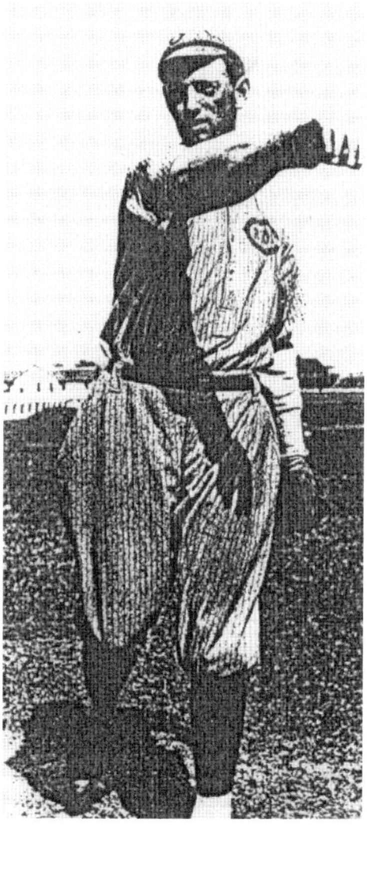

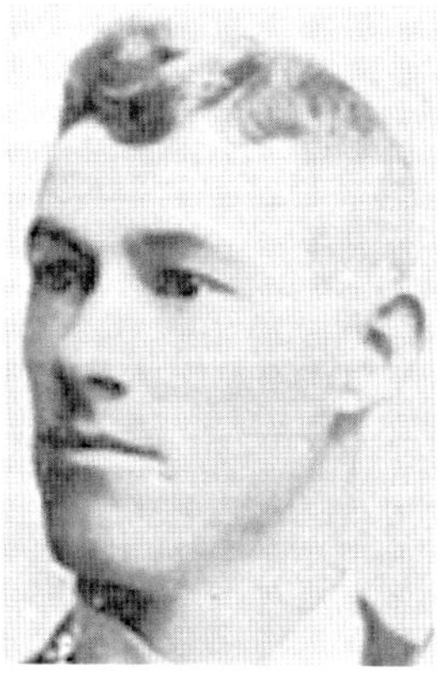

Thomas Jefferson "Buttermilk Tommy" Dowd (1869–1933)
He was Holyoke's first player for the Boston Reds in 1891. He was an American Major League Baseball outfielder and second baseman. He also played for the Washington Senators, St. Louis Browns, Philadelphia Phillies, and Cleveland Spiders in the National League and the Boston Americans in the American League. He was a right-handed batter with a career batting average of .271, and he stole 366 bases. He played until 1901 and then returned to Western Massachusetts to coach at Amherst and Williams College. He also studied law at Georgetown University. He passed away in an accidental drowning on the Connecticut River in Holyoke at the age of 64. (Both images courtesy of the Holyoke Public Library.)

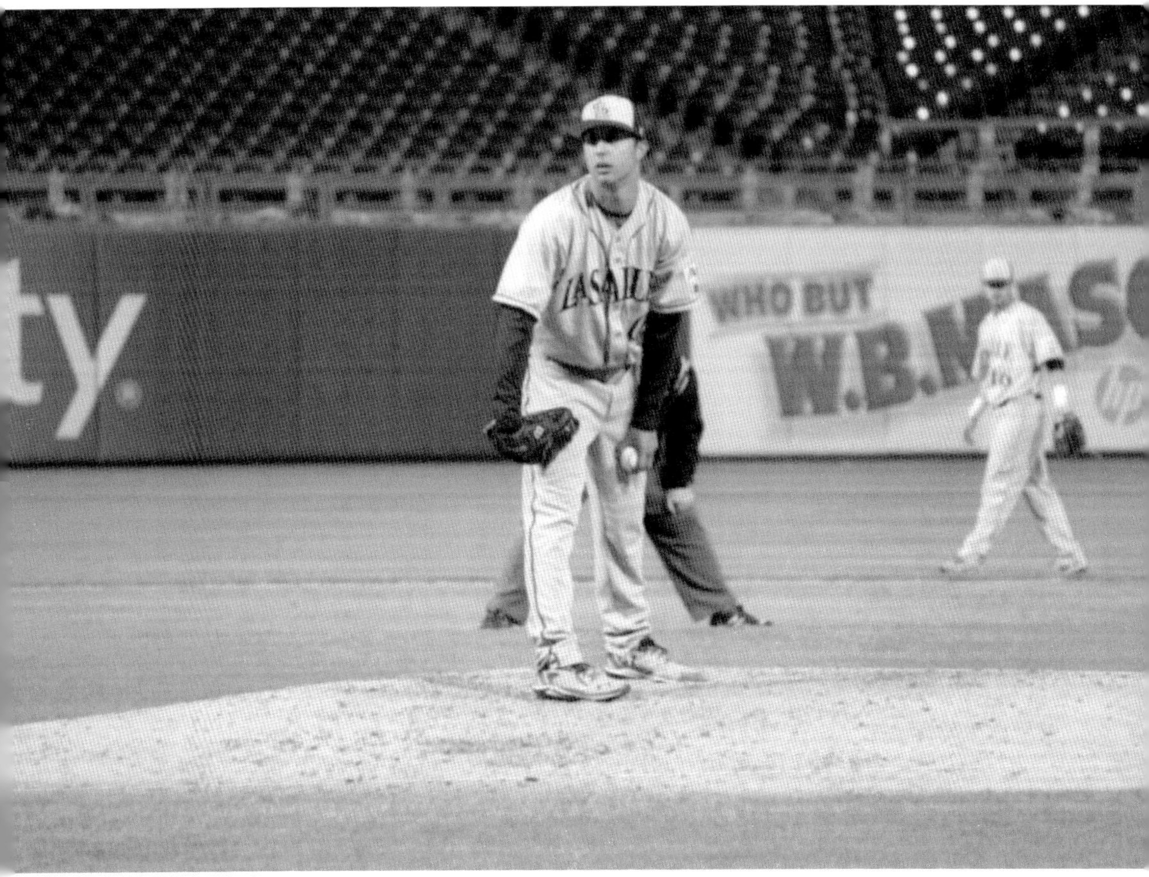

Freddy Andujar (1994–)

He was raised in Holyoke and was an outstanding athlete and student at Holyoke High School. He played Division I baseball his freshman year at the University of Hartford, Connecticut. He had to move back home with his parents because his scholarship did not cover all of his school expenses, so he attended Holyoke Community College, the Cougars, for his sophomore year. He is known as an ace Cougar pitcher and has been named a first-team All-American by the National Junior College Athletic Association (NJCAA). He was number one in the NJCAA Division III in strikeouts per game in the 2013 season, averaging 16.17; second overall with 97 strikeouts; and 39th in earned run average at 2.50. He was a team Most Valuable Player for the Holyoke Community College Cougars baseball team. His coach at Holyoke Community described Andujar as a "once-in-a-lifetime kid to come walking through here" and said, "Division I prospects don't usually wind up in our lap." This very talented 5-foot, 9-inch, 165-pound young man signed a letter of intent to play Division I baseball for LaSalle University in Philadelphia with a full scholarship. He is an honor student at Holyoke Community College with a 3.67 grade point average and is majoring in criminal justice. (Courtesy of LaSalle University.)

CHAPTER FIVE

Notable Businesses

To be successful, you have to have your heart in your business, and your business in your heart.

—Sr. Thomas Watson

Boty Almonte is a hardworking businessman committed to his family and friends, as is handyman, historian, and businessman Harry Craven, who continues to give back to Holyoke. Robert Grenier worked for years getting just the right shot and making his mark—like the Dwight family, who documented Holyoke's past and present with pen and ink. Jennifer and Kevin Chateauneuf are committed to keeping Nick's Nest a unique destination, as Romeo Grenier did in the Odyssey Bookshop that he opened in 1963. Morton "Morty" Haberman's hearty smile and knowledgeable advice made even a broken or lost part seem insignificant. John Hazen, the technically adept owner of Hazen Paper Company, is putting the shine in advertising and moving Holyoke's youth forward. The amusing and creative Hebert brothers continue to entertain. William Rogalski makes all the difference managing the Holyoke Mall and encouraging children to be committed to their education. Rafael Fernandez keeps people coming back for more of his delicious food and his faithful commitment to the community. Somewhat like what Edna William's warm and inviting Log Cabin restaurant did for the community. Charlene Fantakis, owner of Manny's Pizza, supplies people with a smile and a helping hand. Whether on foot or on his bike, Craig Della Penna always shows people the best in the Pioneer Valley. Hidden in James Curran's The Wherehouse? Building or displayed on a wall, Holyoke's amazing past is safe and sound. In Charles Dinn's eyes, his popular trophies made people all worthy of award, as Jacob L. Barowsky's cleaning solvent LESTOIL assured people that the attire was neat and clean. All of these businessmen and businesswomen have served the community well and have left an indelible mark on the city of Holyoke.

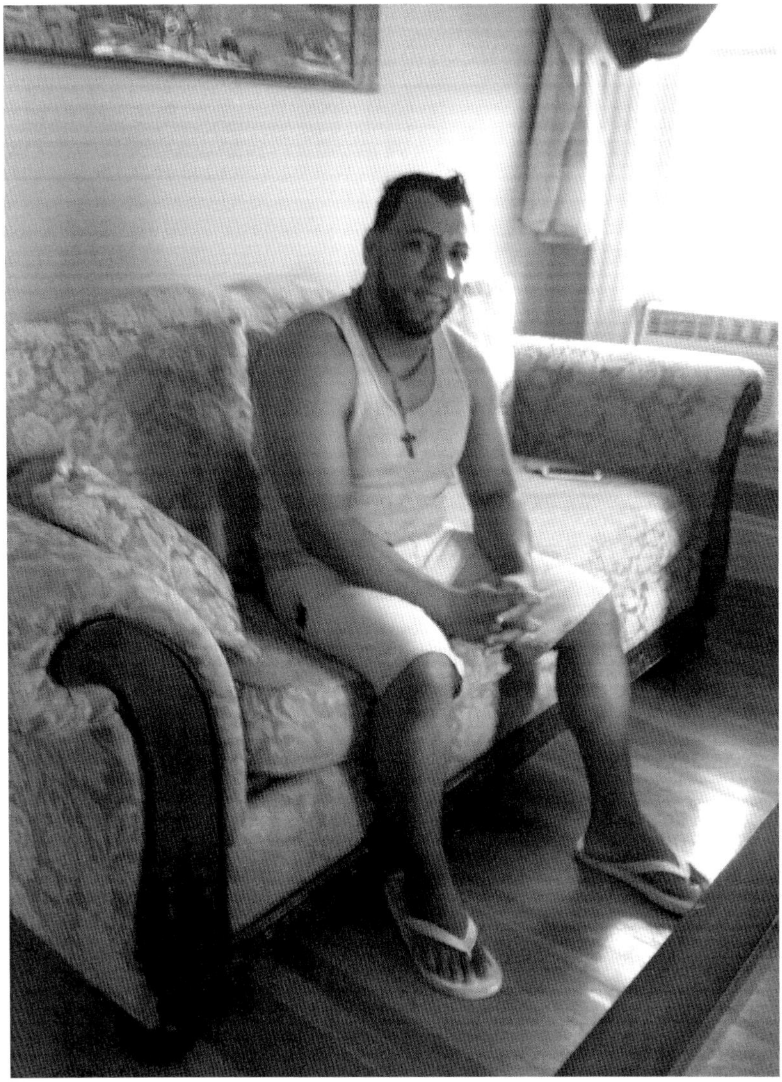

Boty Almonte, Almonte Market

Boty Almonte is from the beautiful Dominican Republic. Almonte worked for his uncle in Verns Market in Springfield until 1997 when it was destroyed by a fire. He and his brother Hose opened the Flats Market; unfortunately, this market also sustained water damage from a fire. They lost everything, but the community rallied around them, helping them to rebuild the new Flats Market. Almonte believes, "Our customers are our loving family, and that just because we had a fire, there is no truck dropping off money; we had to work hard and help ourselves." The Almonte brothers Hose, Rony, and Boty bought another store in Springfield called the North Bridge Mini Market. Today, Rony solely owns the store. Hose and Boty also bought a five-story building next to the fire-damaged Flatts Market that houses the new Flatts Market. In 2002, the two brothers opened up the Almonte Market on South Bridge Street, and in 2003 the Almonte Market 2 on Sargeant Street in Holyoke was opened, and the brothers purchased another store called Manny Market in Chicopee. Boty Almonte has come from humble beginnings and has succeeded beyond his dreams here in the United States. To him, his family members—especially his mother—are like a beautiful tree, all encompassing and loving, and no matter what happens to them they will always take care of each other. (Courtesy of Boty Almonte.)

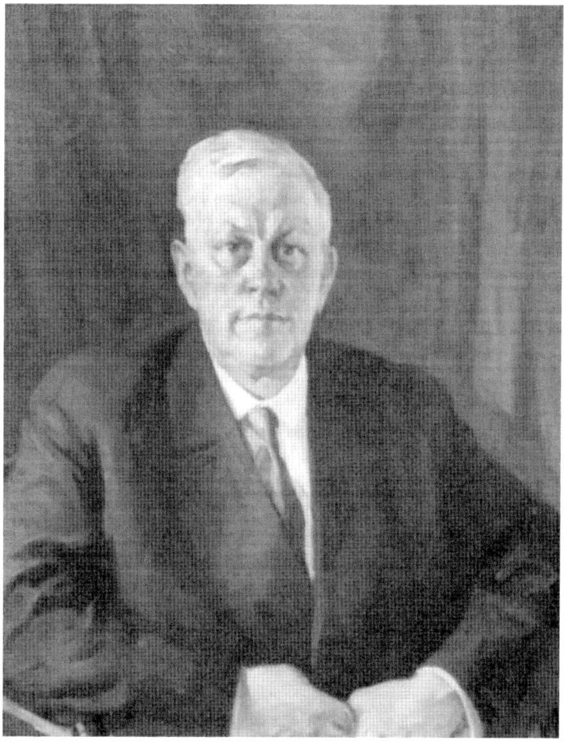

William G. Dwight, *Holyoke Transcript* Newspaper
William G. Dwight (1859–1930) was born in Bernardston, the former home of North Amherst in Massachusetts. He attended public schools and the Powers Institute and graduated from Amherst College in 1881. He bought half of the *Holyoke Transcript* newspaper with William Loomis in 1882, and in 1926 he completed the acquisition, changing the name to the *Holyoke Telegram* daily newspaper until 1993, when the paper was closed. The *Holyoke Telegram* covered the city of Holyoke and Hampshire and Hampden Counties. (Courtesy of the Holyoke Public Library.)

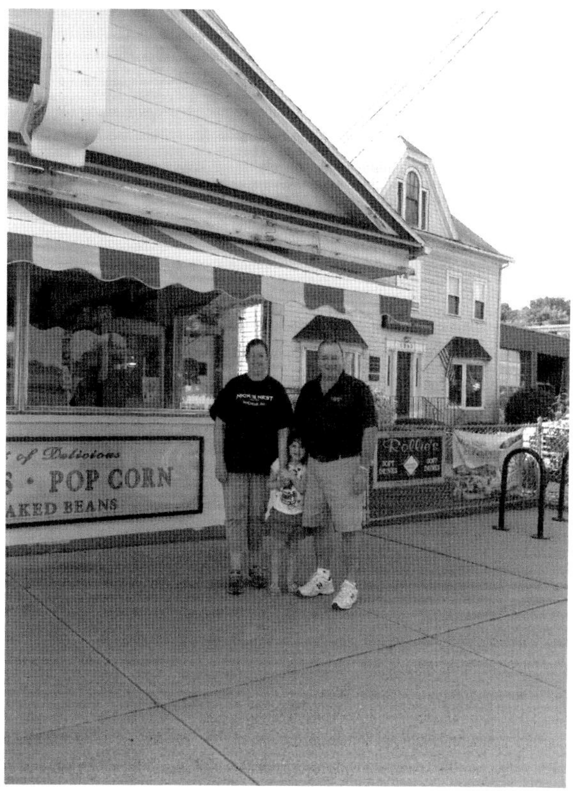

Jennifer and Kevin Chateauneuf, Nick's Nest
Jennifer (1972–) and Kevin (1962–) Chateauneuf both worked in the food business, and in 2005, they purchased a 121-year-old Holyoke institution, Nick's Nest, located on Northampton Street and originally owned by Nick Malfas. The legendary Malfas family built up a loyal clientele that still frequents the restaurant today. The Chateauneufs attribute their customers' loyalty to staying true to the original formula of the hot dogs and keeping the interior and the facade the same as it was the day it opened, including the whimsical miniature band in the upper left-hand corner and the quirky manual door opener. (Courtesy of Chateauneuf family.)

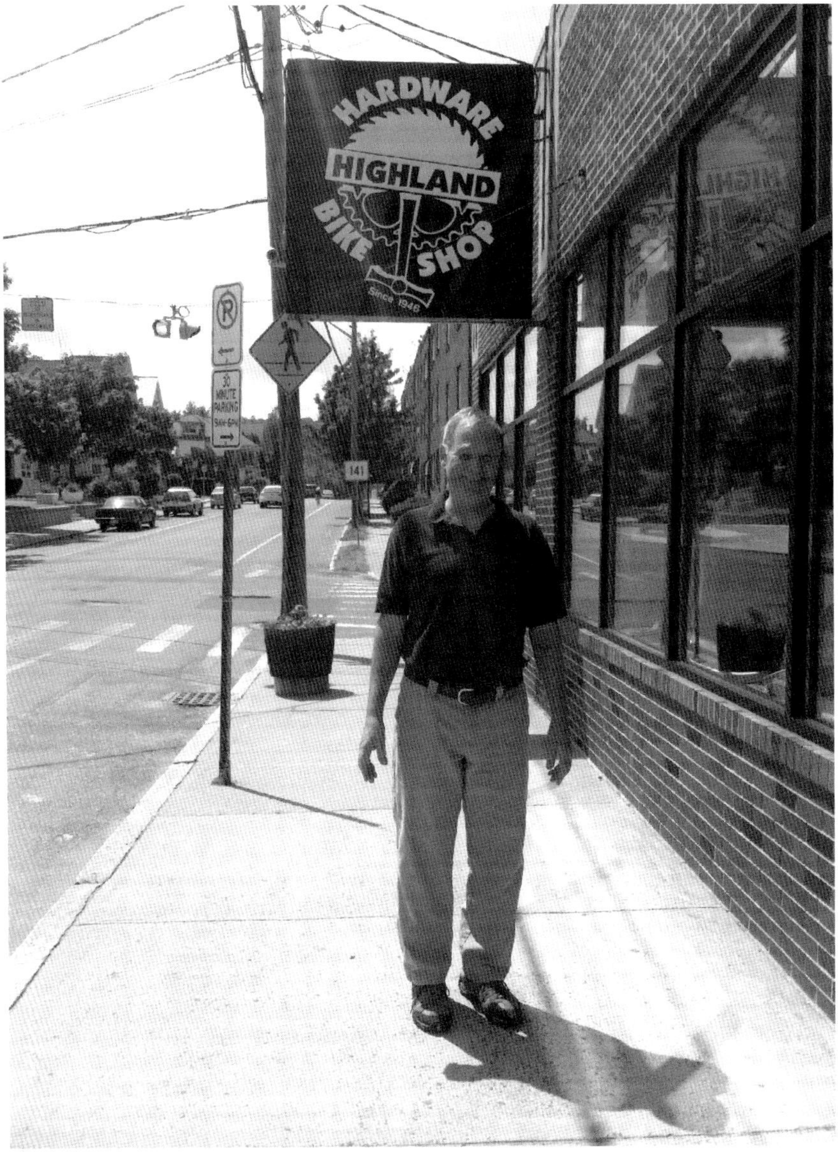

Harry Craven Jr., Highland Hardware and Bike Shop

Harry Craven Sr. opened the Highland Hardware and Bike Shop in 1946, and his son Harry Craven Jr. took over the business 20 years ago. He is a handyman, historian, a philanthropist, and an avid biker. Harry Craven Jr. supplies the community with a myriad of unique hardware and quality bikes. If you can't find a tool or the bike, don't worry. Harry Jr. or his sons will find it. Harry has made the store a place where the community comes together to appreciate the past. He has a unique collection of Holyoke memorabilia, including framed photographs and postcards of residents, landscapes, and historic buildings beautifully displayed throughout his store. In 2000, he was given an award from the Holyoke Historical Society for the preservation of Holyoke historical memorabilia, and in 2003 he was awarded a plaque from former mayor Michael Sullivan for the safekeeping and preservation of some rare Holyoke photographs and memorabilia. He also sells calendars that portray Holyoke's amazing past to benefit local charities. (Courtesy of Harry Craven Jr.)

Robert Grenier, The Greniers Studios

Robert Grenier (1929–) was born on a kitchen table in a cold-water flat with the help of two midwives on South Bridge Street in Holyoke. He is the 9th of 10 children. Grenier was a photographer, and his goal in his work was to find the essence of his subjects through the lens of his camera. In 1946, he worked for Lucien Ducharme in the Ducharme Market (among many other menial jobs) until Lucien's camera caught his attention. As his fascination grew, he worked long hours to save up money for his own camera. Finally, with camera in hand, he immediately started taking pictures of the kids on his block and selling the pictures for 50¢ each. While attending Holyoke High School, he was given a national photography award from the New York Institute of Photography. After graduating from high school, he went into the National Guard in 1948 and served for 10 years. In the same year, he opened the Grenier-Ducharme Studios with Lucien Ducharme. In 1956, the company was the first to use colored pictures in the Holyoke Catholic High School yearbook. In 1965, Lucien retired, and the business name was changed to the Greniers Studios. He and his clever wife, Helene, ran this professional well-liked local institution for 48 years. As a matter of fact, his children Larry, Dan, Marc, Chris, and Lisa were all instrumental in building the business. He was active in many organizations, including the Beavers Club, the American Cancer Society, and the Providence Ministries of the Springfield Dioceses, where he faithfully advocated for addicts and alcoholics and feeding the poor. He was awarded the 1979 Citizenship Award from the St. Patrick Day Parade Committee; the Sr. Agnes Broderick, of the Sisters of Providence (SP), Justice & Peace Award in 2003; and the Human Relations Award from the Greater Holyoke Council of Human Understanding and many other prestigious awards too numerous to mention here. (Courtesy of Helene Grenier.)

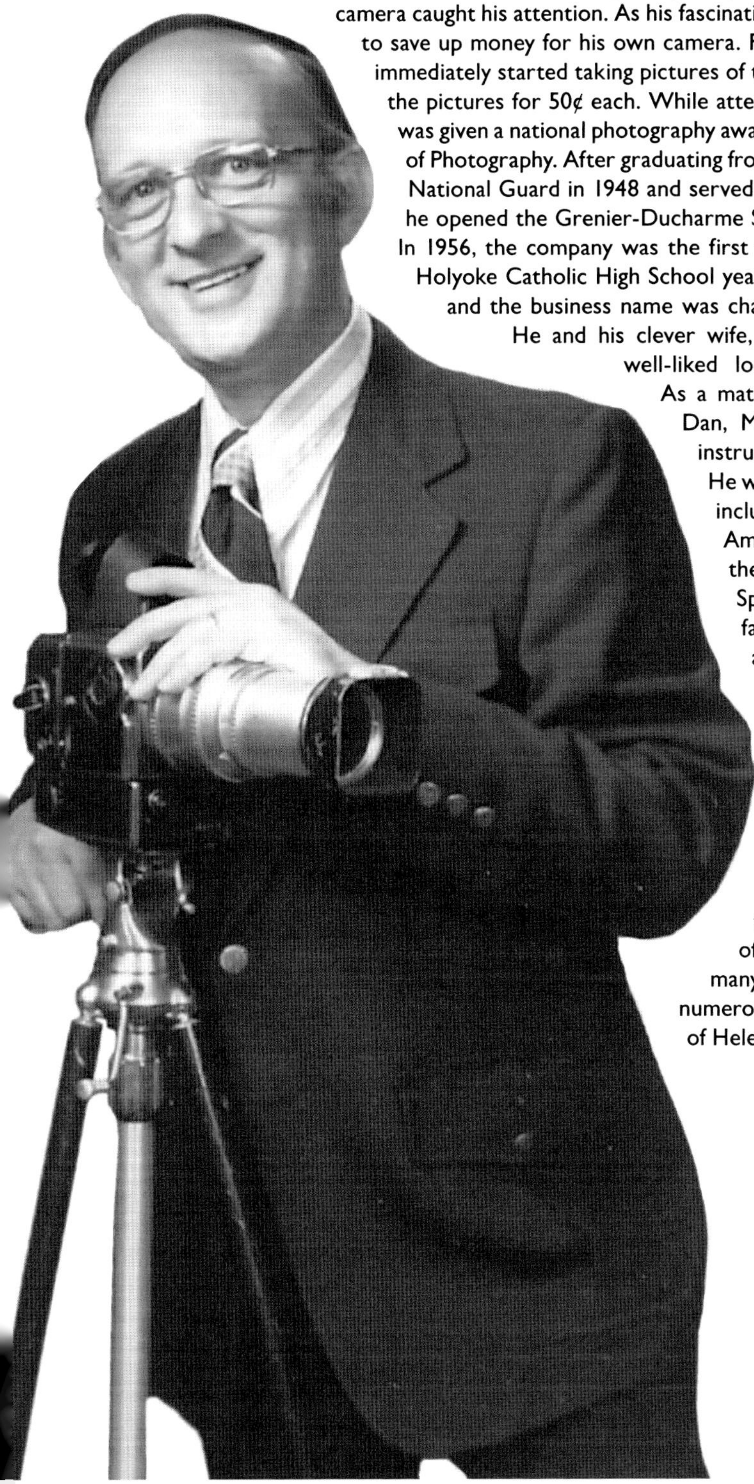

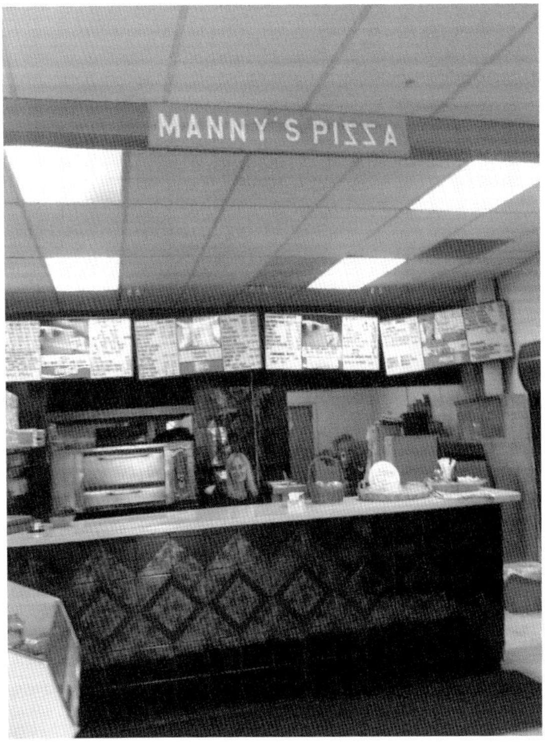

Charlene Fantakis, Manny's Pizza
Charlene Fantakis (1964–) and her husband, Evangelos "Van" Fantakis, (1965–2009) bought Manny's Pizza from Manny Murkoulakis in 1989; Manny originally opened the restaurant in 1975. In 2009, Van passed away from cancer, leaving Charlene to raise their children and run the restaurant on her own. Since that time, Manny's, a local institution, has thrived, as have her children. This courageous and generous businesswoman graduated from the University of Massachusetts and donates her time and food to the Westfield YMCA and other local organizations. She believes that "It's not just about making food; it's about the people, the customers." (Courtesy of Charlene Fantakis.)

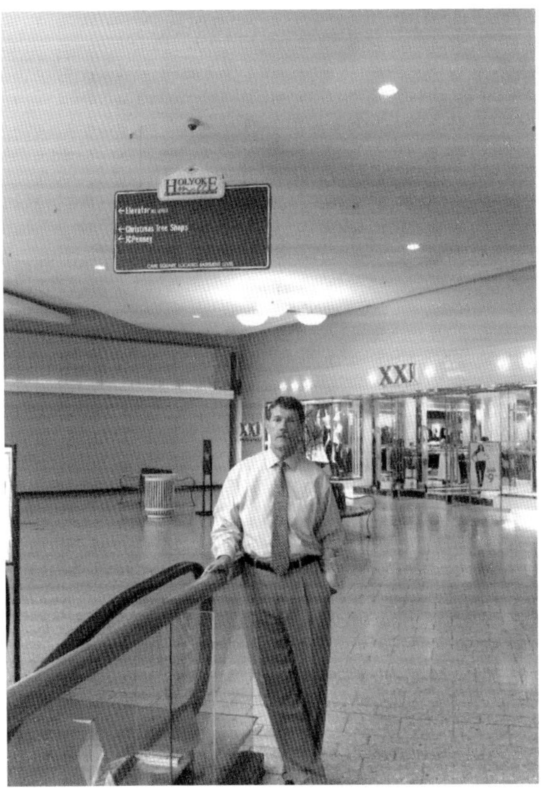

William Rogalski, Holyoke Mall at Ingleside
Growing up in Westfield, William Rogalski was always a hard worker. He earned his bachelor's of arts in marketing at the University of Maine in 1980 and went on to work at Windsor Marketing Group and then the Kasendorf Company. In 1985, he moved to San Francisco to help run a family business called Angeles Fruit Market. It closed in 2002. He started working at the Holyoke Mall at Ingleside in 2002 and has actively been helping people in Holyoke since then. He has served on the boards of the Holyoke Rotary Club and the Holyoke Visiting Nurse Association. (Courtesy of William Rogalski.)

Romeo Grenier, Odyssey Bookshop

Romeo Grenier (1910–1997), the brother of Robert Grenier, was a French Canadian immigrant who worked hard to purchase books to quench his inquisitive and fervent mind. He attended Holyoke High School and served in the US Navy during the World War II. He became a pharmacist and, in 1957, purchased the Glesmann's Pharmacy across the street from the prominent Mount Holyoke College in South Hadley, Massachusetts. As his customers waited for their prescriptions to be filled, he overheard their spirited discourse about some of the books they were reading and other poignant contemporary subjects. He realized that his customers would benefit from and appreciate a book department, so he purchased 500 Penguin titles for the drugstore. In 1963, the Mount Holyoke College community moved many boxes from his drugstore to his new store that was appropriately named the Odyssey Bookshop. In the 1980s, the store had two major fires. By this time, the store had become a popular meeting place and valuable resource for college students, the faculty of Mount Holyoke College, and the surrounding area. The community helped to rebuild the store, as did his dedicated staff. In 1991, Romeo's daughter Joan Grenier was instrumental in relocating the store to its current location in the beautiful Village Commons in South Hadley. Today, the Odyssey hosts over 150 author events a year, provides textbooks for Mount Holyoke College, and offers a highly regarded Signed First Edition Club. The store maintains a full-service website and provides an extensive selection of books and gifts. If Grenier could see now what he began over 50 years ago, he would marvel at how the Odyssey Bookshop provides the community with an impressive selection of books filled with knowledge that would take a lifetime to read. Through his hard work and unyielding dedication, he made it possible for all inquisitive minds to read and behold. (Courtesy of Joan Grenier.)

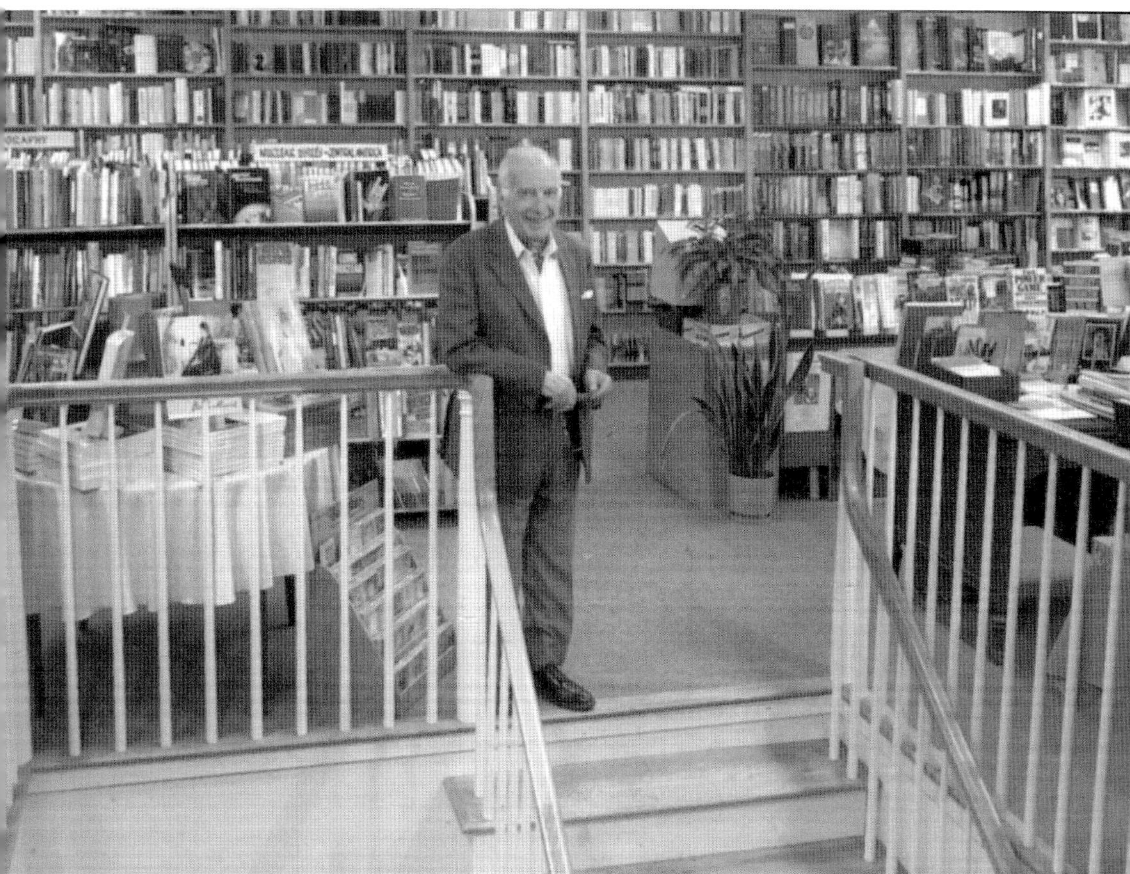

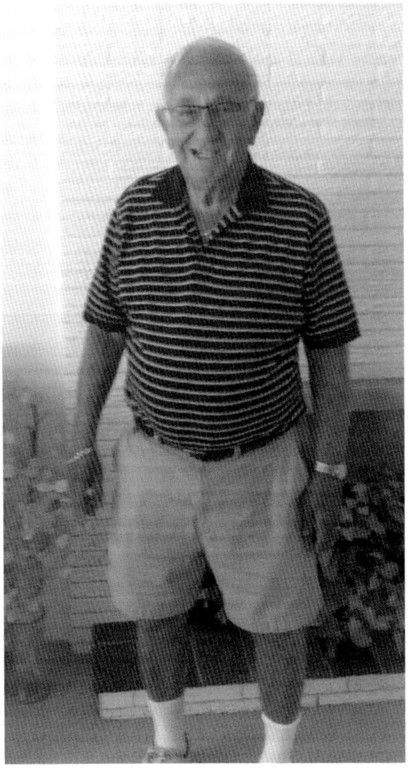

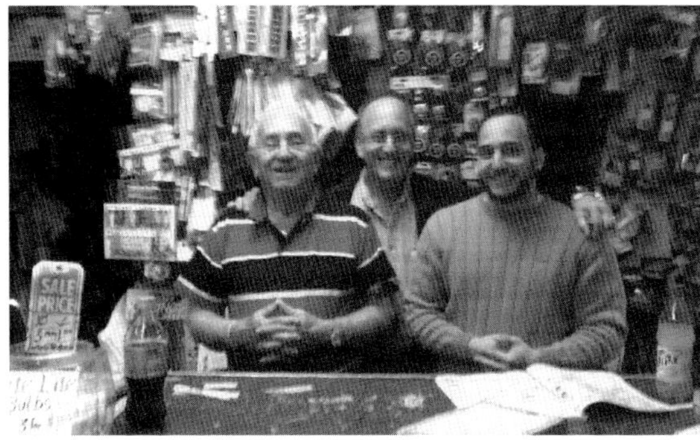

Morton Haberman, Haberman Hardware Corp.

Morton "Morty" Haberman (1929–) is the son of Esther Smargonsky and Russian-born Herman Haberman. The Haberman Hardware Corp. has become a local intuition. Employees help customers with a smile and the famous Haberman motto, "We got it, if we can't find it, then it's just not available." They had some hard times over the years, including a devastating fire in 1968. Haberman's son Hal, the president of the company today, continues his father's distinctive customer service and dedication to the community with a smile and a helping hand. The Habermans contribute to the Diabetes Association. (Courtesy of Morton Haberman.)

John Hazen, Hazen Paper Company

John and Maria Hazen established the Hazen Paper Company in 1925. They passed the company down to their son Thomas N. Hazen and his cousin Edward, also known as "Ted," who operated the company for 40 years. Today, John Hazen (1961–), the current president, runs the company with his cousin Bob. Hazen Paper is a world-class paper convertor that specializes in custom holographic originations, film, foil, and paper laminations. The Hazen Paper Company offers the Holyoke Public School System the World Is Our Classroom, Inc., program, which encourages children to think about mathematics, technology, engineering and science in real time. (Courtesy of John Hazen.)

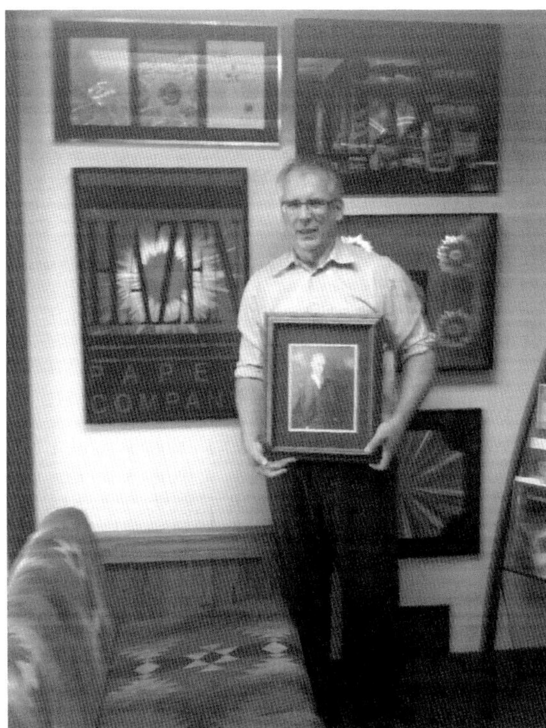

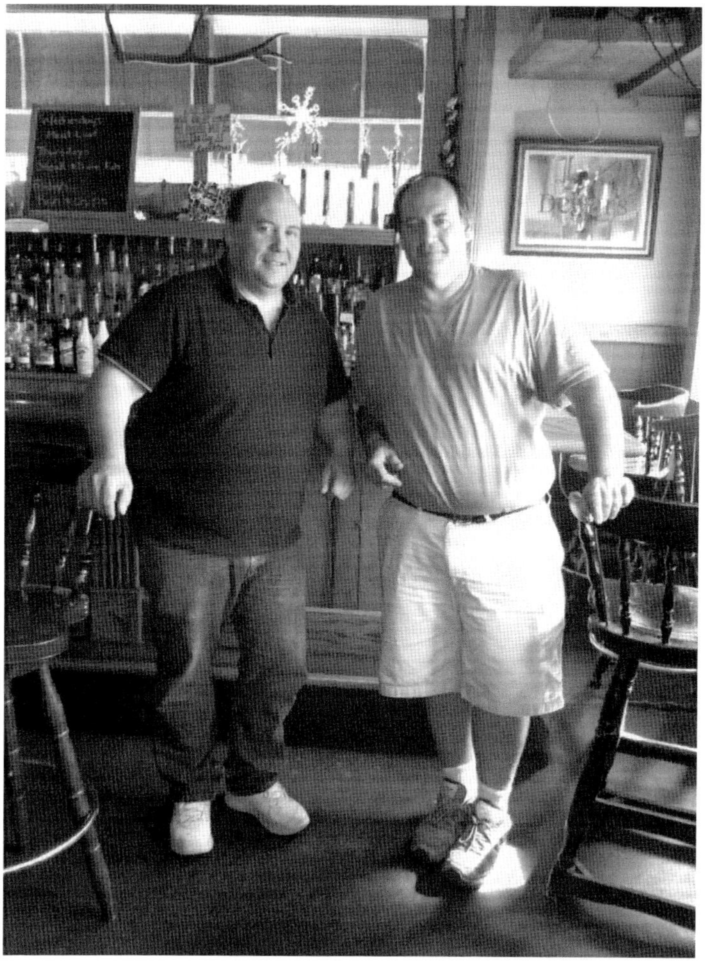

Hebert Brothers, Pioneer Valley Amusement Company
Marc (1957–), Jay (1961–), and John (1964–) Hebert (pictured on the left) have been successfully running a business since 1986 in an old manufacturing warehouse on Cabot Street in Holyoke. While Marc has gone on to other endeavors, his brothers Jay and John continue to run the Pioneer Valley Amusement Company that their father, Roland, started in the 1950s. He originally sold snacks such as peanuts and popcorn; today, they primarily sell jukeboxes and pool tables. In 1995, Jay began brewing his own beer as a hobby. Within a year, he had transformed the fifth floor of his warehouse into a federally and state-approved microbrewery. In November 1996, the Paper City Brewery brewed its first beer called Holyoke Dam Ale, in honor of the dam that was built in 1901 that still provides ample power to the city of Holyoke today. They also have historical Holyoke names for their brews, such as Ireland Parish Golden Ale and Riley's Stout. Tapping into another historical treasure, Jay and John are currently renovating and preserving the integrity of an existing theater in their Cabot Street Warehouse, where 3,000 employees of the Farr Alpaca Company manufactured wool. The owners of Farr Alpaca Company, Herbert Marshall Farr and co-owner Joseph Metcalf, provided their employees with benefits unheard of in the 1800 and 1900s, such as a stage/theater/cabaret space. The space has been used for women's basketball games, musicals, and as a skating rink. Currently, the Holyoke Community College Cultural Group utilizes the space. Today, these two innovative entrepreneurs have and continue to make a positive impact on the city of Holyoke by donating to Holyoke Boys and Girls Club, Wistariahurst Museum, the Holyoke Senior Center, and Holyoke High School. (Courtesy of the Hebert family.)

Craig Della Penna, Sugar Maple Trailside Inn

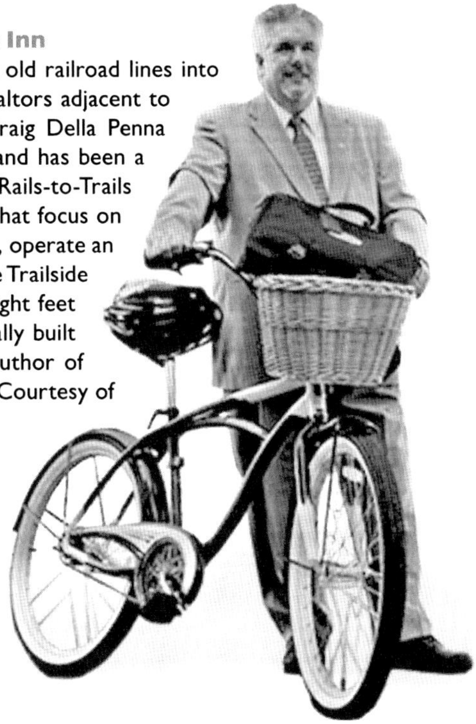

Combining his love for riding his bike, converting old railroad lines into bike trails, and selling real estate for Murphys Realtors adjacent to rail trails, greenways, and conservation lands, Craig Della Penna has succeeded in developing idyllic communities and has been a legislative agent and political organizer for the Rails-to-Trails Conservancy. He is the author of several books that focus on old rail line conversions. He and his wife, Kathleen, operate an 1865 restored bed-and-breakfast called Sugar Maple Trailside Inn in Northampton, Massachusetts. The inn is eight feet away from southern New England's first municipally built and operated rail trail. Della Penna is also the author of Arcadia Publishing's Images of America: *Holyoke*. (Courtesy of Craig Della Penna.)

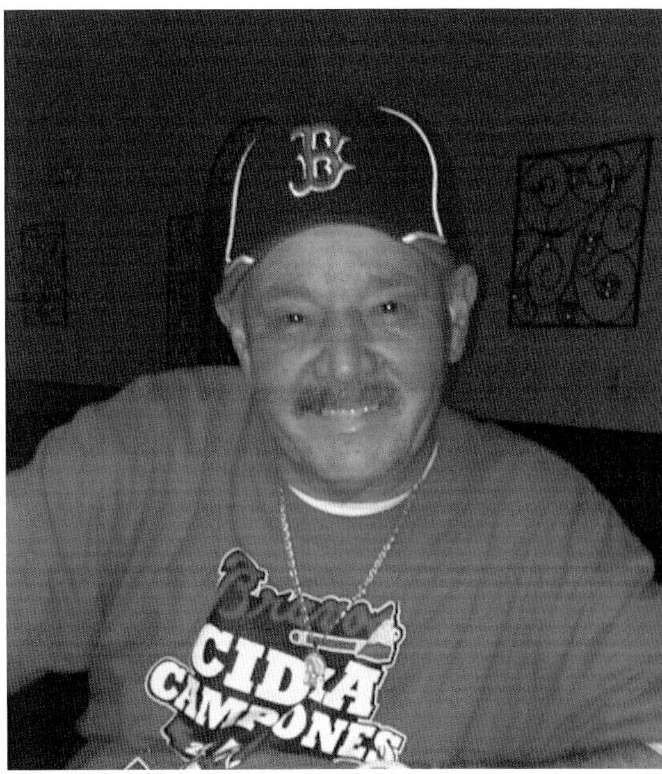

Rafael Fernandez, Fernandez Family Restaurant

Rafael Fernandez (1953–), owner of the Fernandez Family Restaurant on High Street, opened his ever-popular eatery in 1988 to the pleasure of Holyoke residents and surrounding communities. He has raised a hardworking family that has all worked in the restaurant at one time or another, including his daughters Jackie, Ada, and Iuy. Fernandez donates food to the homeless, especially at Christmastime. Recently, he opened another business in South Hadley, which is solely a banquet space specializing in wedding receptions, at his daughter Aida's direction. The Fernandez family proudly continues the tradition of bringing authentic Puerto Rican food to the citizens of Western Massachusetts. (Courtesy of Rafael Fernandez.)

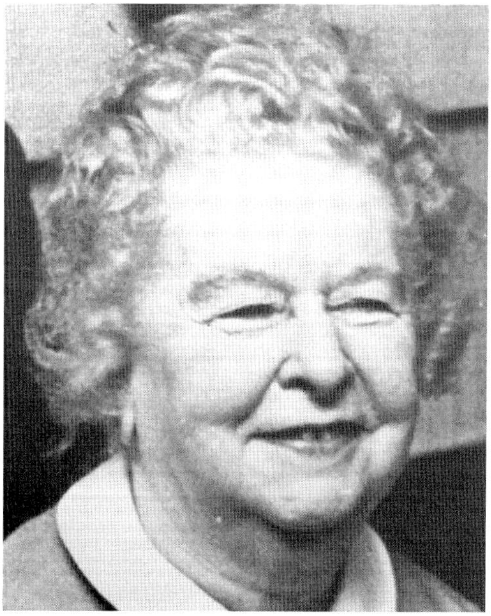

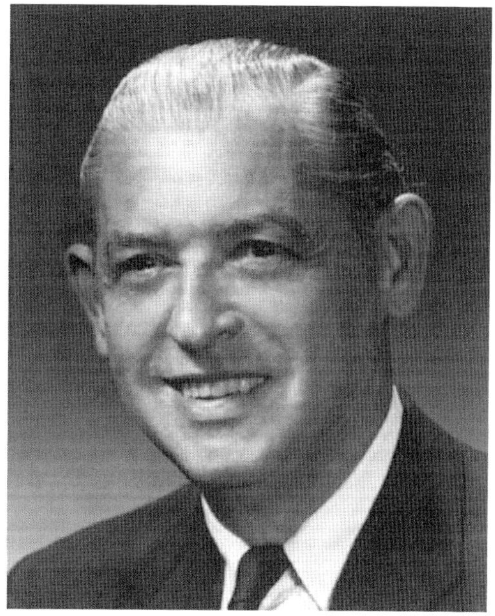

Samuel Resnic and Edna Williams, the Log Cabin Restaurant
Samuel Resnic (1899–1988) and Edna Williams (1903–1997) opened the Log Cabin Restaurant over a cup of coffee while sitting in Gleasons on Suffolk Street in 1953. They continued to meet at their new restaurant a few times a week for 30 years, discussing issues that would improve and sustain the popular restaurant. Resnic practiced general law, managed multiple properties, financed many important businesses, and served as mayor of Holyoke, while Williams, known to have a quirky sense of humor and a pleasant personality, ran the restaurant. Williams received the Holyoke St. Patrick's Parade Citizenship Award in 1975, and Resnic received the same award in 1968. The award is presented to a person or organization that may be of non-Irish descent that has made substantial contributions to the Parade and/or the Parade Committee. (Left image courtesy of Harry Craven Jr.; right image courtesy of Burton Resnic.)

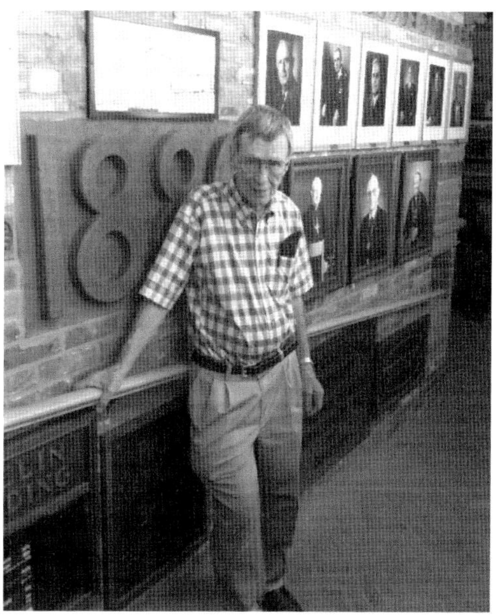

James Curran, The Wherehouse? and Curran Construction
Curran (1934–) grew up in Holyoke, graduated from the Holyoke Vocational School, and volunteered for the Korean War. Upon his return, he worked in the mills and for the Daniel O'Connell Company. He opened the Curran Construction Company in 1957 and The Wherehouse? in 1977. The Wherehouse? is a successful banquet facility and home to some of Holyoke's precious memorabilia, including signs, machines, facades of defunct businesses, and a very unique trolley car No. 144 and so much more. Curran has generously donated his heavy machinery, construction expertise, and labor to the city of Holyoke on numerous projects. (Courtesy of James Curran.)

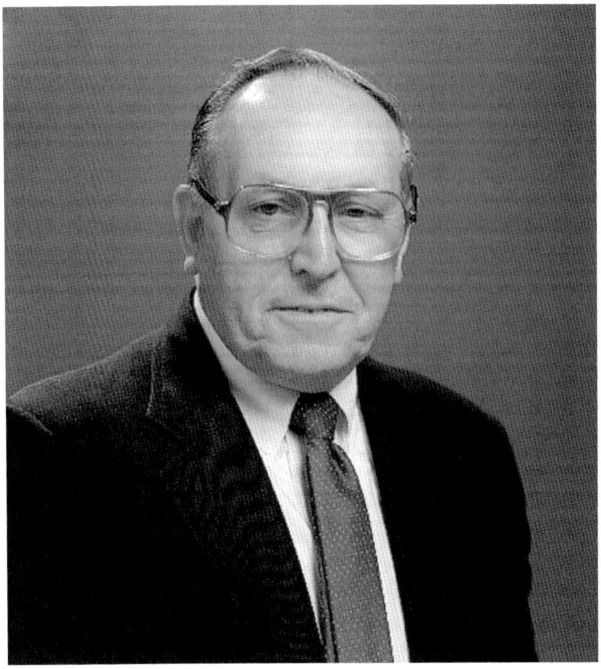

Charles "Bill" Dinn, Dinn Brothers Trophies
Charles "Bill" Dinn (1931–2013) grew up on Hillside Avenue in Holyoke. After graduating from Holyoke High School in 1950 and attending Bryant and American International College, he went into a business he never even considered until his brother was asked to engrave a trophy for a soldier at Westover Air Force Base in Chicopee. Together, they started Dinn Brothers Trophies. Today, after years of hard work and determination, the Dinn family continues to operate this fully automated and nationally respected business that has been going strong since 1956. (Courtesy of Paul Dinn.)

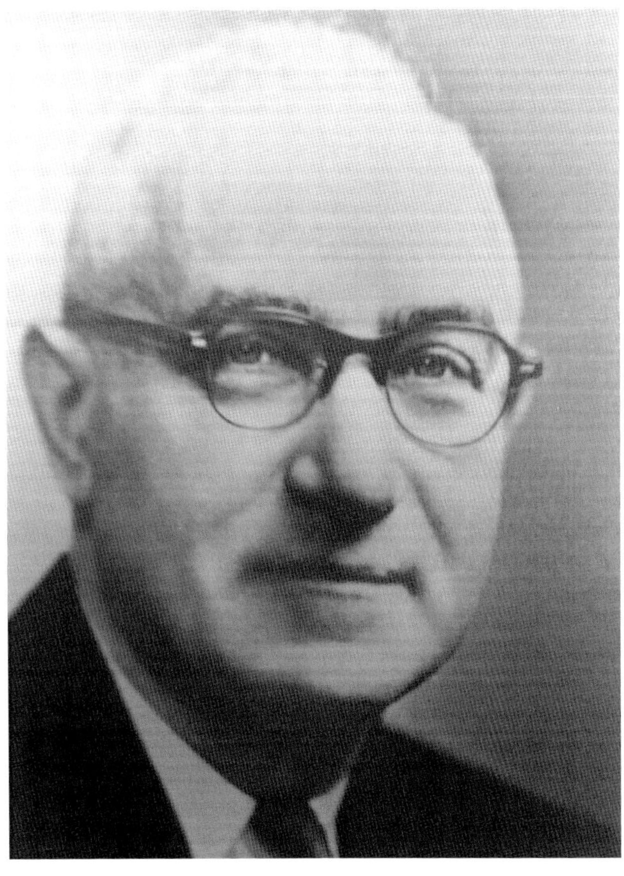

Adell Chemical Company
Jacob Barowsky attended Holyoke Public Schools and earned a bachelor's of arts from Harvard College. He worked in the paper mills, manufactured metal products, and sold real estate until 1927, when he started working with his brothers at General Cleaners and Dyers. In 1933, he formed the Adell Chemical Company and named his cleaning agent LESTOIL in 1936. He sold his company to Standard International Corporation of Andover, Massachusetts. He settled on the company due to its family-orientated policies and their promise to adhere to his company's management style and participation in Holyoke community affairs. (Courtesy of the Holyoke Public Library.)

CHAPTER SIX

Unique Artists

One ought, every day at least, to hear a little song, read a good poem, see a fine picture, and, if it were possible, to speak a few reasonable words.

—Johann Wolfgang von Goethe,
Wilhelm Meister's Apprenticeship

To be a talented artist one must be born that way, right? Maybe, but not necessarily, a person will never know until he or she tries, as they say. But what if it is just like learning another language? Art is a visual language, one of the heart and hand joined together through endless hours of passionate study and practice, one that the following artists have mastered on a legendary level. George Murphy lights up a room with his wit and good will, and Jim Donohue's clever combination of words and colorful lines delight and amuse our senses. Tom Browne, a professional whistler, had a talented mouth that has been heard by vast crowds, and Jerome Connor let his skilled hands chisel emotional features into stone. William Churchill Hammon has delighted countless audiences by playing his organ. "Ziegfeld girl," Eva Tanguay sang and danced her way into the hearts and minds of many. Jeffrey Bynes portraits are fresh and clean while his Holyoke shots are filled wonder and reflection. Raymond D'Addario photographed London for 18 months in World War II and documented the Nuremberg trials, while his brother Vincent D'Addario, who also had a professional career in photography, captured his subjects in the Western Massachusetts. Douglas John "DJ" Garritty is a sculptor who gives his subjects a voice and a prominent place on which to stand. Master painter Vitek J.P. Kruta has dedicated his life to creating, restoring, and teaching art. Mary Jo Maichack, an international award-winning singer storyteller and teaching artist, continues to touch hearts and tickle funny bones, while her very talented husband portrait artist, Gregory Maichack, teaches how to find the essence of subjects in the paint. Phillip de Fremery teaches his students how to express themselves through classical guitar at Holyoke Community College and surrounding institutions, and there is also the hilarious T.J. Jagodowski, a successful improvisational theater actor.

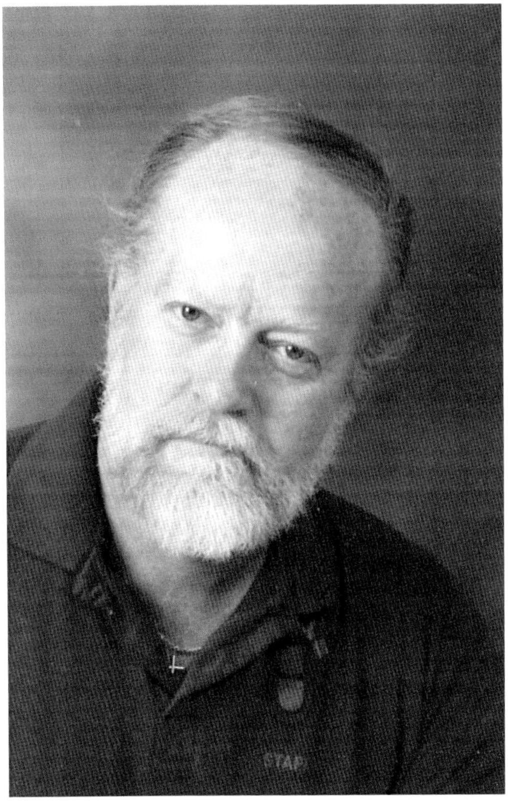

George Murphy
Born and raised in Holyoke, he attended Holyoke High School. He performed in community theater and in a role on the Emmy-nominated children's program called *Odyssey* on WWLP in the 1960s. He was the host for the popular show *Making it Here* on WGBY, a community-supported PBS member television station where he entertained and enlightened people with his whimsical commentary and insightful observations. (Courtesy of George Murphy.)

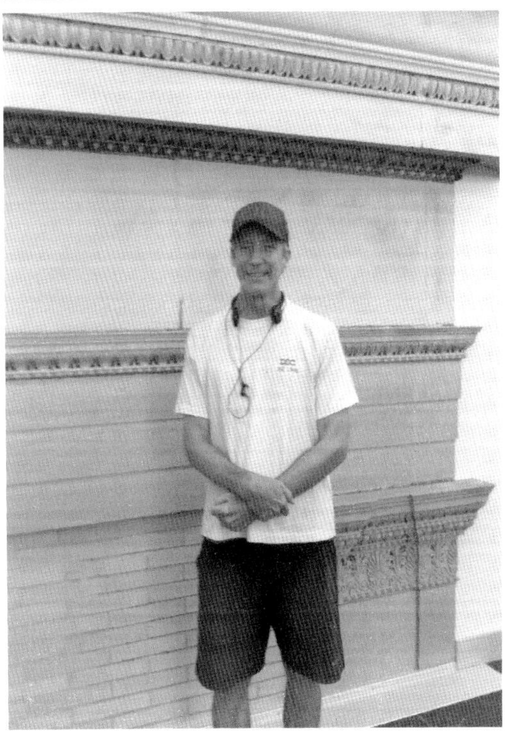

Jim Donahue (1949–)
Arriving in Holyoke in 1973, he taught English as a second language, beginning literacy, adult basic education (ABE), and pre-GED at the HALO (Holyoke Adult Learning Opportunity) Center in Holyoke. Since his retirement in 1994, he has frequented Holyoke Public Library, delving into a myriad of books utilizing his boundless language acumen to create fascinating cards that are filled with color and extraordinary associations of ancient dialogue and modern usage. (Courtesy of William James Donahue.)

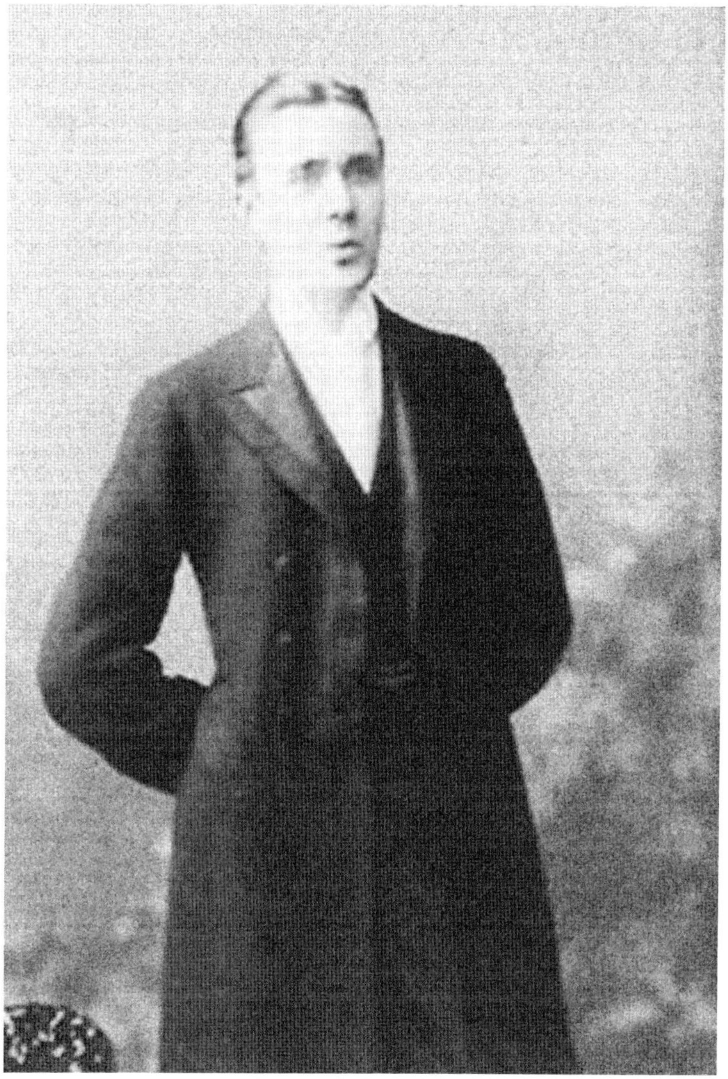

Tom Browne (1865–1912)
He was born in Adams, Massachusetts. His father came to Holyoke to find work when he was a child. After attending Holyoke public schools, he enrolled in the Hinman's Commercial School to better his bookkeeping skills. Utilizing his newfound accounting skills, he worked for a furniture company for 10 years, until his natural whistling talent took him in a whole new direction. In 1892, he initially worked with the Bryne Brothers in Eight Bells. After a year in the company, he was introduced to J.B. Carroll of Springfield and to Patrick Collins of Boston, who was the consul general to Great Britain. Soon after, he was contracted to tour through England and Europe and was invited to perform for the king of England who was the prince of Wales at that time. He performed throughout Europe, including Germany, France, and Switzerland. When he returned home, he became a member of the Zig Zag Company in a booth with Peter and Dan Daly and was in the Trip to Chinatown Company, which made a record-breaking run in the Madison Square Theater in New York. In his later years, he was engaged in vaudeville performances in Western Massachusetts. Browne was a well-liked man in the city of Holyoke whose engaging whistling still echoes through the streets of Holyoke today and beyond. (Courtesy of the Holyoke Public Library.)

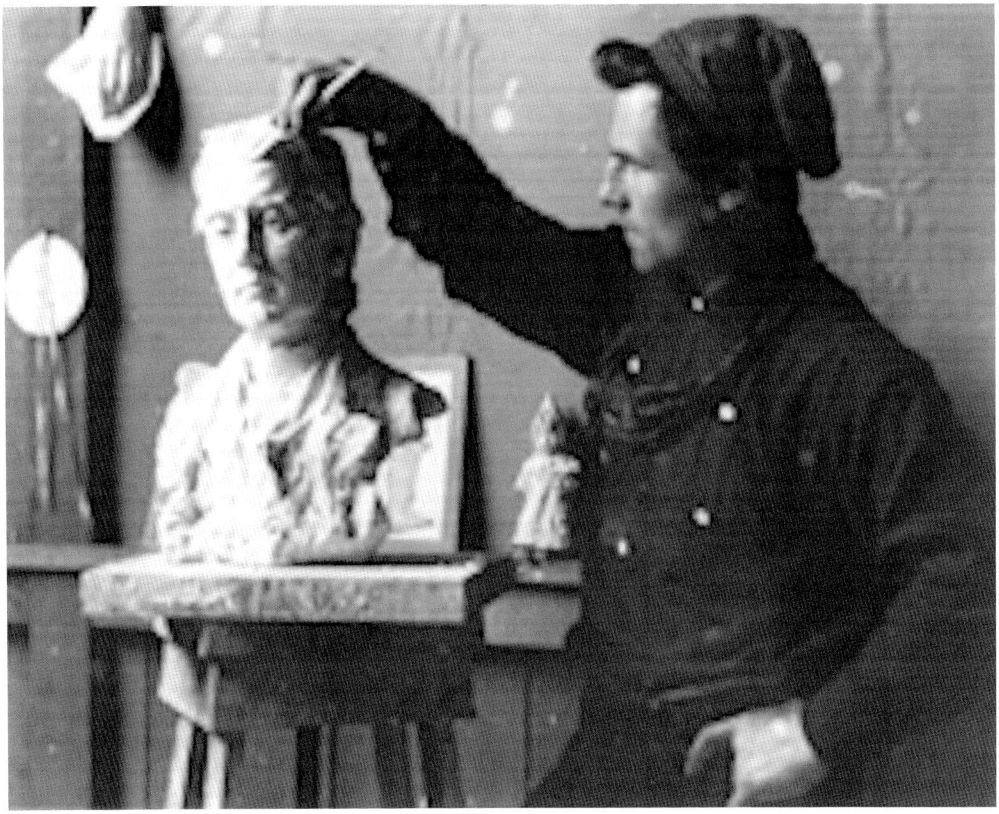

Jerome Connor (1874–1943)
Moving from his family farm in Annascaul, County Kerry, Ireland, at the age of 14 to Holyoke in 1888, Connor stated, "My father was a master of four trades, and it was the inheriting of those tendencies, along with a little extra will all my own, that enables me to do this work. I am self taught . . . when I was a boy I used to steal my father's chisels and carve figures on the rocks in Kerry." In 1899, he assisted in the manufacture of bronzes such as the Fountain of Neptune bronzes at the Library of Congress in Washington, DC, and the Civil War Memorial in South Hadley, Massachusetts. He went on to mold 200 of his designs, including small portrait heads to relief panels and large civic commissions of major monuments in the United States and Ireland. (Courtesy of Jerome Connor.)

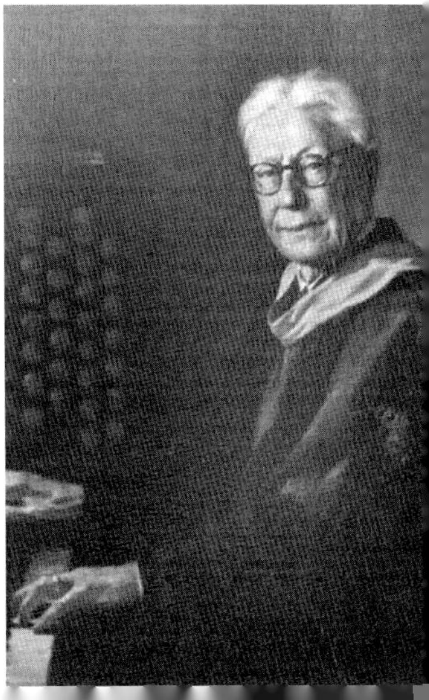

William Churchill Hammon
Holyoke was fortunate to have Hammon, a talented and generous organist. He was an outgoing, jovial organist for the Holyoke Congregational Church. Citizens from all over Holyoke came to hear him play. By the closing of the recital season of the spring of 1912, he had given 550 free public recitals. Some say that the recitals attracted some 250,000 people annually. He was the head of a college music department and would play the organ at both the Holyoke Congregational Church and at the Mount Holyoke vesper service on Sunday. He was also a teacher and in the choir administration. (Courtesy of the Holyoke Public Library.)

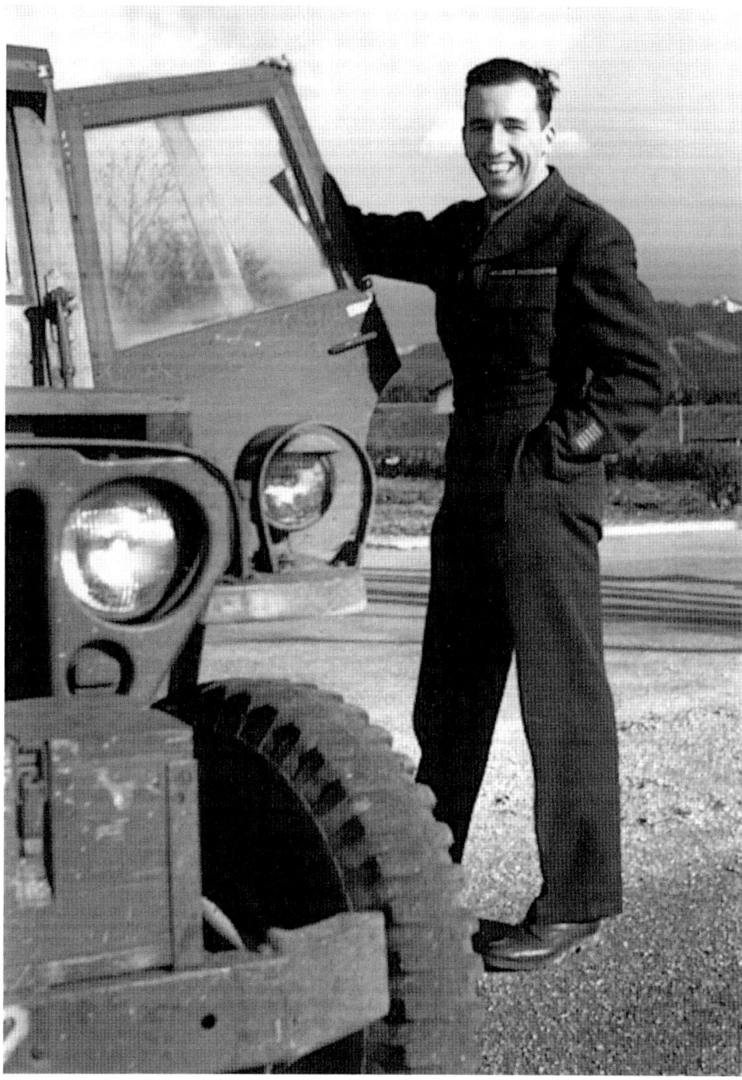

Raymond D'Addario (1920–2011)
Raymond D'Addario was born in Holyoke and graduated from Holyoke High School in 1938. After the attack on Pearl Harbor on December 7, 1941, he volunteered to serve in the Army. He was assigned to the Army Pictorial Services in London for 18 months. He stayed in London for three years and became the chief photographer of the Nuremberg trials, of 12 later trials, and one of the few people to participate in all 13 trials. He also documented the devastation of the city from the war and returned 20 years later to see the city reconstructed and documented the recovery through his thoughtful and steady lens. He published the pictures in a book called *Nuremberg Then and Now*, which is in its seventh printing in Germany. He also photographed "Nuremberg after 1945" and "Der Nurnberger Prozess" ("The Nuremberg Trials"). He returned to Holyoke on 1949 with his wife, Margarete, who was a translator at the trials. They opened D'Addario's Camera Shop on Maple Street and then on High Street. They added stores in Westfield and Hadley. He was a president of the Lions Club for 50 years and was elected a Melvin Jones Fellow, the highest recognition offered by the club. He was know by his family and friends to have a great sense of humor, a positive attitude, and appreciated the simple things in life. (Courtesy of the D'Addario family.)

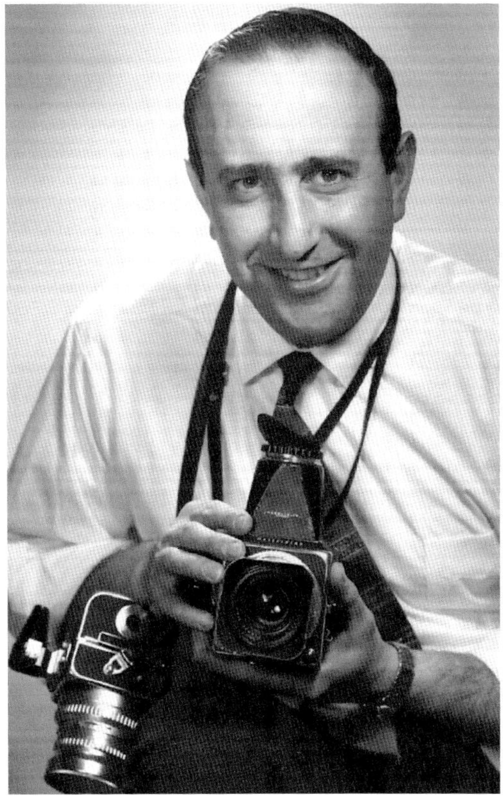

Vincent D'Addario (1930–2011)
Like his famous and talented brother Raymond, he was born in Holyoke and graduated from Holyoke High School. He joined the Army and was stationed in Biloxi, Mississippi, where he attended a photography school. He worked as a freelance photographer and was on the staff of the *Springfield Republican* newspaper. He has won countless awards for his professional photographs from the Boston Press Photographers Association, United Press International and Associated Press, National Press Photographers Association, and *Look* magazine. He was also given a Lifetime Achievement Award from the Valley Press Club. He has photographed some very famous people, including Muhammad Ali; John F. Kennedy and his wife, Jacqueline Kennedy; Martin Luther King; Richard Nixon; and Norman Rockwell. He also took the first scenes of Ted Kennedy's plane crash in Southampton and many other important pictures of residents in Western Massachusetts. (Courtesy of the D'Addario family.)

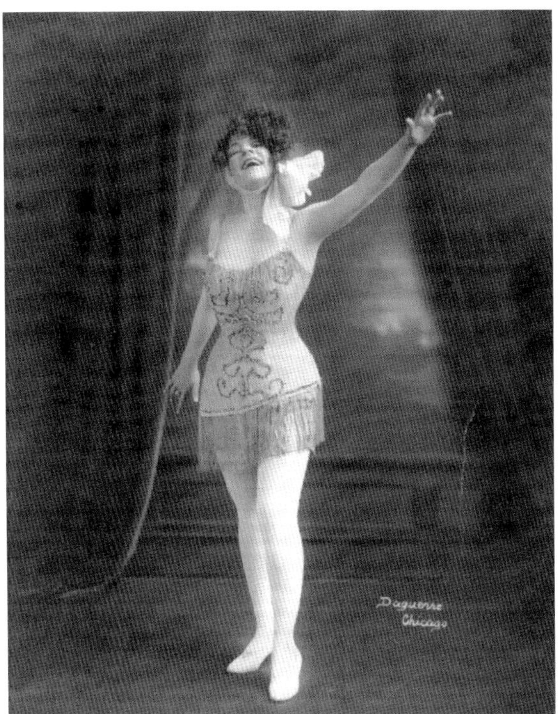

Eva Tanguay (1878–1947)
Born in Marbleton, Quebec, Canada, she came to Holyoke with her family in 1880s. She was discovered after winning a dance and voice contest. She became known as "the Queen of the Musical Comedy Stage" due to her vivacious and energetic personality. Eventually, she became a "Ziegfeld girl," earning $3,500 a week in 1905, making her one of the highest-paid vaudeville performers at the time. She made a couple of successful silent movies in the 1920s and did well on Broadway. (Courtesy of the Holyoke Public Library.)

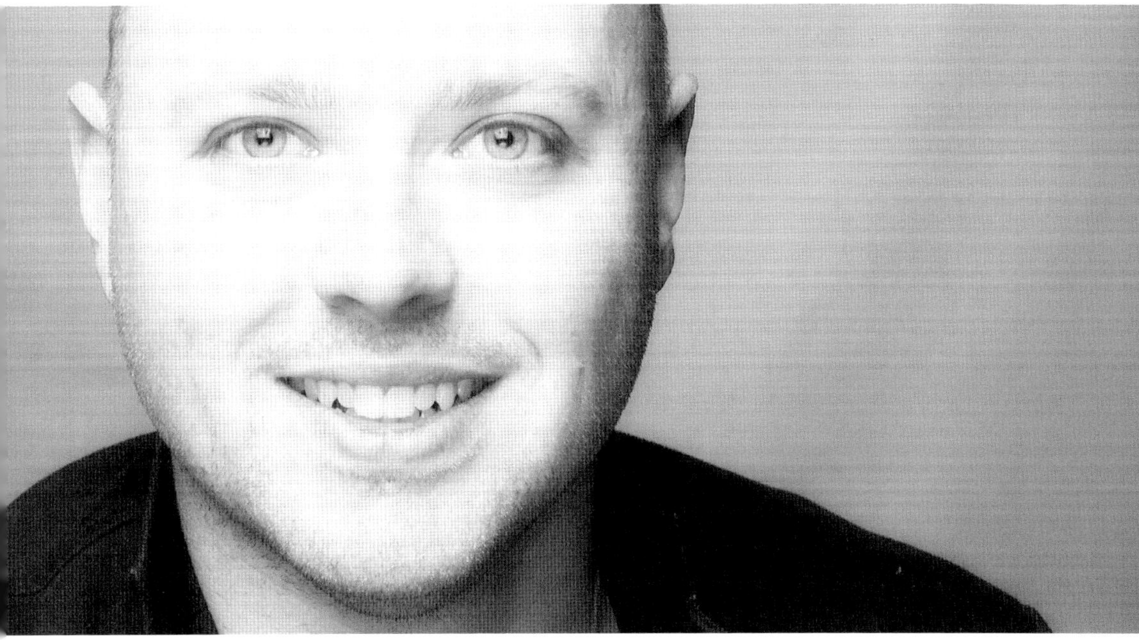

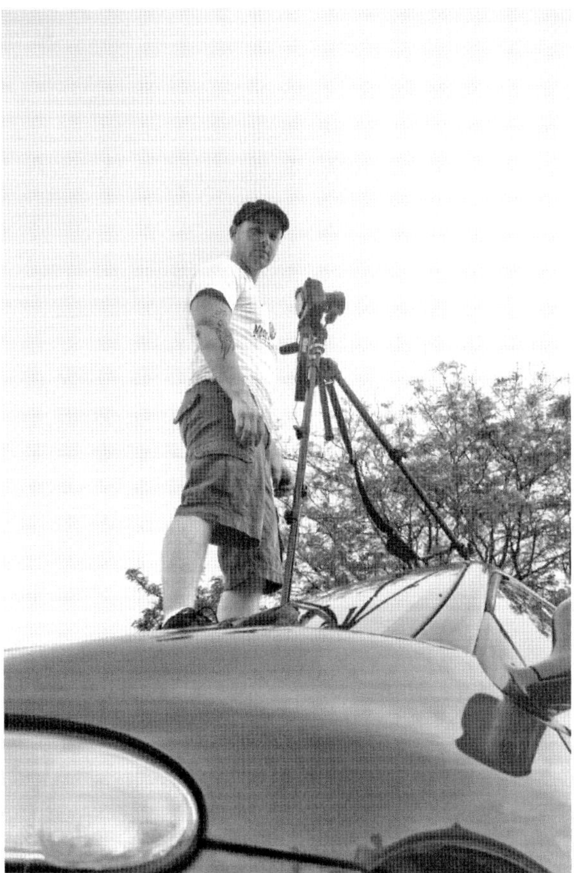

Jeffery Byrnes (1983–)
He earned a degree at Holyoke Community College in visual arts in 2008 and graduated from University of Massachusetts, Amherst, in 2012. He is a professional photographer with a studio on Race Street. He runs two businesses, one that specializes in wedding photography, called Portrait Mill, and one that is called JeffreyB Photography, which covers a wide range of subjects old and new. He strives to show people the hidden beauty that Holyoke has to offer and has raised funds for the renovation of the Holyoke Public Library, among many other important projects for the advancement of Holyoke. (Courtesy of Jeffrey Byrnes.)

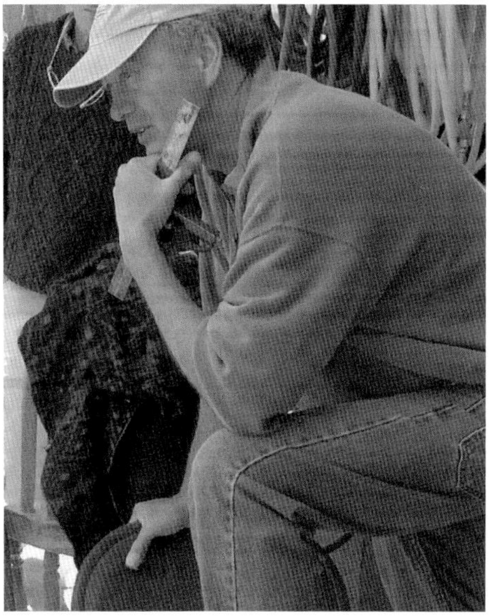

Douglas John "DJ" Garrity (1949–)

Garrity was born in Holyoke and attended Chicopee public schools. He has lived in Ireland, France, and the United States. He teaches sculpting classes in white marble and other pliable stone. When asked about his distinctive artistic style, he says, "My artistic training has been informal and generously influenced by living and working beside men and women in stone yards, quarries, and artistic communities across America and Europe." His unique sculpting skills and meaningful representation of his subjects' struggles encouraged the *Irish America* magazine to include him in their "Top 100 Irish Americans" edition. (Courtesy of Douglas John "DJ" Garrity.)

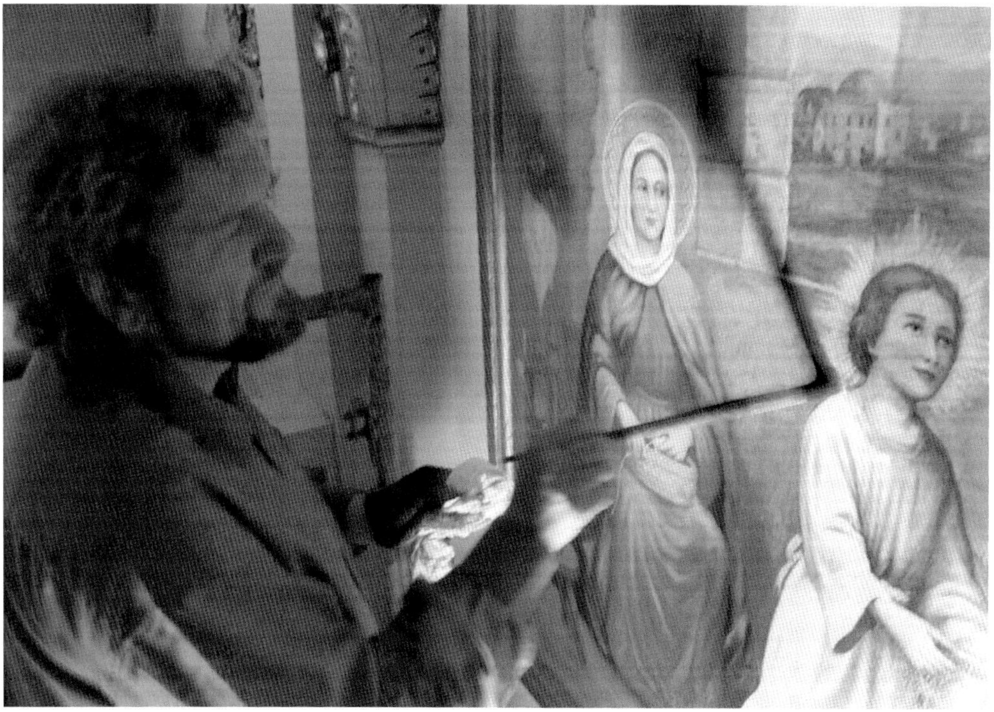

Vitek J.P. Kruta (1962–)

Born in Prague, Czech Republic, Vitek came to the United States in 1991. He has dedicated his life to creating, restoring, and teaching art. Using Old World techniques of fine and decorative art, which he learned in the Czech Republic and Germany, Vitek can transform, protect, or restore murals, paintings, frescoes, furniture, and buildings. Vitek is also a master painter, exhibiting his work in galleries and art shows throughout the country. As a consultant for arts and educational organizations and historical commissions, he shares his vast experience and artistic sensibilities with the community. (Courtesy of Vitek J. P. Kruta.)

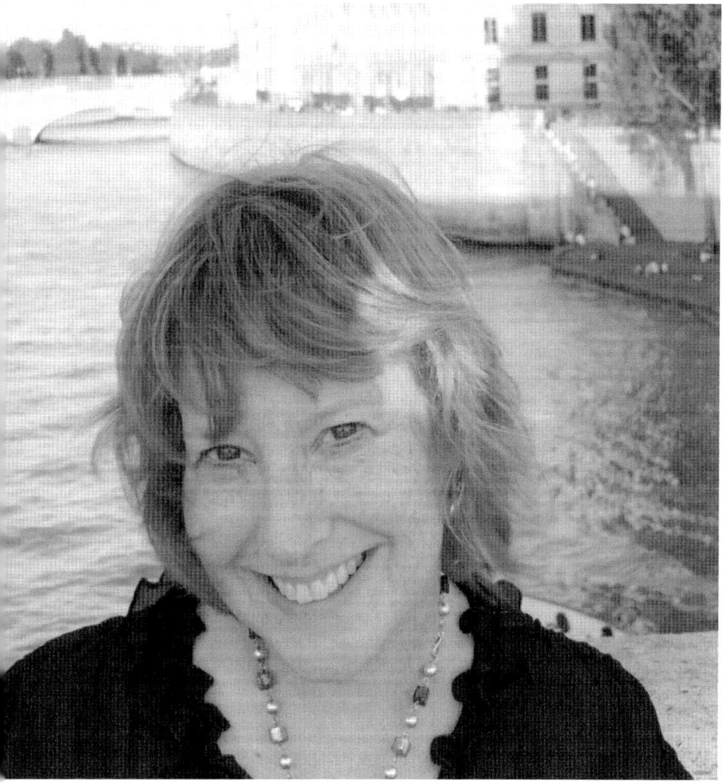

Mary Jo Maichack (1955–)
She can play the violin and guitar as well as sing beautifully. She graduated cum laude from Middlebury College in Vermont with a bachelor's degree in English literature and is fluent in German, French, Italian, and Spanish. She is an international award-winning singer storyteller and teaching artist. She has performed and trained countless children and adults in more than 3,000 sites since 1989 and has traveled throughout the United States and in Europe. She is the recipient of two national awards for her CDs of storytelling and music, including an original tale of historical fiction. (Courtesy of Mary Jo Maichack.)

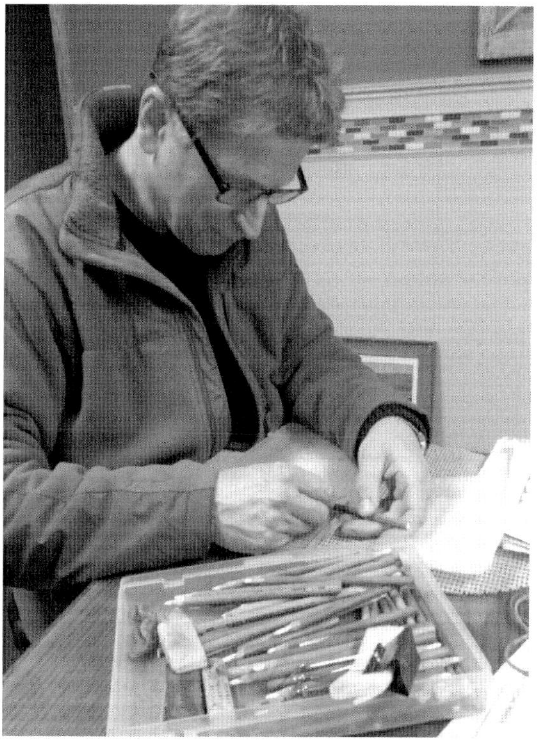

Gregory Maichack (1952–)
Growing up in Bristol, Connecticut, he graduated from College of the Holy Cross in Worcester, Massachusetts, in 1970, majoring in experiential psychology with a minor in English literature. A skilled portraitist and painter working primarily in pastels, he is the recipient of the Massachusetts Cultural Council Gold Star Program Award. He has been in many national juried art shows and has been awarded countless grants. He has also received the Award of Merit from the Bennington Center for the Arts (Impressions of New England Show, 2003) and the Savoir-faire Pastel Award from the Great Lakes Pastel Society, along with many other prestigious art awards. (Courtesy of Gregory Maichack.)

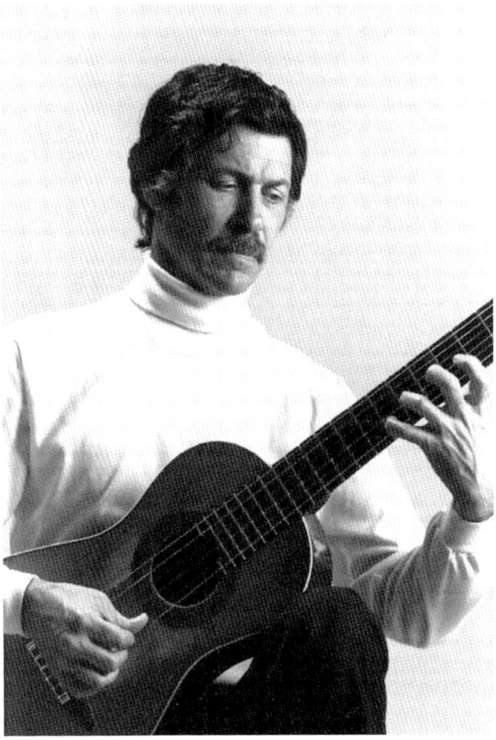

Phillip de Fremery (1948–)
When he was 15 years old, Phillip de Fremery had an accident in his woodshop and lost his right index finger at the knuckle. He studied with renowned guitarist Segovia in North Carolina and in Spain in 1966. He toured the world and settled in the Pioneer Valley in 1986 when he started to teach classical guitar at Holyoke Community College. He also teaches at the University of Massachusetts, Hampshire College, and other important colleges in the area. He received an award for best original music from the Kennedy Center American College Theater Festival, among many other accolades for his outstanding work. (Courtesy of Phillip de Fremery.)

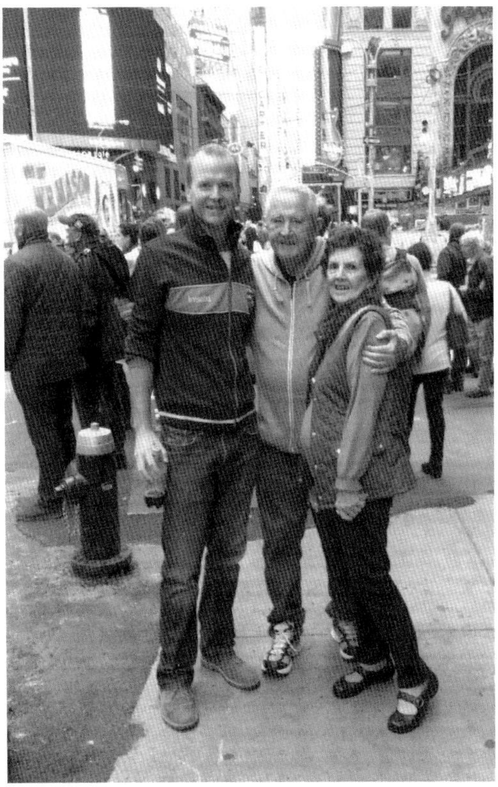

T.J. Jagodowski (1971–)
Jagodowski was born in Holyoke and attended Syracuse University, where he was injured and doctors had to put plates and screws in his leg. Undeterred, he went on to become a successful improvisational theater actor in the 1990s. Gaining notoriety in several Harold teams at iO Chicago in 1997, he went on to open a popular improv theater called the Mission in Chicago with Dave Pasquesi. Jagodowski is one of the "Two Guys," in the Sonic Drive-In commercials with Peter Grosz, and he has been on the well-known NPR news show *Wait, Wait, Don't Tell Me*. (Courtesy of the Jagodowski family.)

CHAPTER SEVEN

Dedicated to Their Community

Never doubt that a small group of thoughtful, committed citizens can change the world; indeed, it's the only thing that ever has.

—Margaret Mead

It all starts with a helping hand, an encouraging word, or just being there for those in need, which is what Mayor Mike Sullivan did for the city of Holyoke without reservation. Franny Rogers did the same for the state of Massachusetts and the community at large. Janet LaLiberte, another selfless individual, taught children how to be confident in their studies, as did Dr. David Bartley, who taught his students how to succeed. Superintendent of the Massachusetts State Police Timothy Alben proudly serves and protects the citizens. After 15 years of working to secure the funds to renovate the invaluable Holyoke Public Library, Maria Pagan succeeded. No matter who needed a helping hand or smile to brighten their day, Jimmy Watson was there, while Maria Dwight has continued to faithfully serve the elderly year after year. Jimmy Lavelle believes that one of the most important jobs he has is providing good service to his Holyoke Gas & Electric customers. An additional benefit for the citizens of Holyoke is director Teresa Shepard, who runs the Holyoke Parks and Recreation Department in a professional and amenable manner. A debt of gratitude is owed to Anna Burns Sullivan for negotiating with management fair wages, hours, and working conditions in Western Massachusetts. Sheryl Young Quinn had her own battle in keeping a senior center open through years of budget cuts and changes in senior care. As an English teacher, Patrick Woods made all the right corrections in his students' academic and long-term aspirations. Another honorable man to remember is Officer John DiNapoli, who was struck down while trying to help a citizen in peril. Carlos Vega helped to elevate and educate immigrants and citizens of Holyoke. Kathy Anderson has helped Holyoke residents live better lives, and let us remember the heart-wrenching story of the brave and courageous Thomas Monahan.

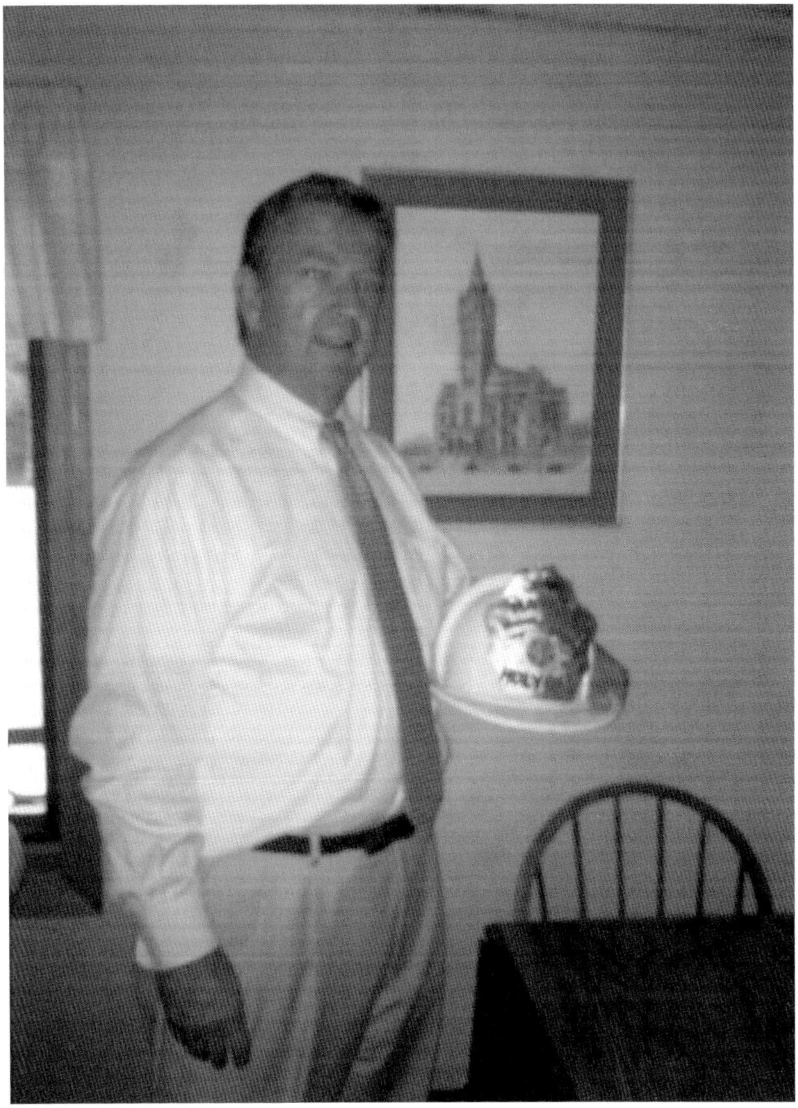

Michael Sullivan (1956–)
Born and raised in Holyoke, Michael Sullivan graduated from Holyoke High School and attended Worcester State College. He bartended and sold for beverage companies from 1978 to 1999. He was a city alderman from 1987 to 1999 and, in 1988, opened a restaurant and bar called Nick O'Neils on High Street in downtown Holyoke. He managed the restaurant until 1999 until he ran for mayor of Holyoke and was elected to become the 42nd mayor. In 2010, he graduated from the University of Massachusetts with an urban studies degree. He went on to work as a town administrator for the City of Maynard, Massachusetts, for three years. In 2013, the Town of South Hadley, Massachusetts, hired him as a town administrator. Asked why he ran for mayor of Holyoke, he points to his fascination with how a community functions, such as its housing, interactions within departments, and social justice issues. Coming from a one-parent home, he remembers how hard his mother's life was and how he had to pay his own way at times. He is well suited to be a public servant due to his compassion for people, 16 years of shrewd municipal experience, and prudent budgetary practices—among the many other reasons he was elected five times to be the mayor of Holyoke. (Courtesy of Michael Sullivan.)

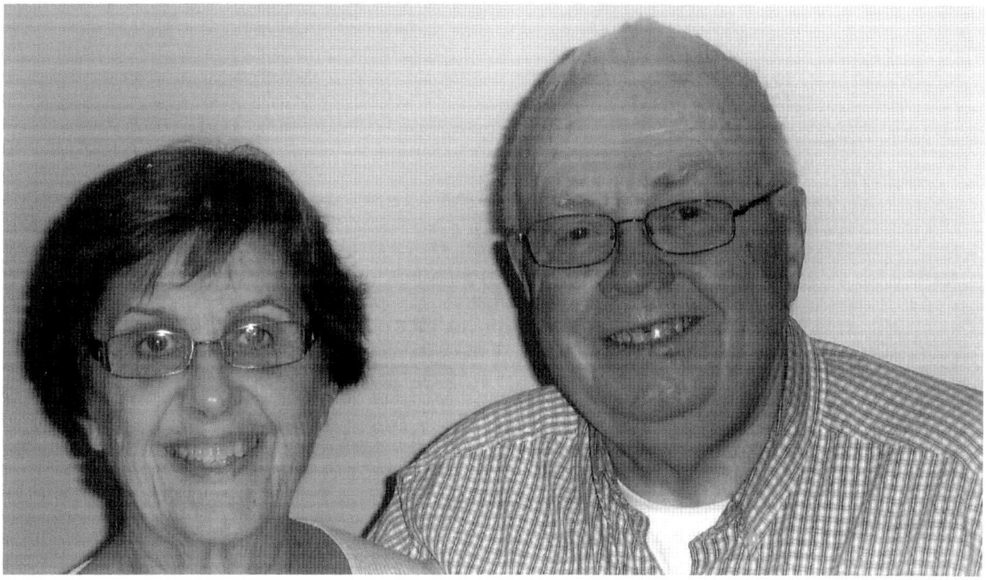

Francis Rogers (1932–)
Always in good humor even when the days were long and hard as he worked as a storage mover for his father's company, Rogers Van and Storage Company, Francis Rogers worked for Daniel O'Connell Construction Company operating heavy equipment machinery until he finally had the opportunity to help the public lead better lives. In 1975, he ran in a special election race for the Massachusetts state representative seat and won. He also worked at the Soldiers' Home in Holyoke from 1981 to 1992, and he was a chairman for the Licensing Board and the Geriatric Authority, and was on the Soldiers' Home in Holyoke Board. (Courtesy of Francis Rogers.)

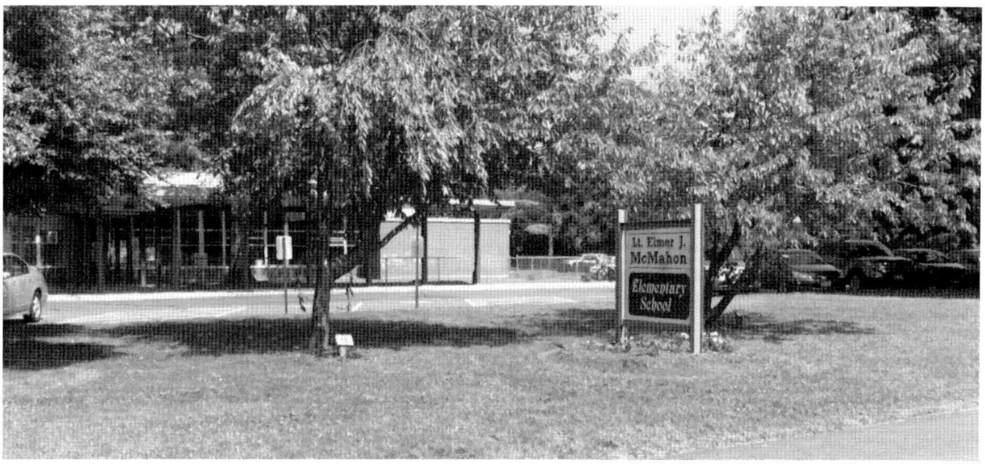

Janet LaLiberte (1929–)
This hardworking professional woman graduated in 1950 from the Westfield State Teachers College and earned her master's degree from Elms College. She taught elementary schoolchildren in the Chicopee and Holyoke school systems for 44 years. Students of this remarkable educator knew that she meant business and that she was there for them with a kind smile and a corrective pen, one that was not jagged or harsh—rather consistent and fair. Asked about the hundreds of children she so astutely taught, she said, "I was fortunate for the most part; the kids were all decent." (Courtesy of Holyoke Public Schools.)

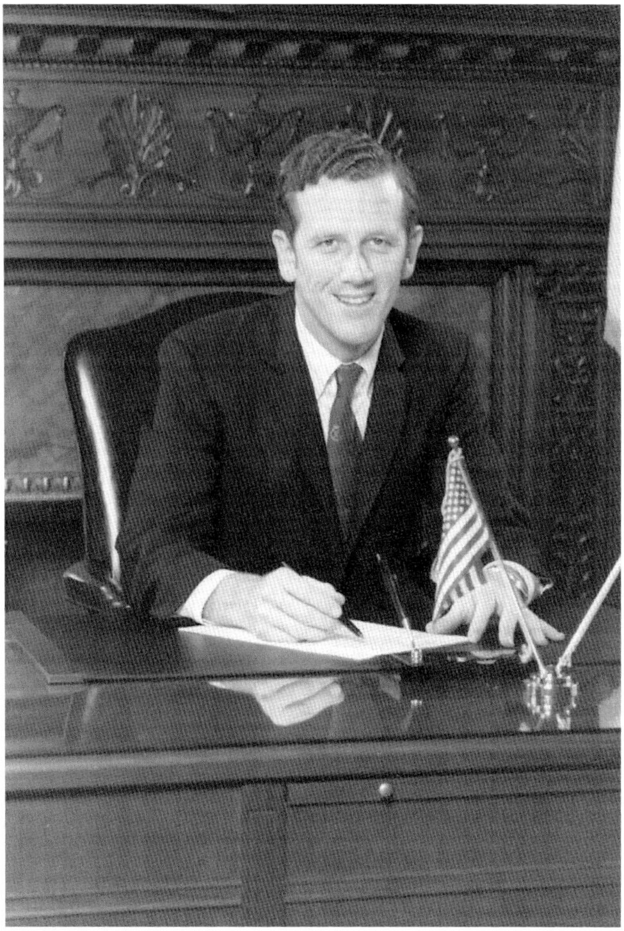

Dr. David Bartley (1935–)
In 1954, Bartley attended Holyoke Junior College (which eventually became known as Holyoke Community College due to the efforts of George Frost, a mentor of Bartley). He earned a bachelor of arts degree in government from University of Massachusetts, Amherst, and returned to receive his master's of education and his doctorate in education. He taught for five years in the Springfield public school system. In 1963, he was elected to the House of Representatives, where he was quickly elected to the majority leader position in 1965 and then as Speaker in 1969. He fulfilled that post until 1975. In that same year, he was appointed to be the president of Holyoke Community College, becoming the longest-serving president of a community college in Massachusetts and the only Massachusetts community college president to preside over his alma mater. Holyoke Community College thrived under his leadership, with triple enrollments and increased course offerings. A new athletic and recreation center was named after him called the Bartley Center. He was also instrumental in planning the existing business center, called the Kittredge Center. Through his astute and long-term planning, Holyoke Community College and the Commonwealth of Massachusetts continues to benefit and prosper from his enduring and sound leadership. One of his greatest triumphs, among many, was in the House of Representatives. He proposed a new law allowing children with disabilities to attend school. After a two-year, hard-fought battle, Chapter No. 766 was implemented in 1974. Due to his noble and compassionate efforts, special-needs children now must be acknowledged and accepted in the Massachusetts school system Since the law was enacted in Massachusetts, it has been enacted in states around the country. (Courtesy of Dr. David Bartley.)

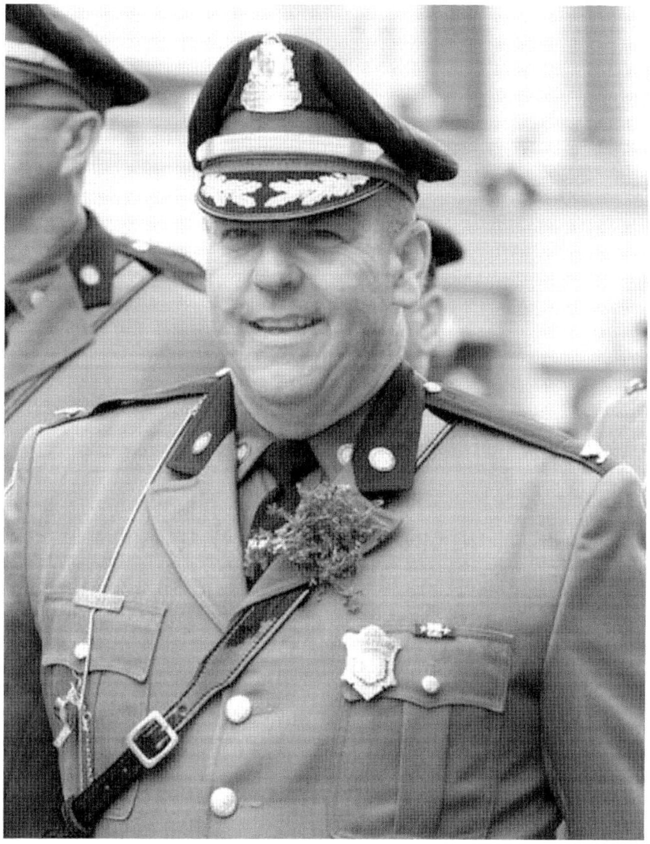

Timothy P. Alben (1959–)
After faithfully serving in the Massachusetts State Police for 30 years, he was promoted to one of the highest positions in the Massachusetts State Police. Prior to his promotion, he investigated mafia cases that entailed illegal gaming, racketeering, and extortion. He also investigated homicides, child abuse, violent, and white-collar crimes, among many other horrific illegal acts. He successfully solved many of these cases due to his penchant for detail, unrelenting perseverance, patience, and calm demeanor. In 2010, he was promoted to lieutenant colonel and commander of the division of field services, where he headed the Massachusetts State Police with some 1,500 uniformed Massachusetts State Troopers and 39 facilities statewide. After Alben successfully led the organization, Gov. Deval Patrick appointed him to be lieutenant colonel/superintendent of all of the 2,300 Massachusetts State Police on July 13, 2012. He earned a bachelor's degree in criminal justice from Westfield State University, a master's degree in criminal justice administration from Western New England University, and a master's degree in security studies (homeland defense and security) from the Naval Postgraduate School in Monterey, California, in 2007. He also graduated from the FBI National Academy and the National Preparedness Leadership Initiative at Harvard's Kennedy School of Government. He is a second-generation Massachusetts state trooper. His father, Albert Alben, also served while his grandfather, considered a helpful and well-respected officer, loyally served the city of Holyoke. Lieutenant Colonel / Superintendent Alben believes that "having been raised in a family where both my father and grandfather were law enforcement officers, choosing such a career path was easy for me. Growing up, they stressed the importance of accountability, sound decision-making and just being a good citizen. My grandfather, in particular, was always motivated about doing good for others. I saw that and wanted the same sense of service and reward for my life. I've never once regretted the decision." (Courtesy of Timothy P. Alben.)

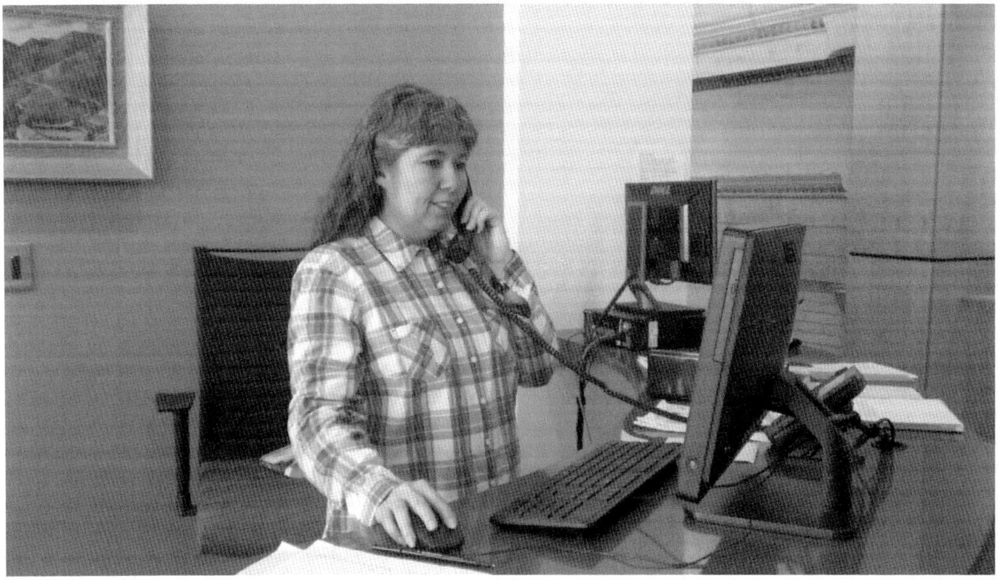

Maria G. Pagan (1946–)
Pagan, the director of the Holyoke Public Library, was instrumental in bringing a long overdue $14.5-million renovation project to fruition after working diligently at raising funds through writing grants, initiating public outreach programs, and many other creative projects for 15 years. In doing so, she successfully protected 20,000 important books from succumbing to ruin from dampness and decay. Through Pagan's hard work, tenacity, and foresight, the Holyoke Public Library continues to provide a vital public service to the citizens of Holyoke and Western Massachusetts. (Courtesy of the Holyoke Public Library.)

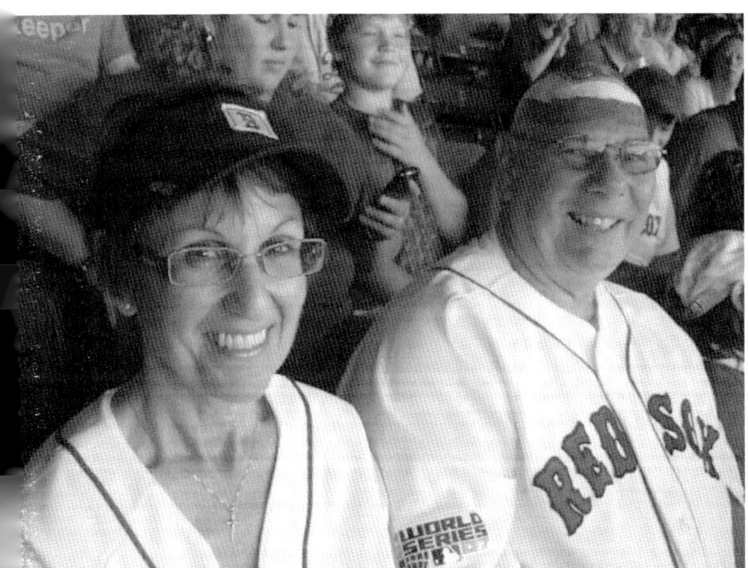

James "Jimmy" Watson
A dedicated employee of the Holyoke Gas & Electric Company for 20 years, Watson strives to bring humor and kindness throughout the year by dressing for the season and wishing all well. At Christmastime, he plays Santa Claus bringing cheer to the disadvantaged children with developmental disabilities at the Second Congregational Church, and when a single mother needs heat or if someone needs something to be moved, he will be there with his truck. (Courtesy of Jackie Watson.)

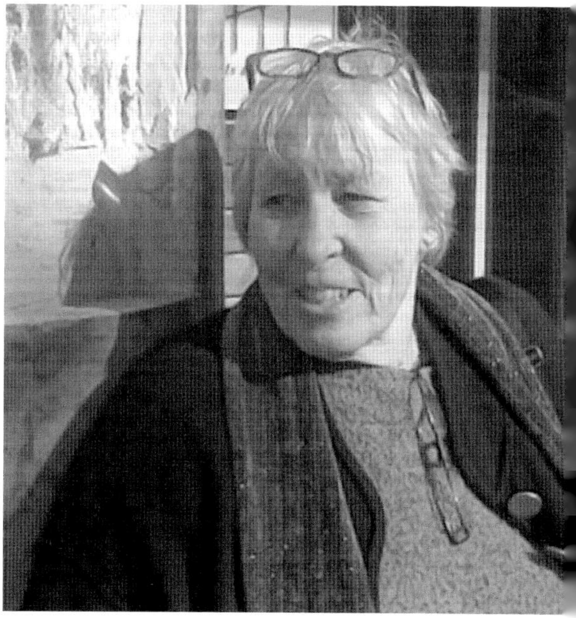

Maria Dwight
She is the president and founder of Gerontological Services, Inc., in Los Angeles, California. She has been working in planning facilities that serve older people, focusing on interrelationship of housing, social services, and health. She earned her undergraduate degree from Hampshire College and her master's degree from the Leonard Davis School of Gerontology, University of Southern California. She has served on many important nonprofit organization boards, including the Center for Healthy Aging Santa Monica, California; Alternative Living for the Aging in Los Angeles, California; and Stonewall Communities of Boston, Massachusetts. The Maria B. Dwight Building where Holyoke Geriatric is located was dedicated in her honor in 1977. (Courtesy of Maria Dwight.)

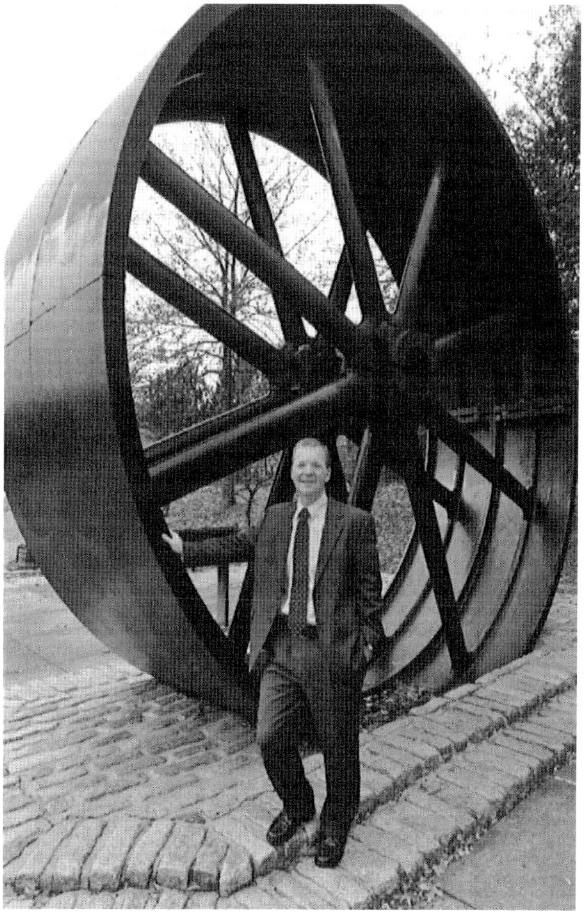

James Lavelle (1964–)
Born and raised in Holyoke, he earned a bachelor's degree in mechanical engineering and a master's degree in business administration from the University of Massachusetts, Amherst. He worked for Hamilton Sundstrand, a division of United Technologies Corporation, before becoming the general manager of Holyoke Gas & Electric in 1999. He was instrumental in taking prudent steps to purchase the Holyoke Water Power Company, which included the federally licensed Holyoke Dam, canal system, and a 50-watt hydroelectric generating resource. He has also been involved in many other resourceful cost-effective projects for the customers of the Holyoke Gas & Electric. (Courtesy of James Lavelle.)

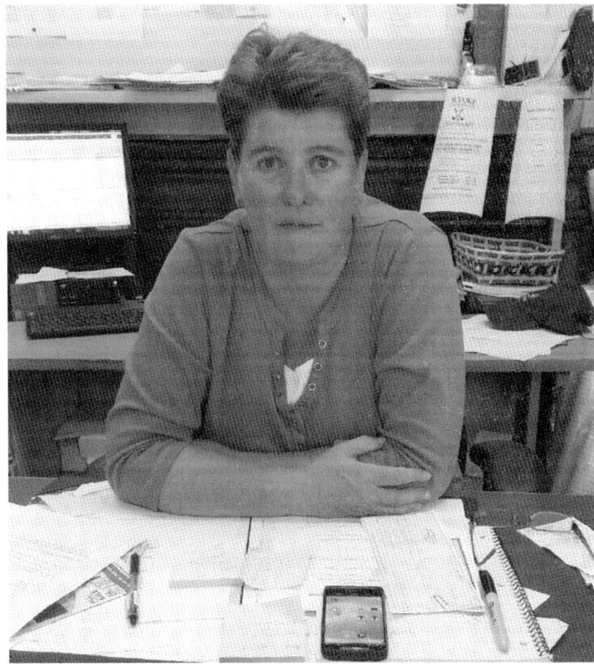

Teresa M. Shepard
Raised in Pittsfield, yet dedicated to Holyoke, this vivacious woman has improved the lives of countless citizens of Holyoke. She graduated from Elms College 1983 and interned at the Holyoke Boys and Girls Club in the social work field. In 1972, she was hired as a secretary and worked her way up to become the director of the Holyoke Parks and Recreation Department in 2007. She received the Citizen of the Year Award for going above and beyond for overseeing and carefully planning renovations of Springdale Park, Community Field, and Veterans Park. (Courtesy of Teresa M. Shepard.)

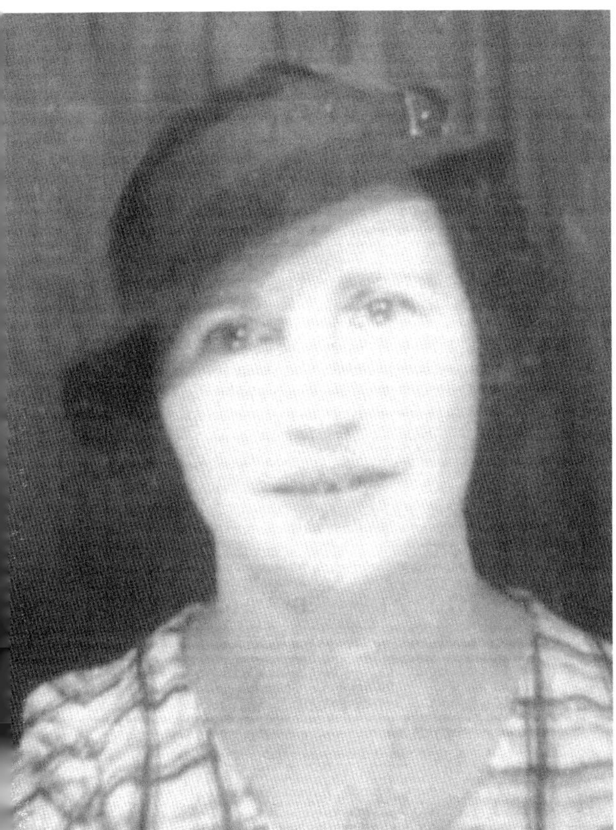

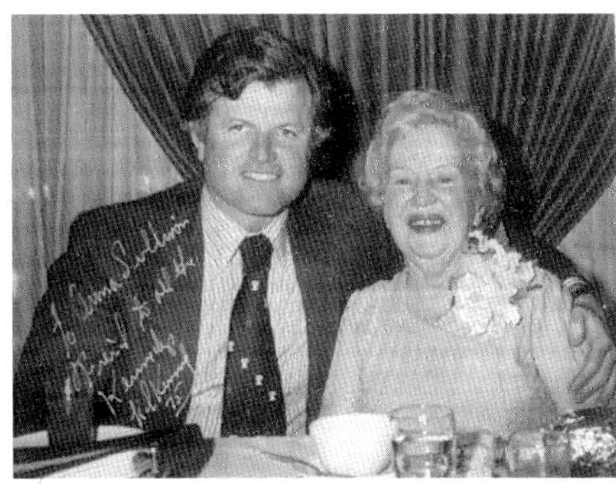

Anna Burns Sullivan (1903–1983)
Born into a family of textile workers, Anna Burns Sullivan believed that people should be able to talk, feel free, and have guaranteed wages, hours, and good working conditions in the Holyoke textile mills in the 1900s. She was known as "tough but fair" and an outstanding organizer and negotiator. She was wholeheartedly dedicated to the 5,000 Western Massachusetts workers that she served as a district manager for the Textile Workers Union of America (TWUA) from 1946 to 1966.

This tenacious maverick was seen passing out leaflets and picketing for free speech in front of a grocery store when she was 77 years old. (Courtesy of Glenn Sullivan.)

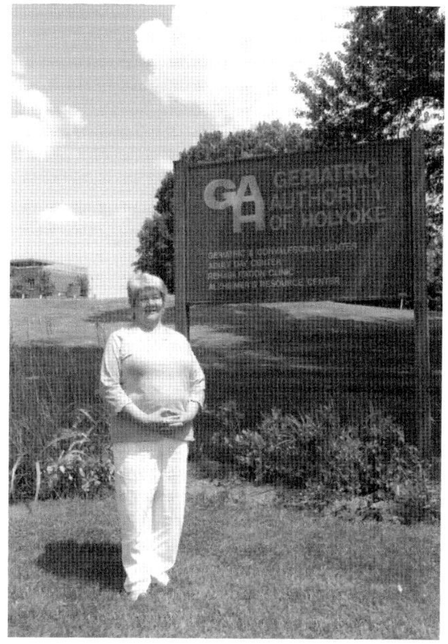

Sheryl Young Quinn (1947–)
She is a sixth-generation descendant of the O'Grady family from Bally Cahane, County Mayo, who immigrated to Holyoke in 1845. Sheryl Young Quinn was born in Holyoke, graduated from Holyoke High School, and attended Holyoke Community College and the University of Massachusetts. A registered dietician, she is also a former executive administrator of the Geriatric Authority of Holyoke, which was started by Maria Dwight. In 1996, she was devastated when the center had to close its doors, knowing full well that it would cause turmoil and disruption in her patient's lives. She reached out to the families and worked hard to help them find suitable accommodations with as little stress as possible. (Courtesy of Sheryl Young Quinn.)

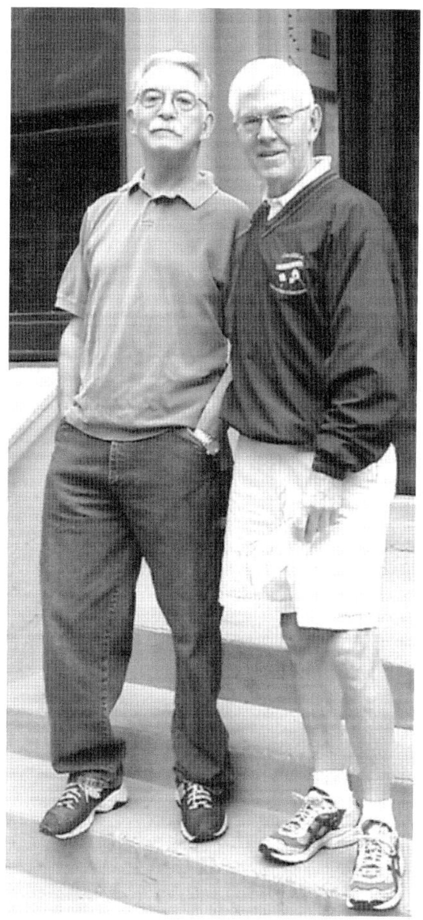

Patrick "Pat" Woods
Pictured at right, Pat Woods was a well-respected English teacher at the Lawrence school and Holyoke High School, and over the intervening years, he assisted his wife, Bonnie, in the operation of the family real estate business, the John B. Woods Company, which was established in 1905. Woods was an avid sportsman, and his students strived to emulate him. One of his students wrote in an essay after seeing him play baseball, "When I'm older, I want to play behind the plate and hit like you." Woods made a lasting impression on his students; he not only taught them to be proficient writers and agile athletes but also encouraged them in a genial and supportive manner to work hard and do their best in all aspects of their lives. (Courtesy of Patrick Woods.)

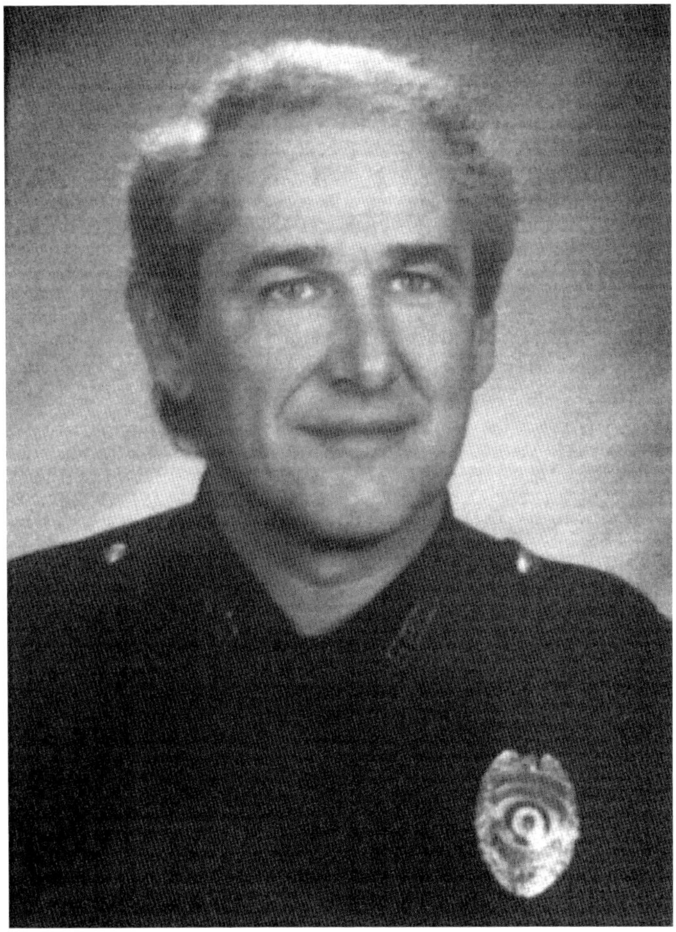

John DiNapoli (1947–1999)
John DiNapoli grew up at 11 Northeast Street and went to the former Holy Rosary School, graduating from Holyoke Catholic High School in 1965. After high school, he worked at a paper mill and at Piels Brewery. He joined the Holyoke Police Department in 1978 in response to his good friend Ofc. James Gatzounas's tragic death from a heart attack in 1997 as he was breaking up a fight in the line of duty. On December 22, 1999, this gentle and good-natured man responded to a disturbance call on Walnut Street in Holyoke. Sadly, multiple gunshot wounds from a drug dealer instantly killed him. He was known to be fair and calm and was always called upon to mediate a disturbance and or to mitigate a fight. DiNapoli was the people's cop; he would rather help than arrest a person. He was especially good to the children of Holyoke, helping them to stay on the right path and listening to them when no one else would. His beloved fiancée, Carol Bevan-Bogart said it best in the *Republican* newspaper: "John chose the life of a police officer because he believed that he could make a difference in people's lives." A beautiful bronze monument has been placed in the front of the Holyoke police station in his honor. Ofc. James Gatzounas and Ofc. John Driscoll, who were also killed in the line of action, also have their names on the monument. The monument depicts DiNapoli sitting with and listening to children. One time, DiNapoli assisted a 15-year-old boy at Dean Vocational High School who got his hand caught in the printing machine in shop class; DiNapoli knelt by his side and never left him until the paramedics arrived. In another horrifying incident, he held a water department employee's head up in a collapsed ditch so that the man would not drown until help arrived. He did so much for the entire community; one could count on Officer DiNapoli; he was reliable; he was always present. (Courtesy of Carol Bevan-Bogart.)

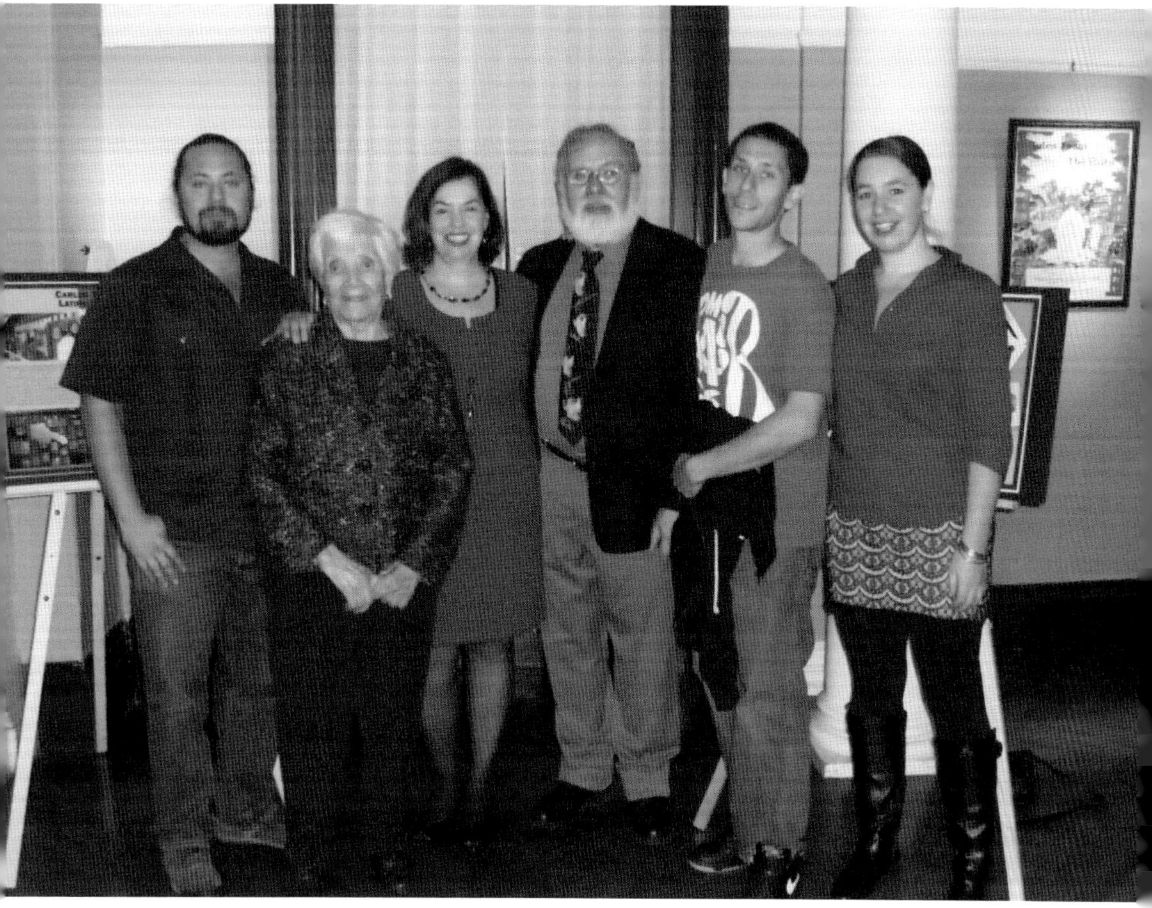

Carlos Vega (1951–2012)

Brought up in the Flats, Carlos Vega (center, in jacket in tie) was born in Ecuador and moved to the United States in 1955 with his family. He worked on a tobacco farm with Puerto Rican families when he was 14 years old. As he grew up, he realized that they were being mistreated and subjected to racism while living in appalling housing conditions in Holyoke and Springfield. Most of these agricultural laborers came to Western Massachusetts due to the encouragement of the Department of Labor. Vega noticed that, by the 1970s, most of the factories that had once thrived in downtown Holyoke had closed and moved their employees and equipment overseas or down south for cheaper labor. It was around that time that he decided to do something to help these men and women by becoming a community organizer. He worked with the Fair Share, Urban Ministry, New Unity, and many other organizations that helped Spanish families. He introduced fair housing laws and the importance of voting and educating children. In 1982, he and other compassionate individuals were instrumental in opening the Nueva Esperanza, a not-for-profit community development organization that restores and maintains old and decrepit buildings in South Holyoke. The organization saved 30 buildings, developed small business spaces, and provided 400 units of affordable housing. Vega, as the executive director of the Nueva Esperanza, proved over and over again how important Spanish citizens were to the city of Holyoke. He stood up for them in the 1970s in a desegregation lawsuit and fought for many other human rights issues throughout his life. Unfortunately, in 1995, he was diagnosed with brain cancer that he fought until 2012. In that agonizing time, this tenacious and brave man continued to fight for the human rights and dignity of the Spanish community in Holyoke and in South America. The City of Holyoke renamed Hamilton Street Park to Carlos Vega Park in his honor. (Courtesy of Wistariahurst Museum.)

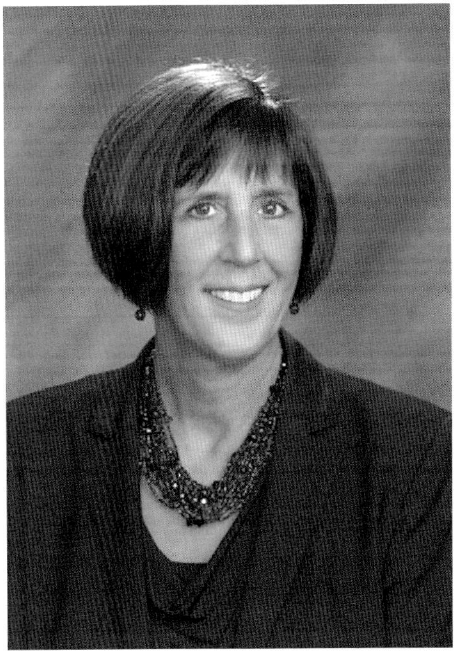

Kathleen Anderson (1957–)
A fourth-generation Holyoke resident, Kathleen Anderson earned an early education degree at Holyoke Community College and a bachelor of arts degree in early childhood and elementary education from Fitchburg State College. She worked for the Holyoke/Chicopee Headstart Program and the Churchill Neighborhood Partnership and was the director of the Planning and Economic Development for Holyoke, among many other constructive positions that have improved the lives of Holyoke residents. Today, she is the president of the Greater Holyoke Chamber of Commerce, where she initiates innovative programs that bolster the community and Holyoke businesses. (Courtesy of Kathleen Anderson.)

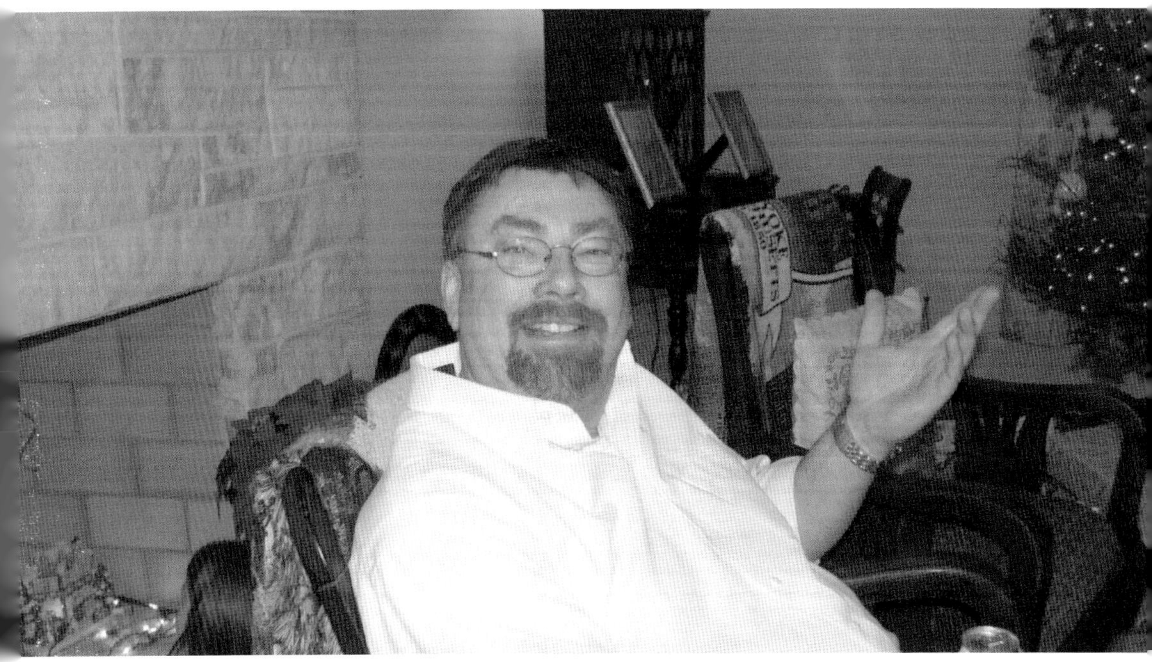

Thomas Monahan (1958–2011)
He was born in Holyoke and attended Holyoke schools and Springfield Technical Community College. On June 4, 2011, this dedicated family man responded to an overturned car that had crashed into a parked car in the front of his home before midnight. In an unselfish act of heroism, he tried to help the victim and was inadvertently hit by another car that slammed into the disabled vehicle. He sustained serious injuries and died two days later. This brave man was known to have helped people in his community and leaves a legacy of grace and kindness. (Courtesy of the Monahan family.)

CHAPTER EIGHT

Trailblazers

I will not follow where the path may lead,
but I will go where there is no path, and I will leave a trail.

—Muriel Strode

Holyoke's unique landscapes and abundant optimists encourage adventure and creativity, especially for the brave and men and women who dared to be first, tried something new, and never gave up. Christopher Clarke is a good example of never giving up; he was known as a public-spirited citizen, allowing future park dwellers to enjoy nature by advocating for the Mount Tom State Reservation in 1903. He made way for the industrious Kathryn "Kay" Burnett, who organized and blazed trails on the spectacular Mount Tom State Reservation. Another dedicated trailblazer was the incorrigible woodsman and historian Robert Schwobe, who hiked and searched for remnants of Holyoke's past in the ridges and fields of the Mount Tom Range. George C. Ewing envisioned utilizing water to power mills that would change the landscape of Ireland Parish. Bearing witness to the plight and journey of modern figures, journalist Barbara Bernard astutely told their stories through a myriad of media outlets, while Ella Merkel DiCarlo documented the lives of Holyoke residents in her book *Holyoke-Chicopee: A Perspective 1882–1982*. Esteemed historian Olivia Davis Mausel continues to profile historical events and people. Keeping the environment protected was the peaceful and inspiring naturalist and conservationist Terry Blunt. Another stalwart advocate of the environment was Gary "Ridesfar" Thabault; he safeguarded the Mount Tom Range. Advocating for children and keeping the United States safe from harm was Willma Jennings, who faithfully served in the US Army and patiently taught young children how to read. Dr. Julia M. Patten helped Holyoke citizens with their health needs, and Elizabeth Towne encouraged a natural diet, exercise, and free thinking in her *Nautilus* magazine. In 1870, Daniel O'Connell also indulged in independent thinking when he started his own construction company with his employees' best interests in mind. Bill Dwight also declared his independence by working hard to improve his life and the lives of those in the community. Dr. Howard Conant, a 35-year Holyoke High principal, and William J. Dean, superintendent of the Holyoke Public Schools, continually advocated for education. Lastly, there was Daniel Shanahan, who published insightful poetry books. All of these trailblazers have made substantial contributions to the city of Holyoke and beyond.

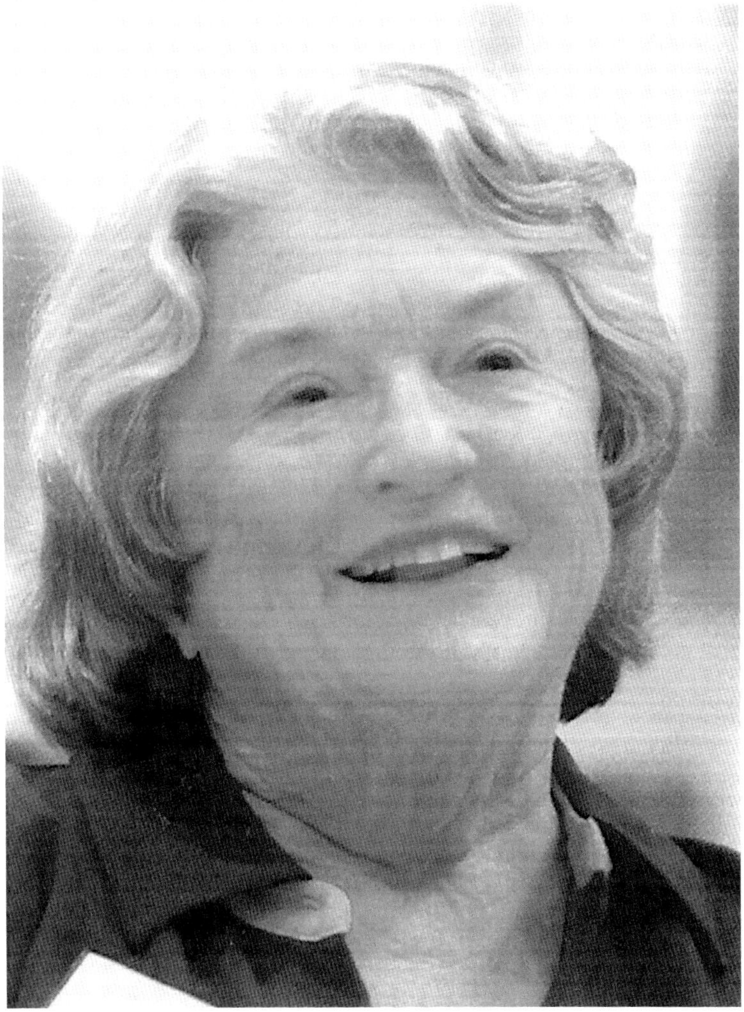

Barbara Bernard (1928–)
This amazing woman is a trailblazer to emulate and respect, due to her outstanding 70 years of professional journalism, public service, and good citizenship. A graduate of Mount Holyoke College, she was a copywriter for WHYN radio, a stringer for the *New York Times,* and was the first woman in Western Massachusetts to have her own television show, *The Barbara Bernard Show,* on WHYN-TV. She interviewed Judy Garland, Robert Goulet, Merv Griffin, Arthur Fiedler, and many other important figures. She was among a select few women who wrote for the *Holyoke Transcript-Telegram* newspaper in the 1950s and found time while raising her children to write copy for some of New York's finest fashion and food magazines. A dedicated advocate of the Golden Age Club, she was instrumental in helping to bring Holyoke's new senior center to fruition. She is the recipient of the esteemed Oldershaw Award for excellence in professional achievements and community service, among many other well-deserved accolades, including the Valley Press Club's Lifetime Achievement Award (the first to be awarded to a woman), the Holyoke St. Patrick's Parade Committee's Citizenship Award, and the Christian Charity Award given by the Ancient Order of Hibernians. Six decades of Bernard's monumental archives can be viewed at the Holyoke Public Library. Today, she continues to entertain, inform, and reassure people in her *Republican* newspaper column. (Courtesy of the *Republican* newspaper.)

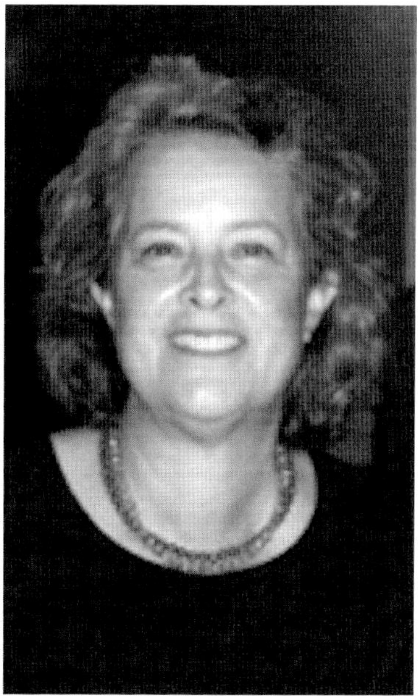

Olivia Davis Mausel
She is a graduate of Oklahoma University and Westfield State College in special education and has taught at Holyoke High School for 18 years. She has lived in Holyoke for 45 years with her husband, children, and grandchildren. She is the chairperson of the Holyoke Historical Commission and has been a member of the Fairfield Avenue Local Historic District Commission since 1994. She received the Paul E. Tsongas Profiles in Preservation Honoree in 2010 from Preservation Massachusetts. Mausel continues to learn and be involved in historical preservation on the state and local level. (Courtesy of Olivia Davis Mausel.)

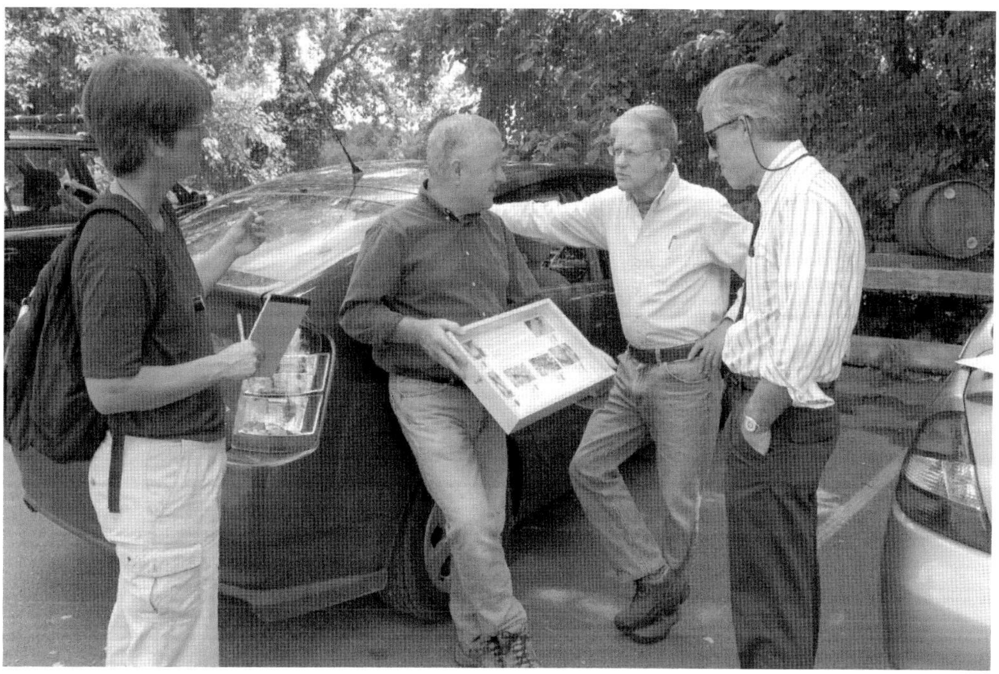

Terry Blunt (1942–2010)
As a trained naturalist and conservationist, Terry Blunt (pictured third from left) managed to save thousands of acres in the Connecticut River valley for future generations. For 25 years, he worked for the Connecticut River Watershed Council and the Department of Environmental Management, acting as the director for the Connecticut Valley Action Program. He was instrumental in protecting the 12-mile Connecticut River Water Trail from Hatfield to Turners Falls, the land on Mount Tom, the Holyoke Range and Skinner Park, and the French King Gorge. He was an avid hiker, boater, and fisherman. (Courtesy of Pete Westover.)

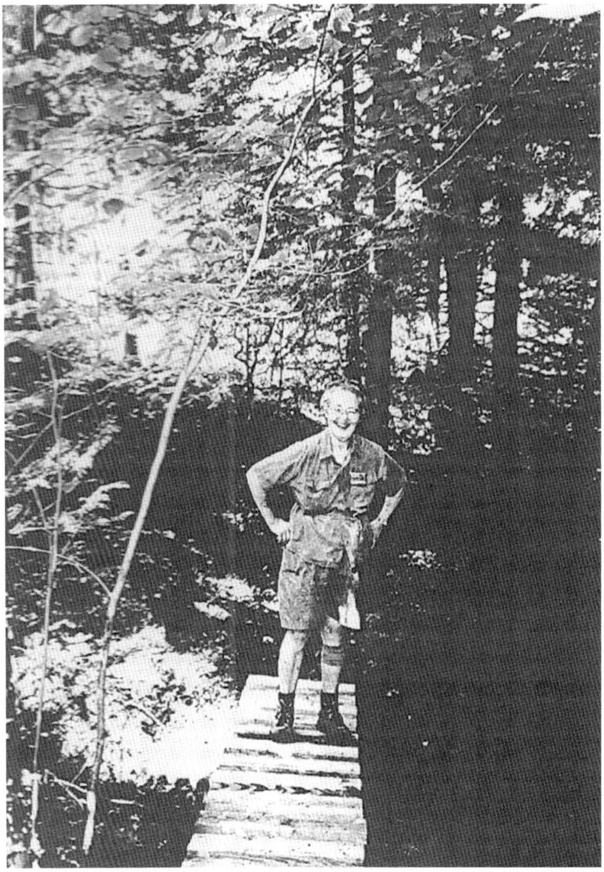

Kathryn "Kay" Burnett (1931–)
She earned her bachelor's degree from Oberlin College and a master's degree from Smith College. Since 1975, she has been a music librarian at Smith College. Nicknamed "the trail lady of the Mount Tom State Reservation," Burnett worked tirelessly for 15 years to organize the Mount Tom trails on the Mount Tom State Reservation. She faithfully served on the Mount Tom Citizens Advisory Committee as the chair for many years. The Hampshire County Commission gave this steadfast lady a Certificate of Merit for organizing, instituting, and maintaining the trail system on the Mount Tom State Reservation. (Courtesy of Mount Tom State Reservation.)

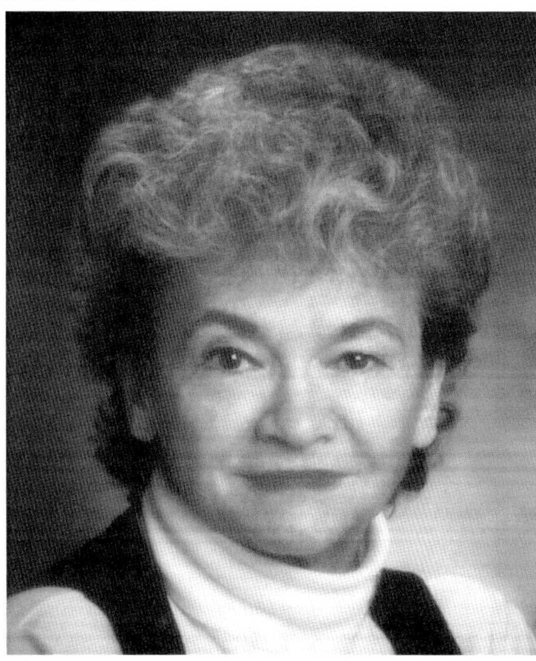

Ella Merkel DiCarlo (1919–1996)
DiCarlo was an author, reporter, historian, and community activist. She wrote for the former *Holyoke Transcript-Telegram* in 1968, became the first female wire editor in New England, was an assistant editorial writer, and won the associated Press Award for the best news story in New England. She served on the Regional Child Care Committee, YMCA, League of Women's Voters, and Friends of the Holyoke Museum. She was the president of the Holyoke Women's Club and the Association for Improvement of Minorities and wrote the histories of the Greater Holyoke Chamber of Commerce and the Holyoke Hospital. Most notably, she wrote *Holyoke-Chicopee: A Perspective 1882–1982*, published by the *Holyoke Transcript-Telegram*. (Courtesy of Sandy DiCarlo.)

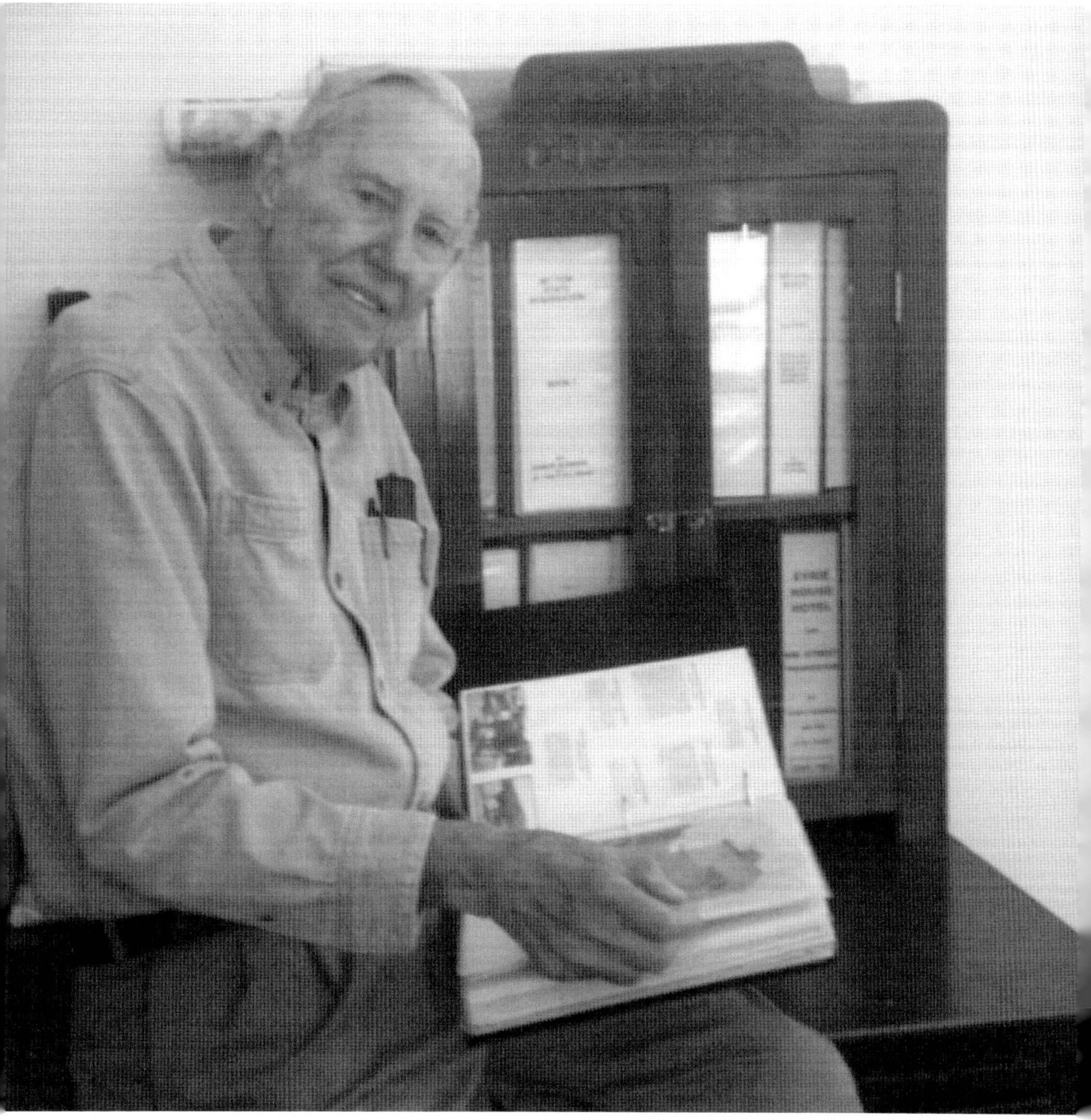

Robert Schwobe (1930–)
Schwobe retired as a Hampshire County corrections officer in his late fifties due to a heart ailment. Though he went home, he did not stay home; he got a walking stick and started hiking on the Mount Tom Range. He did not hike on the beaten path; he set out to find unusual artifacts that were hidden in the fields and ridges on Mount Tom. A well-versed historian and gentleman, he researched and documented information about the Mount Tom Range for 30 years. His impressive collection of 13 historical volumes are being stored in a beautiful wooden cabinet with glass doors that Thomas Scanlon and Kurt Pierce, members of the maintenance team at the Massachusetts Conservation of Recreation Department, constructed for the public to view. They even carved his name on the front upper face of the piece of furniture. One can also view informational CDs that Schwobe has researched and narrated pertaining to the Mount Tom State Reservation. He was also involved in helping to install the B-17 memorial on Mount Tom. (Courtesy of Robert Schwobe.)

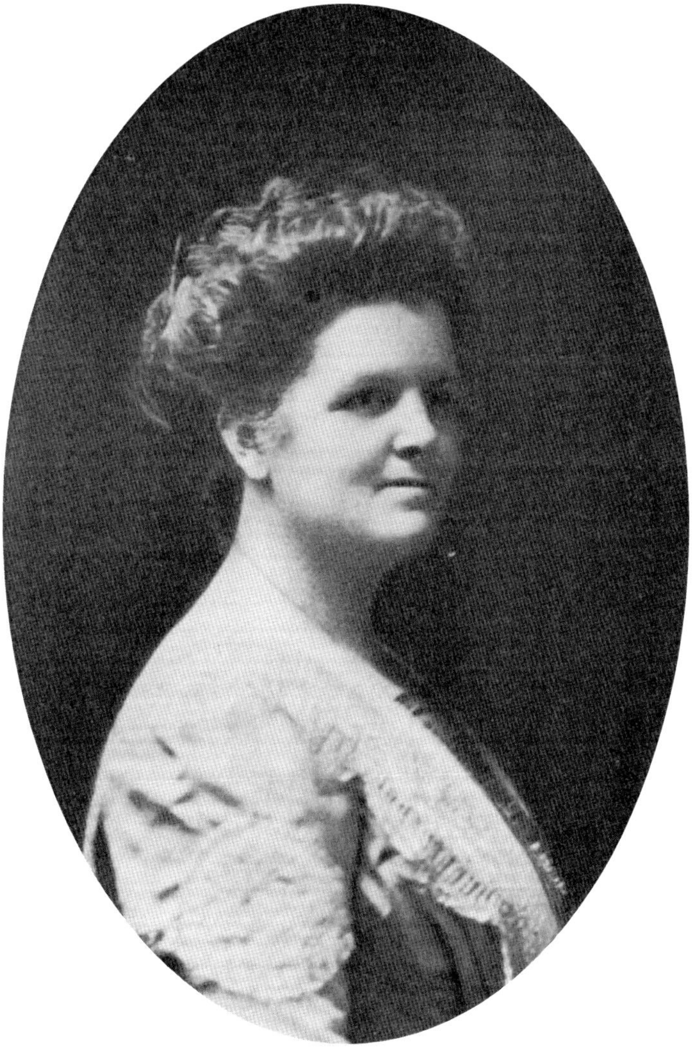

Elizabeth Towne (1865–1960)
She created the metaphysics journal *Nautilus* magazine, in 1898 in Portland, Oregon. Elizabeth Halsey Struble moved to Holyoke in 1880 to marry William Elmer Towne, vice president and secretary of her company called Elizabeth Towne Company, Inc., after her first marriage to Joseph Holt Struble ended. Towne was instrumental in creating the New Thought movement, which centered on the power of self-help, self-healing, and positive thinking. She believed that being a vegetarian, having strong Christian beliefs, and exercising on a daily basis would assure longevity and happiness. The magazine eventually had 90,000 subscribers and was circulated around the world. She was an international lecturer for the International New Thought Alliance and served on many prominent boards and clubs, including the Hampden County Women's Club of Western Massachusetts, the Massachusetts Federation of Women's Club, and the Business and Professional Women's Club. In 1912, she and her husband sat as delegates at the convention of 1916 and was one of the three state committeewomen of the Progressive party in 1913 and served on the board of directors of the Massachusetts Federation of Progressive Women. She was the first woman alderman-at-large in December 1926 and the first woman to declare her candidacy for mayor of Holyoke in 1928. She was known as a pioneer of truth and inspiration for the citizen's of Holyoke and internationally. (Courtesy of the Holyoke Public Library.)

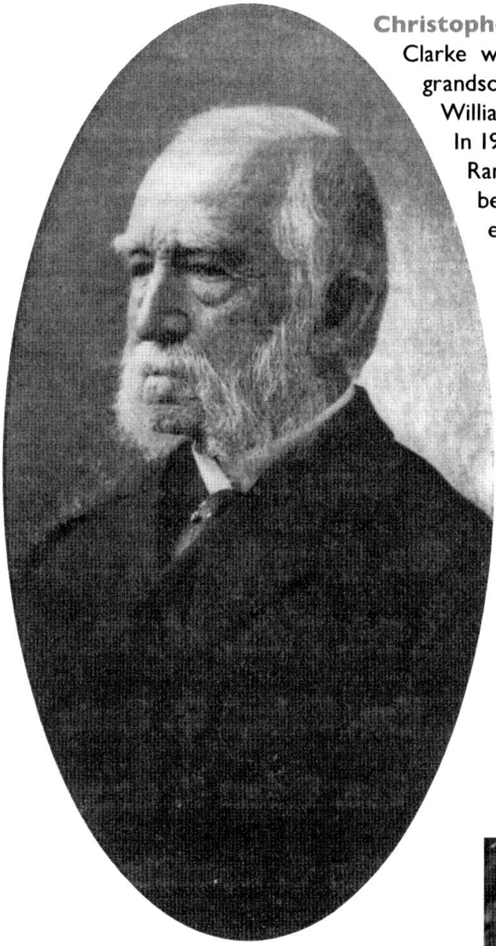

Christopher Clarke (1827–1915)
Clarke was born in Northampton; he was the paternal grandson of Samuel Clarke and the maternal grandson of William Butler, the publisher of the *Northampton Gazette*. In 1903, he sold his 150 acres of land on the Mount Tom Range to the City of Holyoke with the caveat that it be used for a public park. He also planned the now existing four-mile drive (from Easthampton Mountain Road to Holyoke to the Mount Tom railroad station). The public reservation authorities named the road Christopher Clarke Road. (Courtesy of the Forbes Library.)

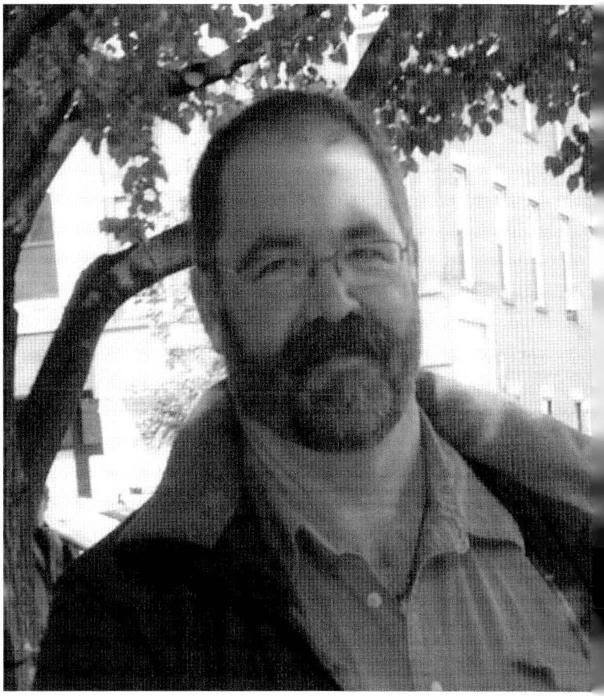

Bill Dwight (1955–)
A descendant of the *Holyoke Transcript-Telegram* newspaper Dwight family, Bill Dwight passed his general educational development (GED) tests 39 years after he would have graduated from Holyoke High School in 1973. Today, he is earning his bachelor's degree at University of Massachusetts, Amherst, in the University Without Walls program in political science with a concentration in film. This affable president of the Northampton City Council made a lasting impression in the community with his arduous effort to earn an education, inspiring people to join the Northampton Literacy Project. (Courtesy of Bill Dwight.)

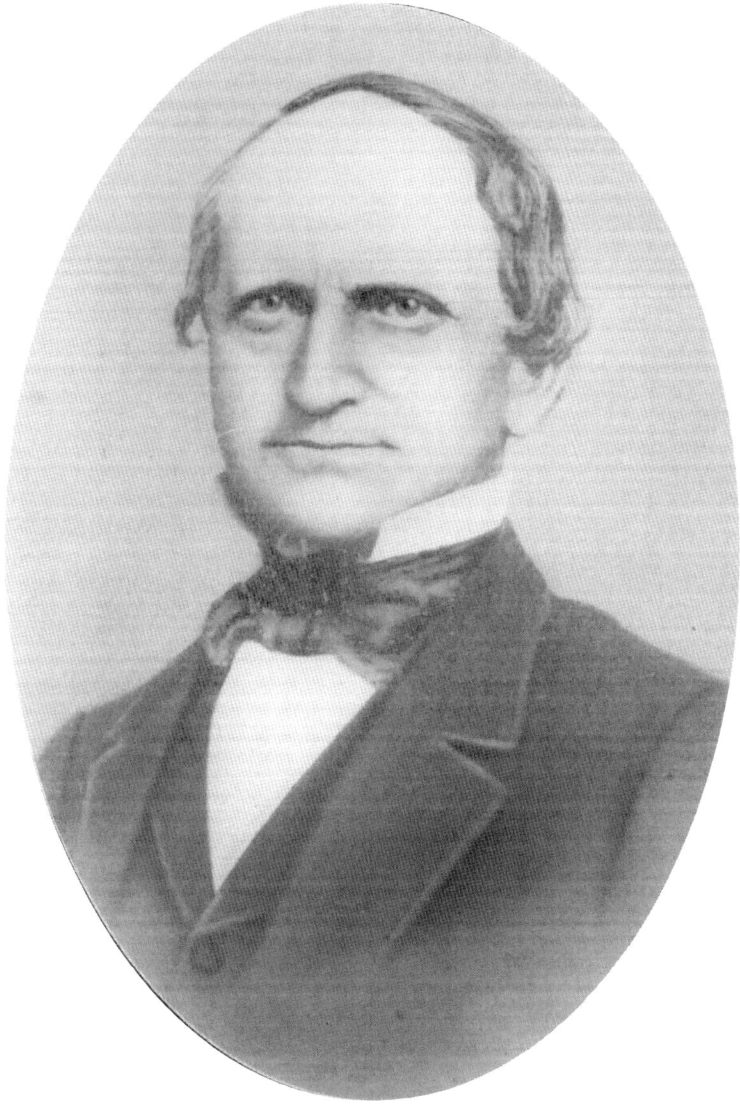

George C. Ewing (1810–1888)
He was born in Hudson, New York, to Miriam and Noble Ewing. Ewing married Lydia Ann Stillwell of Taunton, Massachusetts, and then moved to Littleton, New Hampshire. He owned a carriage manufacturing company and had eight children. He worked as a salesman for the Fairbanks Scale Company in St. Johnsbury, Vermont. On one of his trips to the Holyoke area, he observed rapids in the Connecticut River and a traprock bed between two mountain ranges. He marveled at the wing dam in Lowell, Massachusetts. In 1846, he persuaded businessmen that a dam was a feasible project to power industrial mills. The same year, he was appointed by the Hadley Falls Company to be a land agent responsible for securing 1,200 acres of land along the river. He secured water rights for the project and also purchased a large tract of land of his own in the Dwight Street section that eventually became known as Ewingville. He was instrumental in changing the landscape in Ireland Parish. He served on the board of selectmen, as a town assessor, and was a superintendent of schools. The citizens of Holyoke were fortunate to have Ewing's foresight to harness hydropower for one of the first planned industrial cities in the United States in 1846. (Courtesy of the Holyoke Public Library.)

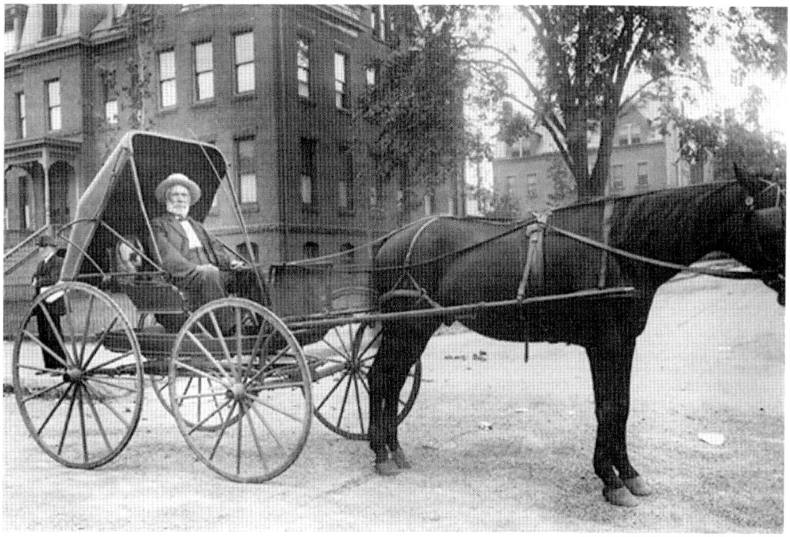

Daniel O'Connell, O'Connell Companies

In 1879, this tenacious man established the Daniel O'Connell Construction Company and hired the men he tried to protect in his former job. The company touts a good work ethic and has the following motto: "Fill your shovel or fill your coat." In 1901, the company built the Holyoke dam that still supplies hydropower to the city of Holyoke today. The company initially offered heavy construction throughout Western Massachusetts for 91 years until the founder's grandson Daniel J. O'Connell realized that the company needed to diversify. Today, the 135-year-old company is called the O'Connell Companies. It offers property management, real estate development, construction management, and contracting services through O'Connell Development Group, Appleton Corporation, New England Fertilizer Company (NEFCO), and a number of O'Connell subsidiaries, including Sealand Enviro. In 1962, the company opened the Mount Tom Ski Area. Unfortunately, it closed in 1998 to the dismay of many loyal patrons. (Courtesy of the O'Connell Companies.)

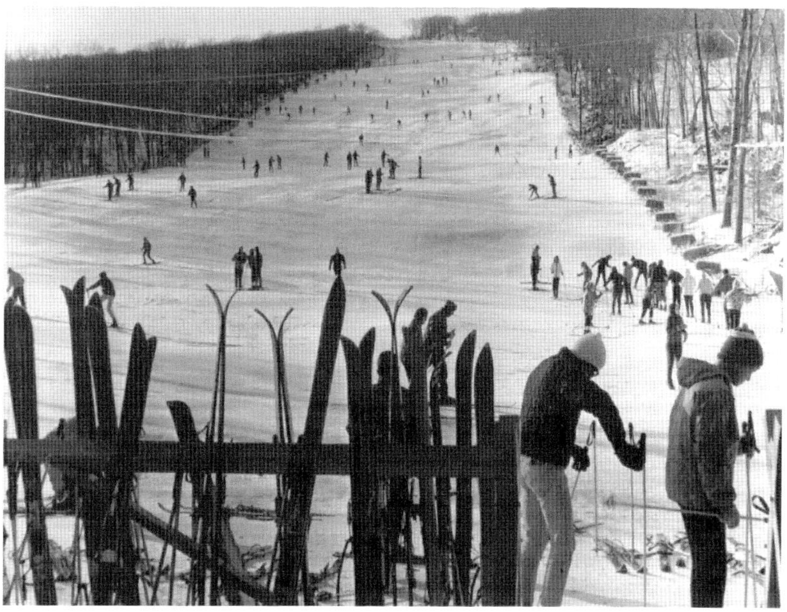

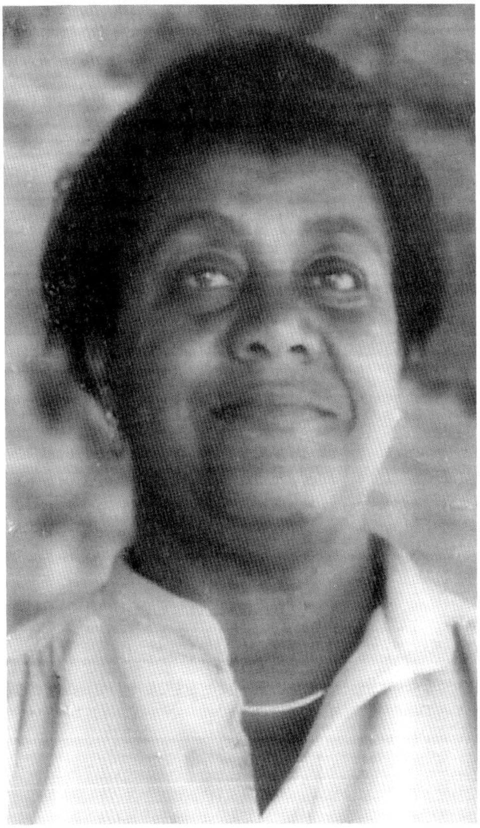

Willma Jennings (1921–1999)

Willma Jennings was born in Pittsburgh, Pennsylvania. She received her bachelor of arts degree in education at the University of Massachusetts and her master's degree in education at Springfield College. She was a teacher at the Humpty Dumpty Preschool and in the Head Start programs and Model Cities. Jennings served in World War II in the 6888th Central Postal Division, the first black women's unit in the Women's Army Corps (WAC) in England and France from 1943 to 1945. Jennings was also the first woman commissioner of the Holyoke War Memorial Building, and she volunteered at the Womanshelter-Compañeras. (Courtesy of Henry Jennings.)

Julia M. Patten (1858–1902)

She grew up in Somers, Connecticut, and graduated from the Westfield Normal School and Chicago Medical College. She studied in Vienna and Dresden and practiced in Holyoke in 1880. She was on the Holyoke City Hospital staff and the House of Providence, making her one of the leading female physicians in Western Massachusetts at that time. She passed away from a heart attack at 43 years of age. Dr. Patten was active in the Young Women's Christian association and Tuesday Club and was a commissioner of the Whiting Fund. (Courtesy of the Holyoke Public Library.)

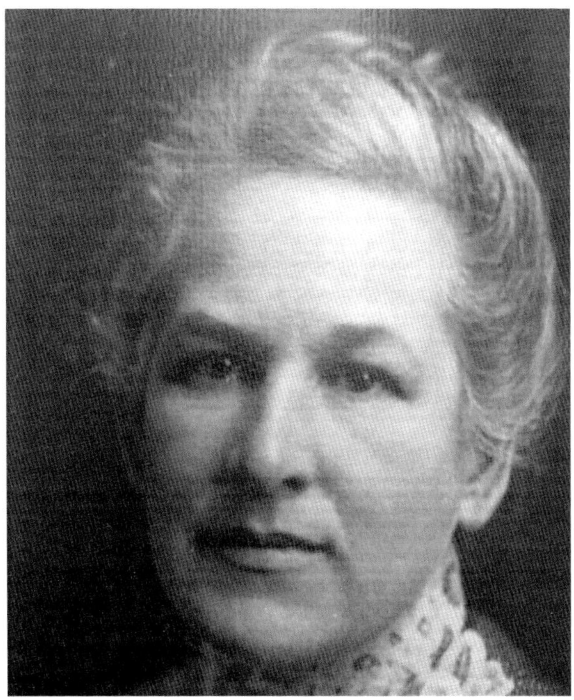

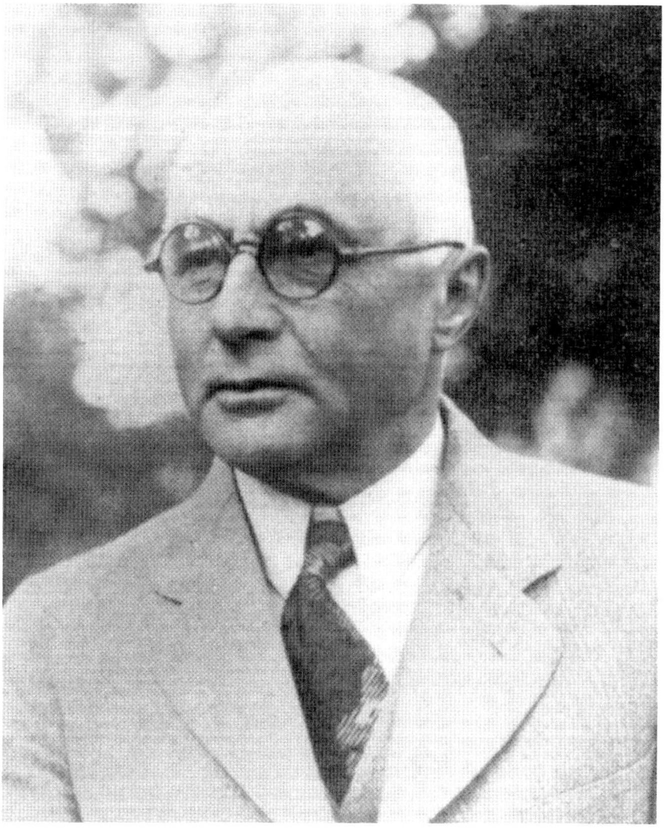

Dr. Howard Conant
Born in Elmira, New York, Conant graduated from Union College in 1892. He was the assistant principal at the Waverly High School and the principal of the PennYan High School in New York as well as at Elmira Free Academy. Starting in 1924, Conant was also a principal at Holyoke High School for 35 years. He was a faithful advocate for his students and the city of Holyoke. (Courtesy of the Holyoke Public Library.)

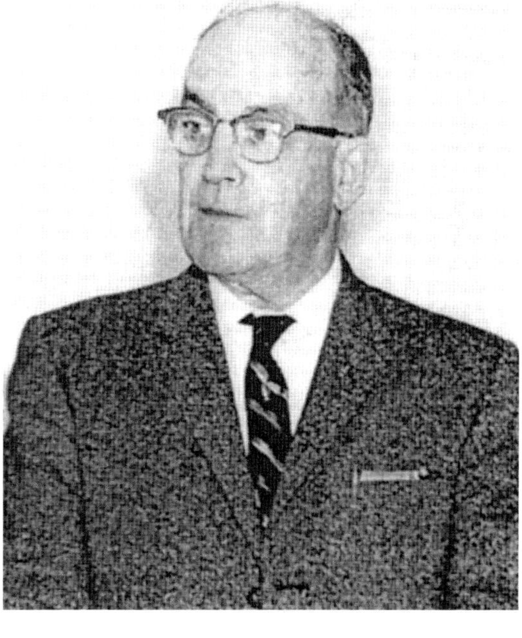

William J. Dean Sr.
Dean grew up in Holyoke, attended the Fordum School, and earned an advanced degree from Teachers' College at Columbia University. He was the principal of the Holyoke Vocational School for 30 years. Dean made it possible for his students to have breakfast through a paper project that raised funds with a periodic collection. In 1962, an addition was added to the school due to over-crowding, and the name was changed from the Holyoke Vocational School to the William J. Dean Vocational-Technical School in his honor. When the new school opened in 1989, they changed the name once again to William J. Dean Technical High School. (Courtesy of the Holyoke Public Library.)

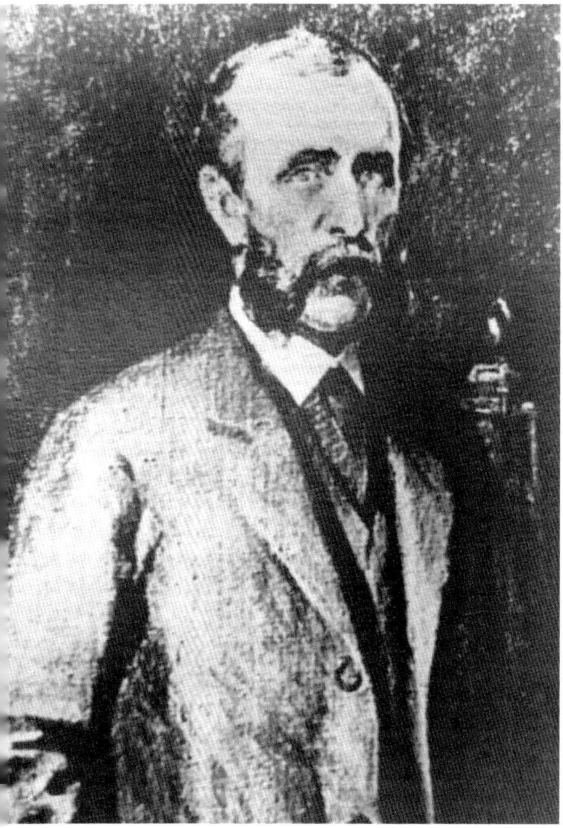

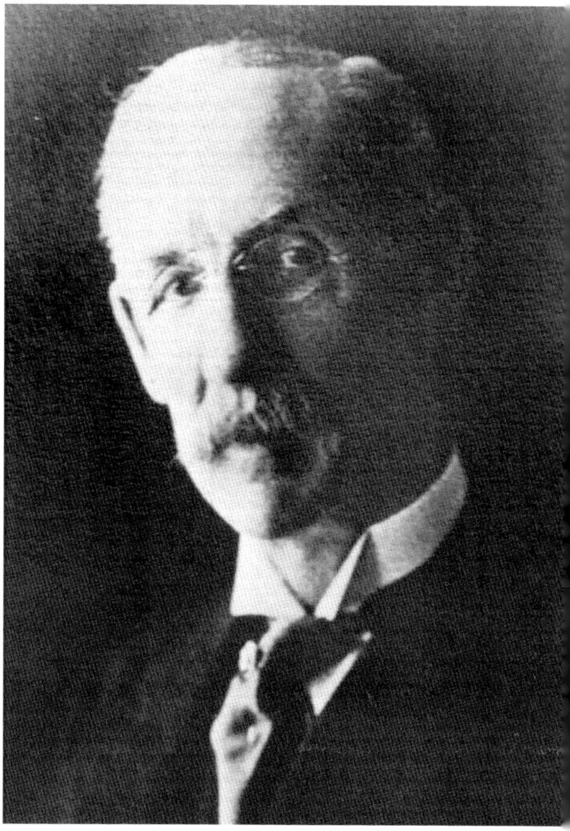

Herbert Marshall Farr and Joseph Metcalf

On November 13, 1873, Herbert Marshall Farr (pictured left) partnered with Joseph Metcalf (pictured right) to establish the Farr Alpaca Company. By 1876, the company had over 3,000 employees whose meticulous labor produced some of the finest cashmeres, serges, and other wool products in the United States and in Europe. Employees were given access to doctors, dentists, and an English teacher to help them get acclimated to the United States. They were also given an athletic field, a community house, and an entertainment venue on the first floor of a factory. This was unheard in the 1800s; Farr and Metcalf were clever industrious men who were not only generous but also ahead of their time. They were progressive thinkers who understood that if a person wants to stand out in a crowd of manufacturers, then he'd better stand up for the people who are manufacturing their products—and they most certainly did! (Courtesy of the Holyoke Public Library.)

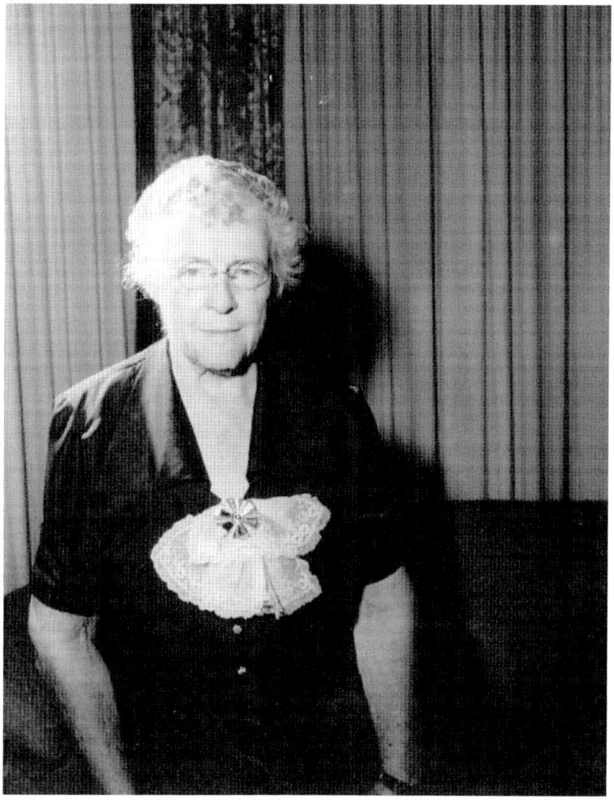

Minnie Ryan Dwight (1873–1957)
Minnie and her husband, William Dwight, published the *Holyoke Transcript-Telegram* together until his untimely death in Fruitland Park, Florida. Prior to his passing they owned a home called Pine Eden and purchased a community center called The Casino, which they donated to the city. She continued to publish the newspaper after her husband's passing. She wrote a column called "Letters from Florida," where she expressed her strong opinions about social issues affecting women and children. She was also involved in helping impoverished children in downtown Holyoke. (Courtesy of the Holyoke Public Library.)

Eric Suhr (1965–)
A successful businessman, Suhr owns ES Sports and many commercial buildings in Holyoke and Northampton. He also owns and runs a whole plethora of successful entertainment venues under the name of the Iron Horse Entertainment Group in Northampton, Massachusetts. Included in this group are the Iron Horse Music Hall, Pearl Street Nightclub, Calvin Theatre, and the Mountain Park Amphitheater on the Mount Tom Range. Suhr is hailed for providing the citizens in Western Massachusetts with employment and safe and well-maintained places for invigorating and relaxing entertainment. (Courtesy of Eric Suhr.)

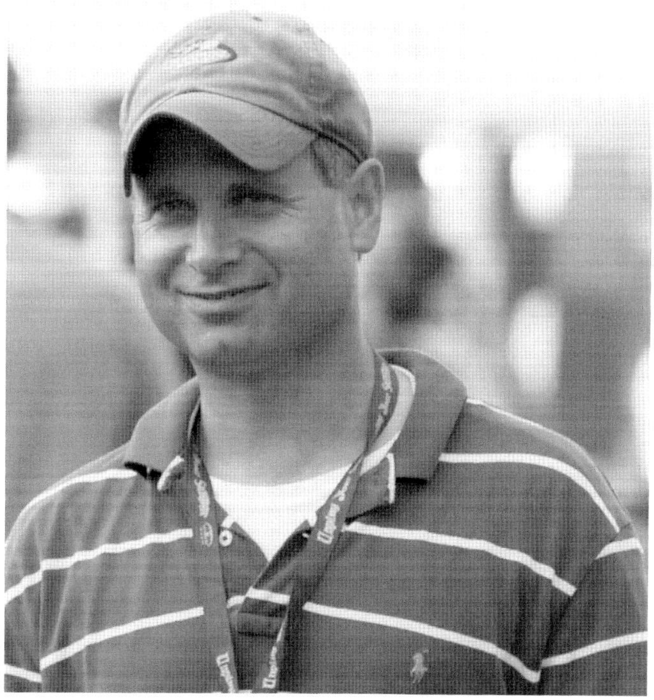

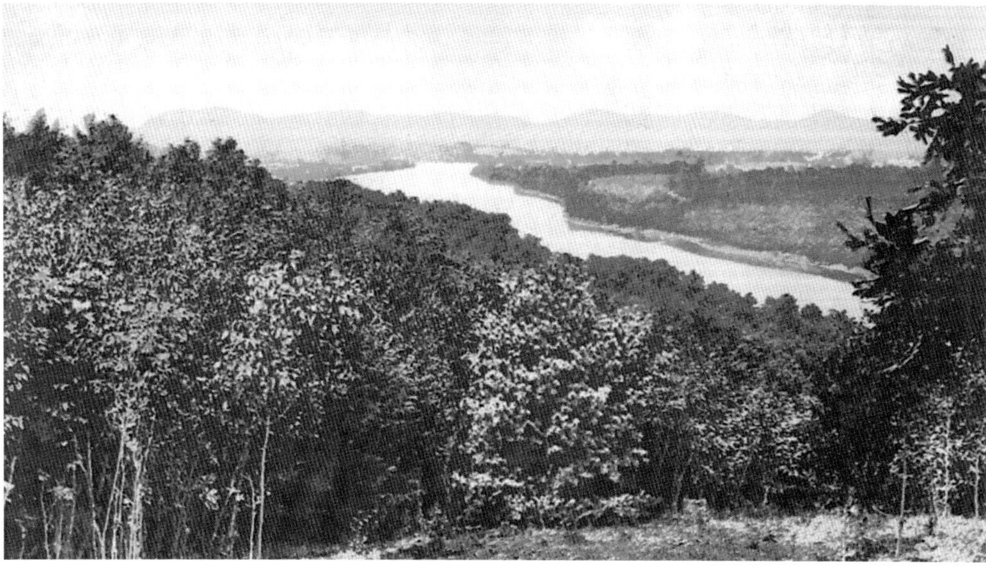

Gary "Ridesfar" Thibault (1953–2001)

Gary Thomas Thibault, also known as "Ridesfar," was a member of the Haudenosaunee (or Iroquois League) Six Nation Confederacy. He grew up in Chicopee and lived on the Mount Tom Range in two tents and a lean-to house in the vacant Mountain Park section of the range in the 1980s for about 10 years. He was a dishwasher at the Bickford's Family Restaurant in West Springfield and a naturalist, artist, and poet. According to his brother Kickapoo Thunder, he would collect plastic bottles and then use the proceeds to feed his cats—the cats would keep him warm by sleeping in his tent.

Sadly, a car with a headlight out on Route 5 never saw him on the evening of July 20, 2001, as he was walking his bike due to a broken chain. When they found him, his bike was unscathed, but he was not as lucky. Kickapoo Thunder called for a traditional Native American Burial Ceremony. Mohawk, Algonquian, Hebrew, and French Canadian Indians attended his burial service; the tribal ceremony, which was usually only for Indian chiefs, had not been performed in more than 250 years. Ridesfar was granted this unique ritual ceremony due to adhering to his traditional Native American Indian practices, such as living in nature and being a good steward to the environment. Chief Randy Joseph (Wampanogg) with assistance from Larry Mann (Nipmuc) performed the sacred ceremony. His brother recited the following poem at the ceremony:

I'm not here
Do not stand by my grave and weep
I m not there. I do not sleep.
I am a thousand winds that blow.
I am the diamonds glint on snow.
I am the sunlight on ripened grain.
I am the gentle autumn rain.
When you awaken in morning's hush
I am the swift uplifting rush
Of quiet birds in circled flight.
I am the soft stars that shine at night
Do not stand by my grave and cry;
I am not there. I did not die.

(Courtesy of Mary Elizabeth Frye)

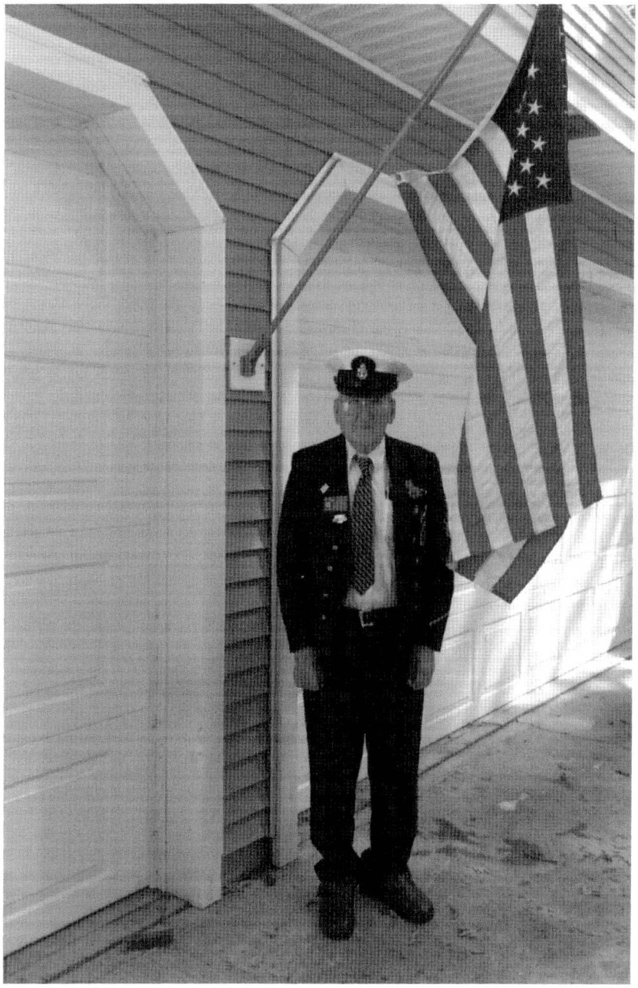

Edward Borucki (1920–)
Edward Borucki was born and raised in Holyoke; he was the fourth of seven children who resided on Lyman Street in Holyoke. He graduated from Holyoke High in 1939 and worked for the Springfield Daily News Company in distribution until he worked at the Armory in Springfield. He enlisted in the Navy in 1940 and was stationed in Hawaii on the USS *Helena* (CL50) at Dock NO. 1010 when the Japanese attacked Pearl Harbor on December 7, 1941. As the chief petty officer, Borucki shut the watertight doors as he heard countless torpedoes, men screaming, and massive guns on the ship trying to shoot down the Japanese planes. He is extremely lucky to be here, especially since a torpedo had destroyed the battle station he had been at 30 seconds after he left it. He was given the grim task of carrying 33 of his deceased comrades off the ship. He returned home to earn his bachelor of arts degree from American International College with the assistance of the G.I. Bill. He taught in the Springfield and Chicopee school systems. Borucki worked for two years to have a bridge named in honor of the Pearl Harbor veterans; the bridge was named Pearl Harbor Veterans Memorial Bridge in Easthampton. He also was the commander of Southampton American Legion Post No. 168 and the district commander for Franklin and Hampden Convention in Hawaii, Chicago, and Miami. Asked why he continues to talk about the attack on Pearl Harbor and why he proudly wears his uniform, he says, "He wants people to never forget about the 2,390 brave men, including his shipmates that were killed and the 1,178 men that were wounded on that fateful day 73 years ago." (Courtesy of Edward Borucki.)

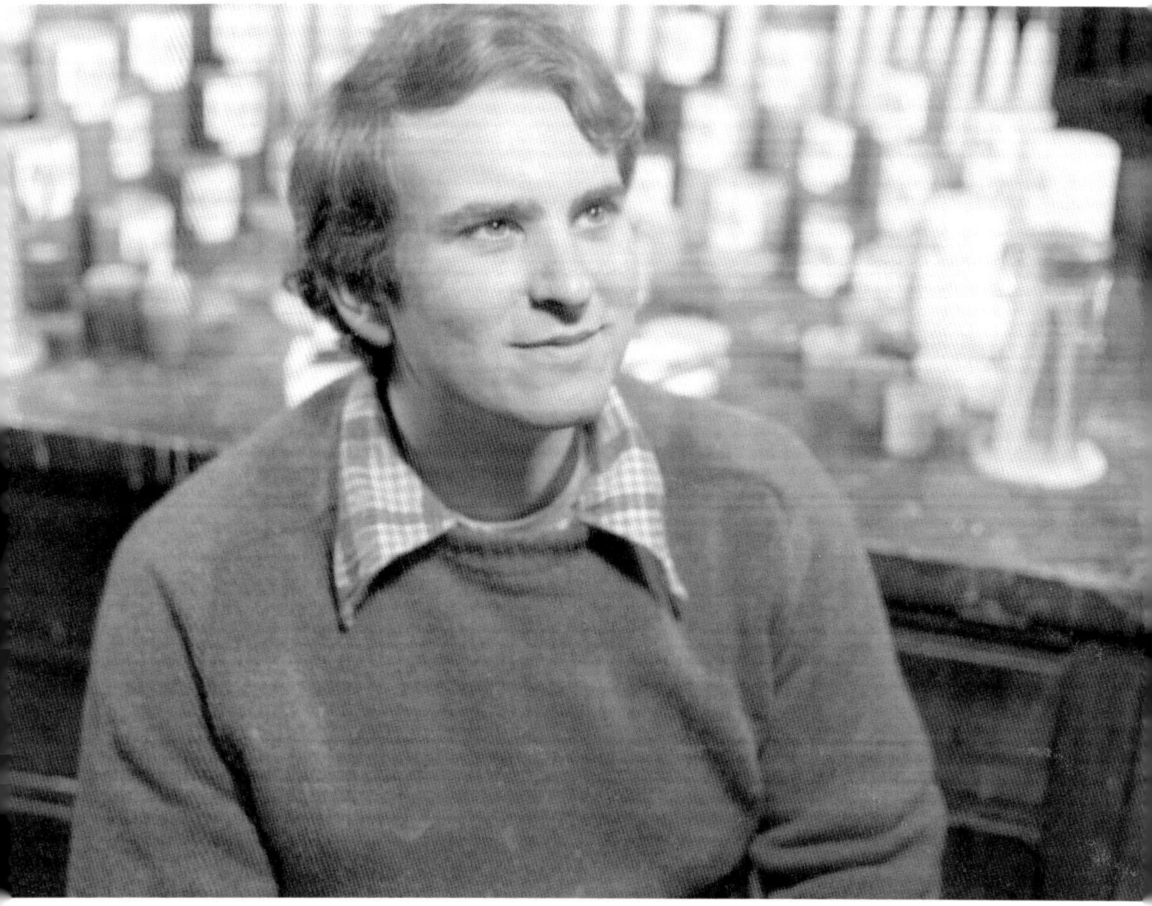

Yankee Candle Company, Michael Kittredge
In 1969, 16-year-old Michael Kittredge (1953–) was attending South Hadley High School and playing a guitar in a band called Bristol Curries. When his band broke up and he needed money to buy a Christmas gift for his mother, he used his imagination. He found some used crayons, a pound of canning wax, and borrowed wicks from existing candles around the house. He added scent and warmed up the crayons in a metal container and poured it into a used milk carton, making his first scented candle. He started selling his popular candles out of his parents' home in 1971, but his parents eventually encouraged him to find another suitable place. In 1979, he rented an old mill in Holyoke, and by 1979, he had 30 employees working for him. The company began distributing his candles nationally. Originally called Candles by Michael Kittredge, he renamed his company the Yankee Candle Company. He ran his company for 10 years in Holyoke until 1983, when he outgrew the building and moved the company up to South Deerfield, Massachusetts. He opened a second store in 1986 in Sturbridge, Massachusetts. In 1993, he opened the Yankee Candle Bavarian Christmas Village, the Yankee Candle Car Museum, and Chandler's Restaurant in South Deerfield. By 1998, he entered into a partnership with the investment firm Forstmann Little & Company, and by 1999, an initial public offering in stock was completed. While Kittredge sold his extraordinary company for $550 million, he has left an enduring legacy that inspires all to believe that anything is possible if one works hard. (Courtesy of the Kittredge family.)

Mark Folta (1958–)

He was born in Holyoke, attended Perpetual Help School, and graduated from Holyoke High School in 1977. He earned his associate's degree at Holyoke Community College in 1980 and his bachelor of arts at Southeastern Massachusetts University in 1982. He was a substitute teacher at Holyoke High School. In 1985, he earned his teaching certificate and went on to get his master's in business management at Cambridge College in 2000. He was a business teacher at Holyoke High School until he was offered a vice principal position at Hampshire Regional High School in Westhampton, Massachusetts. All the while, he has been working at Stop and Shop in the Deli for 32 years. When asked why he reaches out to help people whether at the deli or at school, he says he enjoys helping people and strives "to empower kids to help them solve their problems." (Courtesy of Mark Folta.)

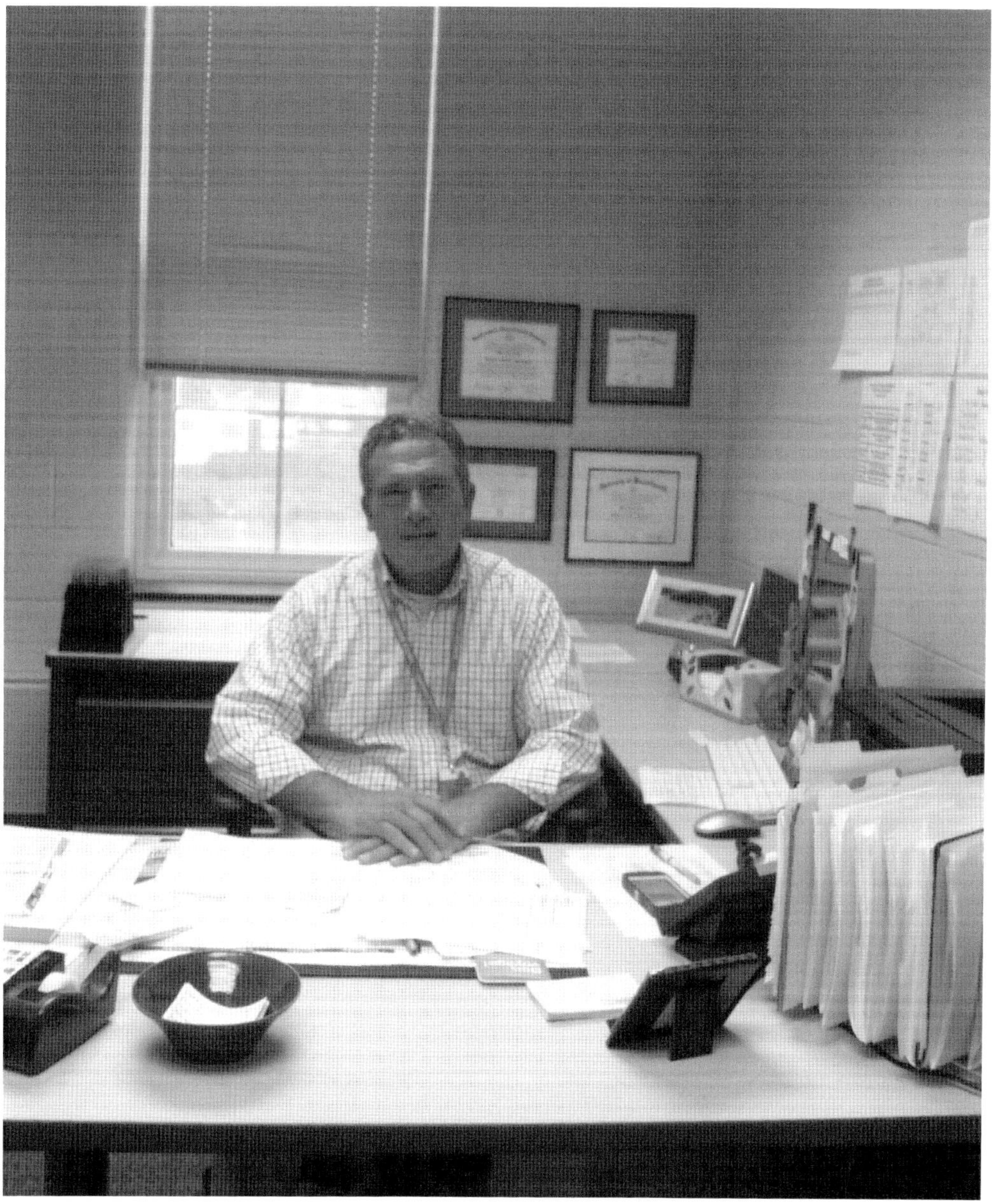

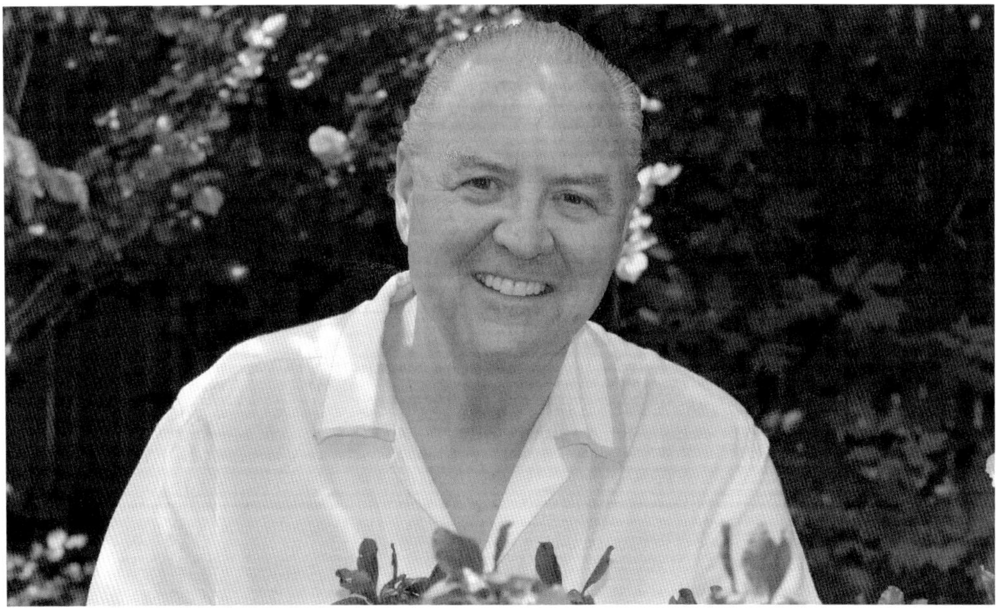

Daniel J. Shanahan

Daniel J. Shanahan worked as a fisherman on Cape Cod, as a welder on a cargo ship in the Quincy Shipyard, as a truck driver, and as a warehouseman on the Alaska Pipeline. Reading the works of Dylan Thomas, T.S. Elliot, and Yeats at the tender age of 15 at the Holyoke Public Library helped him to develop into a talented and intuitive poet. He has lived in Alaska and India, where he learned from the meditation masters. He is a founding member of Stone Soup Poets, which is thought to be one of the longest-running open poetry forums in the United States. He is also the founder of Drumlin, a contemplative performing arts ensemble, and is the sole proprietor of Lotus Seed Poetry. Shanahan is a guest teacher at Holyoke Community College and the city's Adult Basic Education School; he encourages his students to experience a poem as a vital presence in one's imagination. Shanahan has published insightful poetry books, including *The Lotus Seed Poems*, *Alaska Poems*, and *Crystal Lake Poems*. He has also been active in promoting the use of battery-operated cars. (Courtesy of Daniel J. Shanahan.)

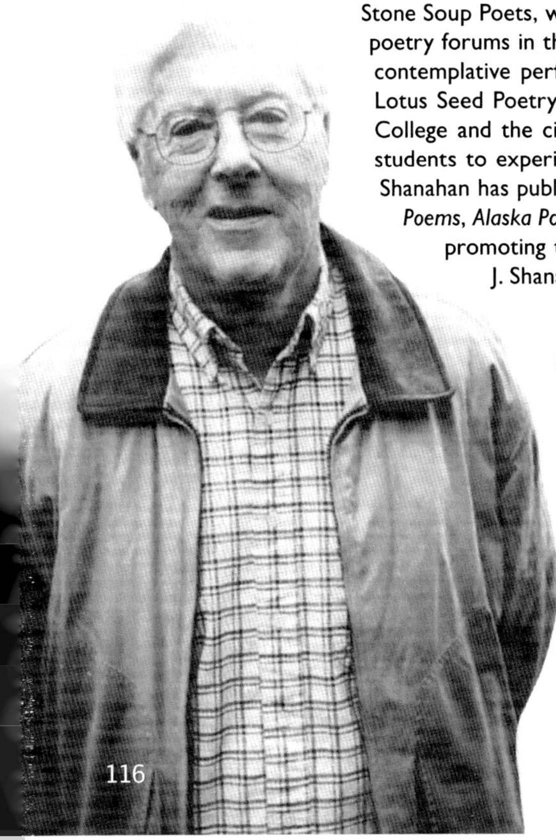

Paul Graves

Born and raised in Holyoke, Paul Graves worked for RCA for 10 years and was a regional sales manager for Magnavox for 15 years. He was instrumental in researching and documenting the history of Holyoke. He was the director of the History Room in the Holyoke Public Library and a 2013 recipient of a Preservation Award from the Holyoke Historical Commission. He organized and inspired the library to purchase an afghan depicting historical scenes and important markers of Holyoke's amazing past to raise funds for the renovation of the Holyoke Public Library. (Courtesy of the Graves family.)

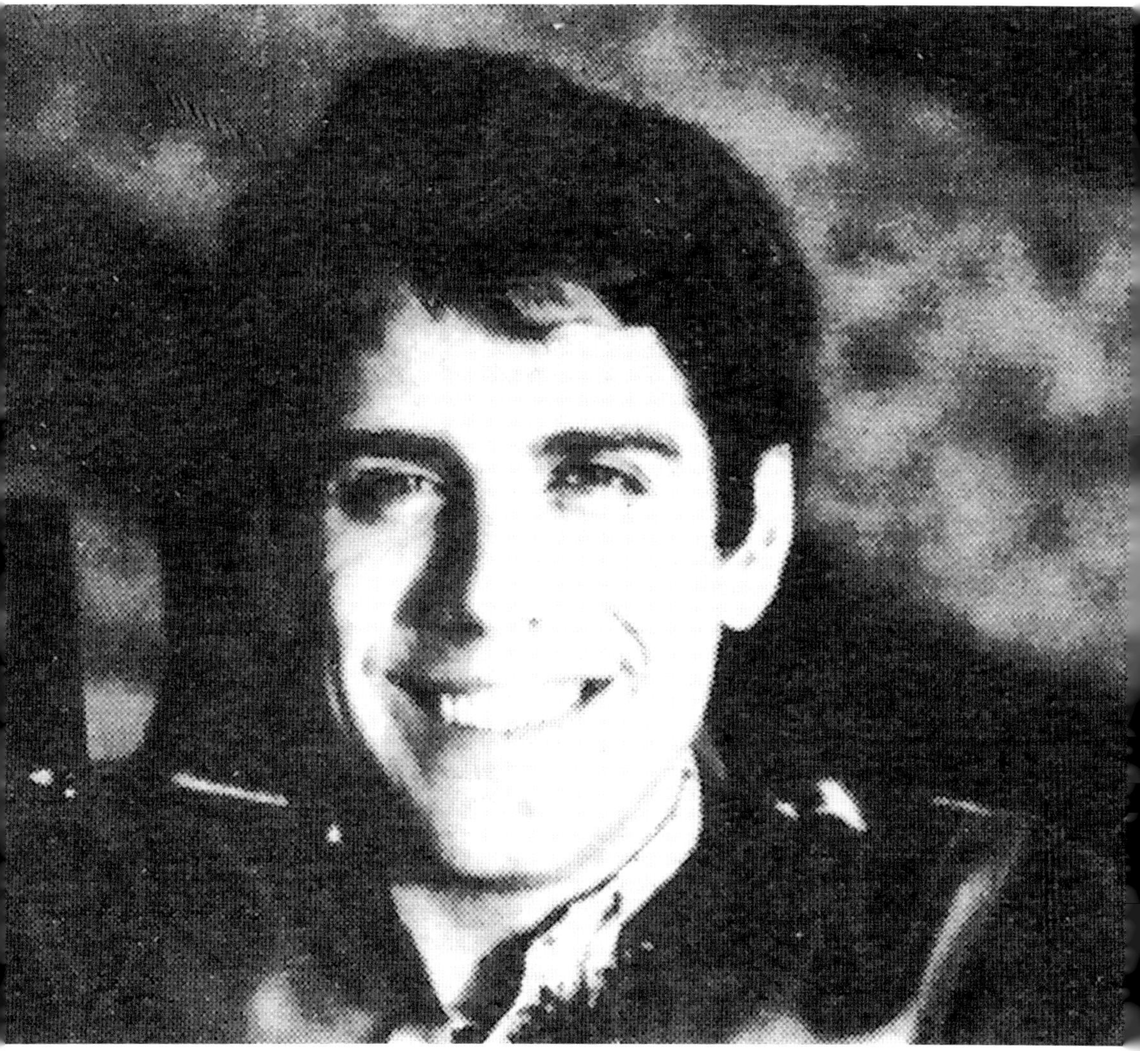

Warren Plaut (1951–1987)
Warren Plaut was born in Chicago but later moved to New York. He graduated from Antioch College in Ohio with a degree in Latin American studies. He worked for the North American Congress on Latin America (NACLA) in New York City. He traveled extensity through Latin American, fostering initiatives to bring reason and peace to the natives. In 1974, the Dennison National Company employed him. He was instrumental in establishing the Massachusetts Coalition for Occupational Safety and Health (MassCOSH) in Boston. Due to his negotiating skills and human rights knowledge, he was elected president of Graphic Communications International Union Local No. 48 in 1985. He worked hard to educate Spanish workers in Holyoke and Springfield about their rights. He passed away in a camping accident in New Hampshire after working hard to finish contract union negotiations for the employees at the Dennison National Company. Plaut's wife, Roberta, and her daughter organized the Warren Plaut Charitable Trust that raises funds and donates to organizations that continue Plaut's social justice work. Today, the trust has three funds called the Warren Plaut Memorial Fund, the Jobs with Justice Fund, and the Union Community Fund. (Courtesy of Jon Weissman.)

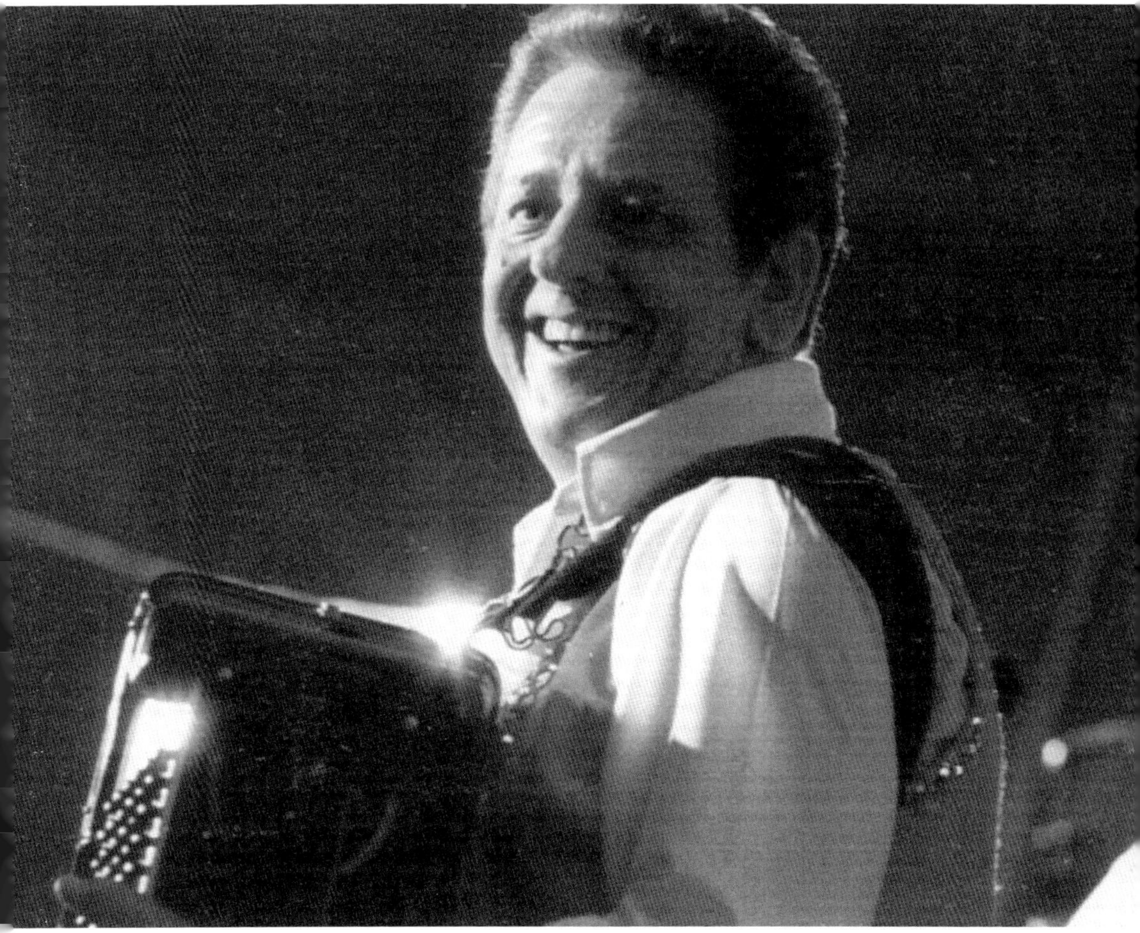

Larry Chesky (1933–2011)

Holyoke-born Chesky was given an accordion when he was only six years old and formed a band with the help of his father, Joe Chesky. They called his first band The Polka Dots when he was 12 years old. By the time he was 15 years old, the band was so popular that they changed the name to Larry's Polka Dots. The band was signed with the Musico Record Company with the help of his mentor and promoter, Joe Tauss, of New York. Chesky formed his "big-band sound" around this time, and his band became a 10-piece orchestra. He changed the name to Larry Chesky and His Orchestra. The band's first major hit was called "Our Gang Oberek." He was ecstatic that people loved his music but knew his education was more important and returned to Massachusetts to finish his education at Holyoke High School and the Hart School of Music. With degree in hand and people clamoring for Larry Chesky and His Orchestra to perform, he played on the eastern polka circuit from New York to Chicago. At one point, he worked with celebrated artists Bobby Vinton, James Darin, Barbara Mandrell, and other famous artists associated with the great Lawrence Welk. In 1974, he formed a company called Modern Mail International to promote Polish heritage through the distribution of "Proud To Be Polish" products. He continued to be very popular, performing at major fairs and parks, like the Eastern States Exposition, the Cobleskill New York Fair, and the Mountain Park Amusement Park in Holyoke. He also performed on countless television and radio programs and was inducted into the Polka Hall of Fame in Chicago in 1985. This talented man made the community happy with his upbeat music and bright smile, a true Holyoke legend. He was also a generous family man and contributed his time to the Shriners. (Courtesy of Linda Chesky Fernandes.)

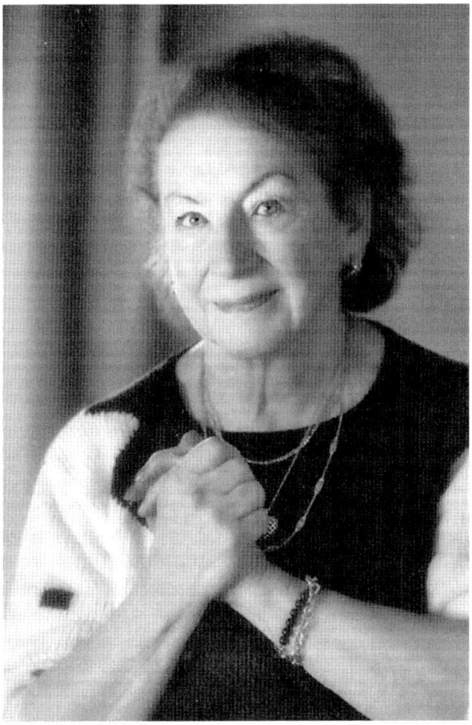

Angela Wright (1935–)
This courageous soul came from West Hartford, Connecticut. She graduated from Holyoke High School in 1952, Holyoke Community College in 1954, and then Boston University. She taught at Holyoke High School. In 1986, she established the Community Adolescent Resource (Care) Center, an alternative education program for pregnant and parenting teens who dropped out of high school. The center continues to help and support teens today. She also served on the boards of the Children's Museum of Holyoke, Junior League of Holyoke, Holyoke Hospital, and the Community Foundation of Western Massachusetts. (Courtesy of Angela Wright.)

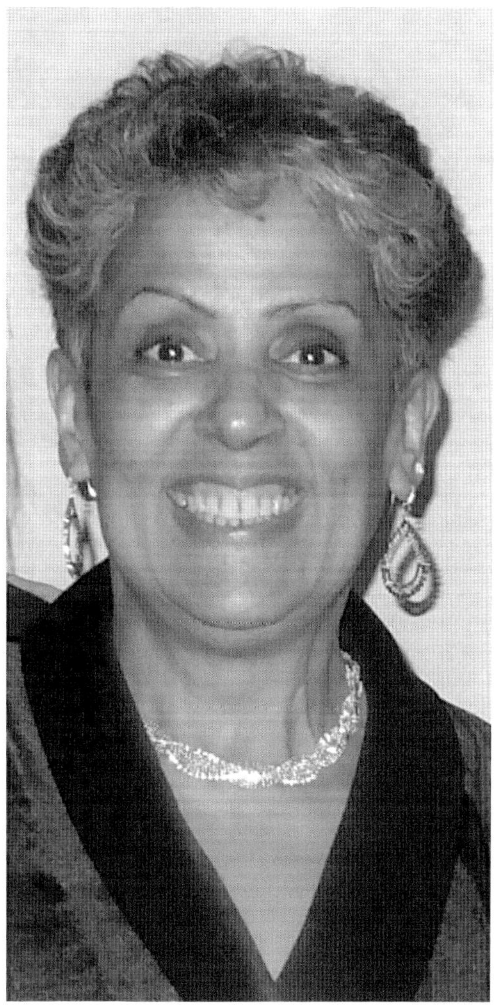

Betty Medina Lichtenstein (1952–)
Born in New York, Betty (Medina) Lichtenstein's family was from Puerto Rico; she moved to Holyoke to help children live a better life. She worked at Baystate Medical Center and was the first female Puerto Rican to be elected to the Holyoke School Committee. Today, she is the executive director of Enlace de Familias (Holyoke Family Network) and is an alliance builder for the Holyoke Unites Organization. She was the recipient of the Sr. Agnes Broderick, SP, Justice & Peace Award, Dora Fuentes Award, and the William G. Dwight Distinguished Service Award. (Courtesy of Betty Medina Lichtenstein.)

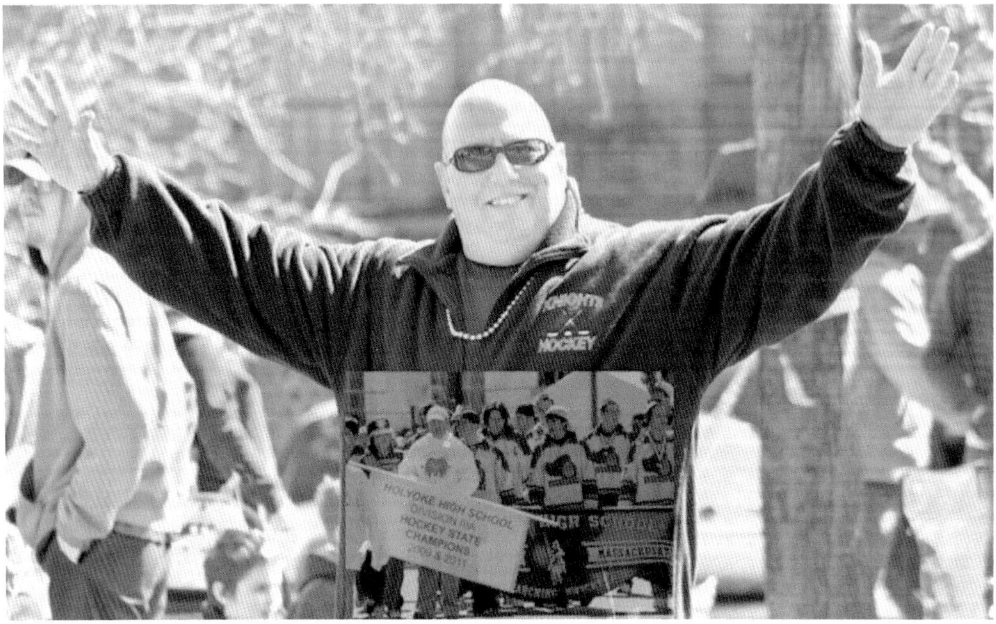

Larry Camus (1961–)
He graduated from Holyoke High School in 1979 and attended Holyoke Community College. He has been a correctional officer for the last 30 years and currently works at the Hampden County Center in Ludlow. Due to his wife's premature death, he has raised his two children and a foster child on his own. He is an assistant coach for the South Hadley–Holyoke cooperative hockey team at the Fitzpatrick Skating Rink in Holyoke, where he has faithfully mentored children and has helped to raise funds for children for the last 16 years. (Courtesy of Larry Camus.)

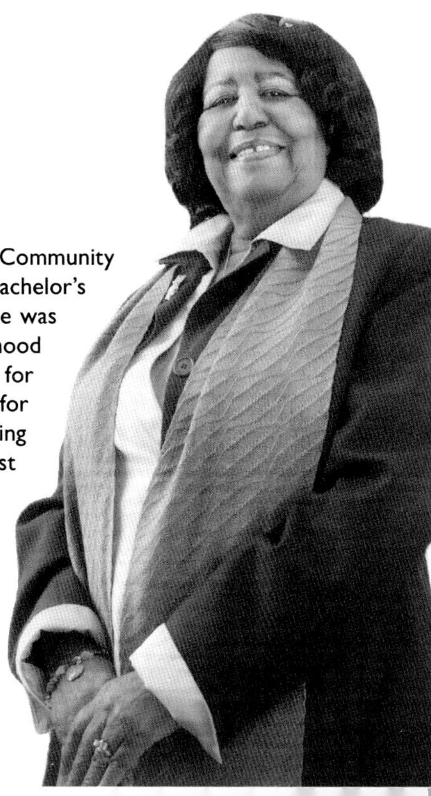

Gloria G. Lomax (1930–)
This tenacious African American woman graduated from Holyoke Community College when she was 45 years old and went on to earn her bachelor's and master's degree in early childhood education in 1970s. She was the first African American woman to teach in the early childhood department at Holyoke Community College and worked there for 27 years. She developed a curriculum and teaching methods for students to overcome prejudices. She also created a "Parenting from Afar" course for incarcerated women and launched the first preschool program in a Massachusetts prison. She is a well-respected member of the community due to her integrity and compassion and was a recipient of the Standing on Her Shoulders Award in 2013 from the Women's Fund. (Courtesy of Robert Charles Photography.)

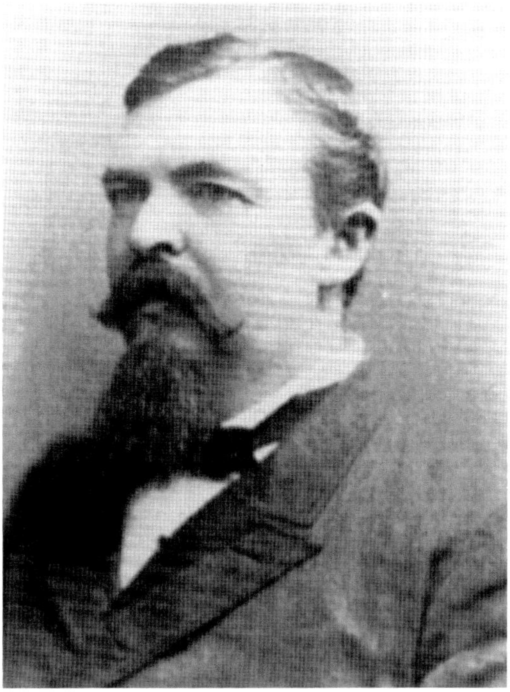

Dr. J.J. O'Connor (1843–1888)
Arriving in Holyoke in 1866, after graduating from Harvard he became a well-liked physician who treated all of his patients with humility and respect. He was the vice president of the Massachusetts Medical Society and served as a member of the State Board of Lunacy and Charity. His early demise of 45 years shook the community due to his profound impact on his patients. (Courtesy of the Holyoke Public Library.)

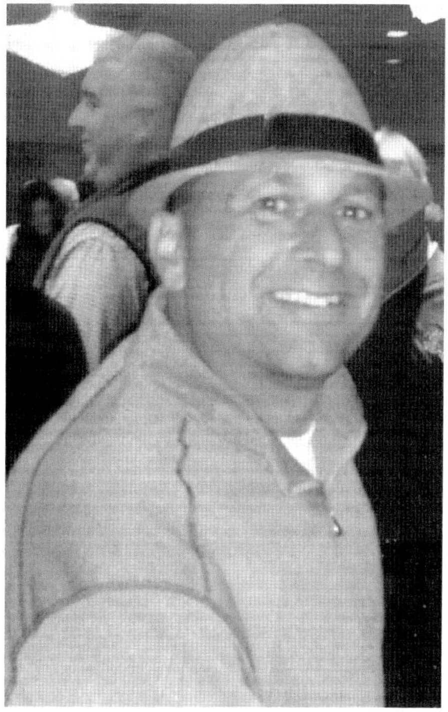

Michael Hamel (1961–)
Growing up in a prominent Holyoke family, Michael Hamel learned his *pépère*'s ideals and values. He graduated from Holyoke High in 1979 and joined the US Air Force in 1981. He earned an associate's degree in business at Holyoke Community College and a medical technology bachelor's degree from Springfield Technical College. While a student, he was asked to cater a social event due to his family's outstanding culinary reputation, and was inspired to open Hamel's Deli Catering in 1990. By 2002, he renamed his business Summit View Banquet & Meeting House and opened it in Holyoke, offering delicious food and excellent service. (Courtesy of Michael Hamel.)

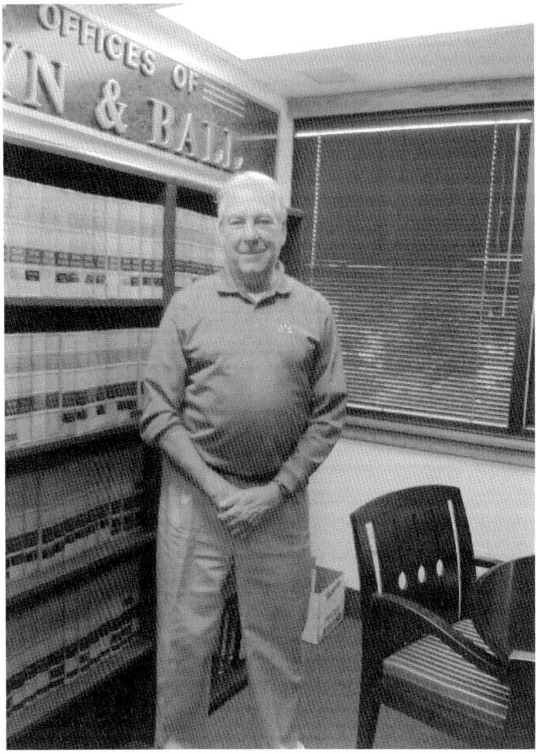

Aaron Wilson (1943–)
He was born in Holyoke and graduated from Holyoke High School and Holyoke Community College. He worked odd jobs until he ran a towing company, served as a Holyoke police officer, an alderman, and in the US Army in 1968. In 1973, he was a probation officer and earned a degree at American International College. He passed the bar in 1975 and became a sought after defense attorney in 1976. He has helped thousands of people in his 38-year criminal justice career. (Courtesy of Aaron Wilson.)

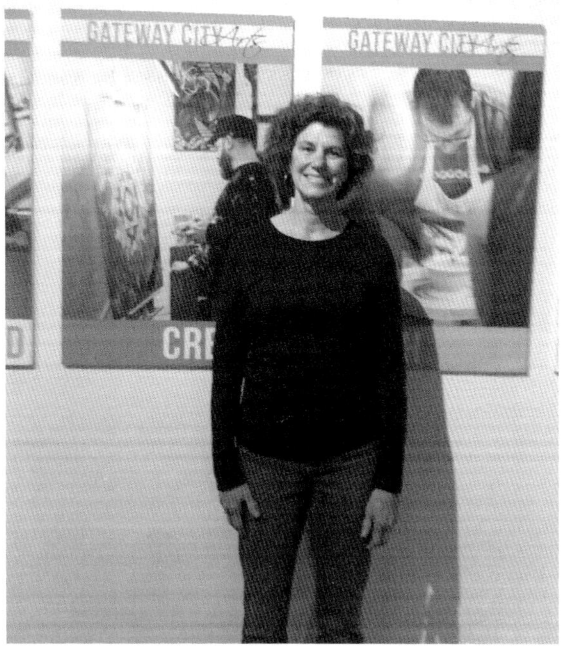

Lori Divine-Hudson (1952–)
Growing up in Minneapolis, Minnesota, she moved to Long Island, attended Boston University and received a BS in Physical Therapy. She also earned an MEd in counseling from UMass / Amherst and continued to work as a physical therapist while raising children and caring for her then ailing husband a professor at Smith College. Beginning in 2001, Lori studied with artist Vitek Kruta, and in 2011 they collaborated to create and renovate a beautiful 40,000-square-foot old mill building into Gateway City Arts, offering event space, artist studios, and ongoing art classes on Race Street in Holyoke. (Courtesy of Lori Divine.)

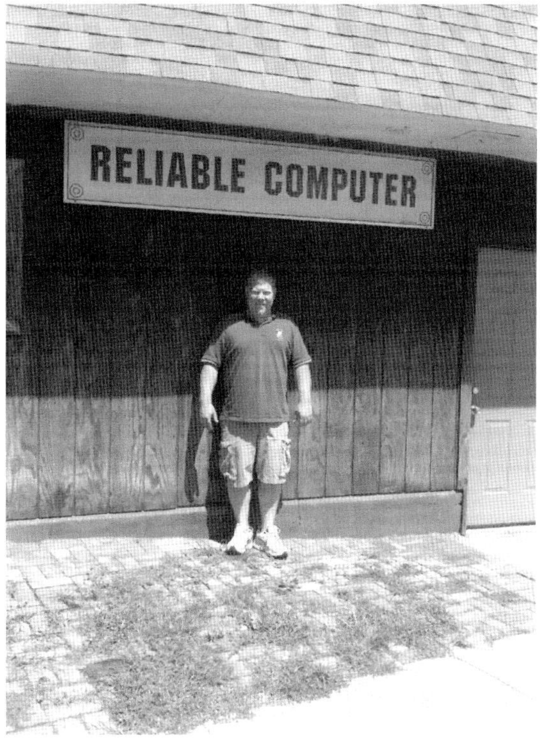

Daniel Deschaine (1973–)
He was born in Holyoke and grew up in Westfield. He attended Holyoke Community College and grew interested in computers after working for a monitor repair company. He graduated in 1995 from the Porter and Chester Institute and opened the Reliable Computer Company in 1996 in Holyoke. This friendly and knowledgeable computer expert has been providing his customers with reasonably priced refurbished and new computers for 18 years. He is the recipient of a certificate of appreciation from the South Hadley Police Association and the Booster Association of South Hadley (BASH) for his generous support; he also received a certificate of appreciation from the Holyoke Fireman's Aid Association, Inc. (Courtesy of Daniel Deschaine.)

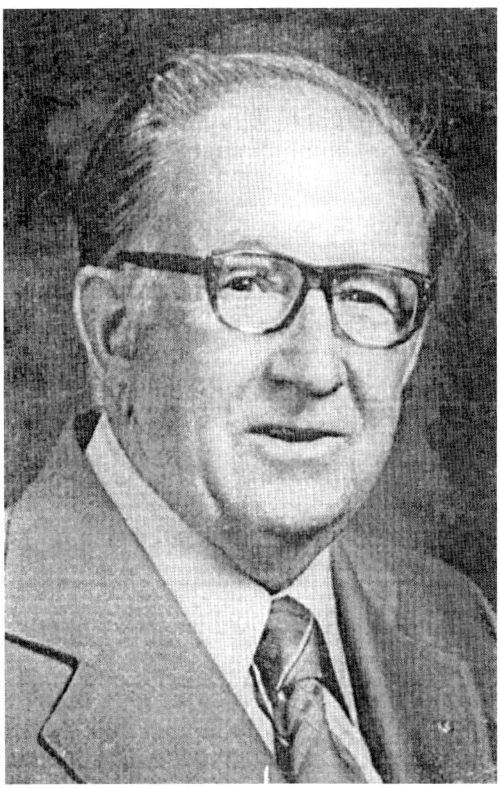

James "Jim" Prentice (1909–2005)
He was born and raised in Holyoke. When he graduated from the University of New Hampshire in 1934, he opened the Electric Game Company. He sold games to the Parker Brothers Company and Macy's department store. He developed over 100 games and employed 140 people; employees were divided into two shifts in the former Mackintosh Building on 109 Lyman Street. He was awarded the Abbot Award in 1993 for being a unique entrepreneur in the American game industry and for contributing games that have a social significance, are easy to play, and display an artistic flare. (Courtesy of Harry Craven Jr.)

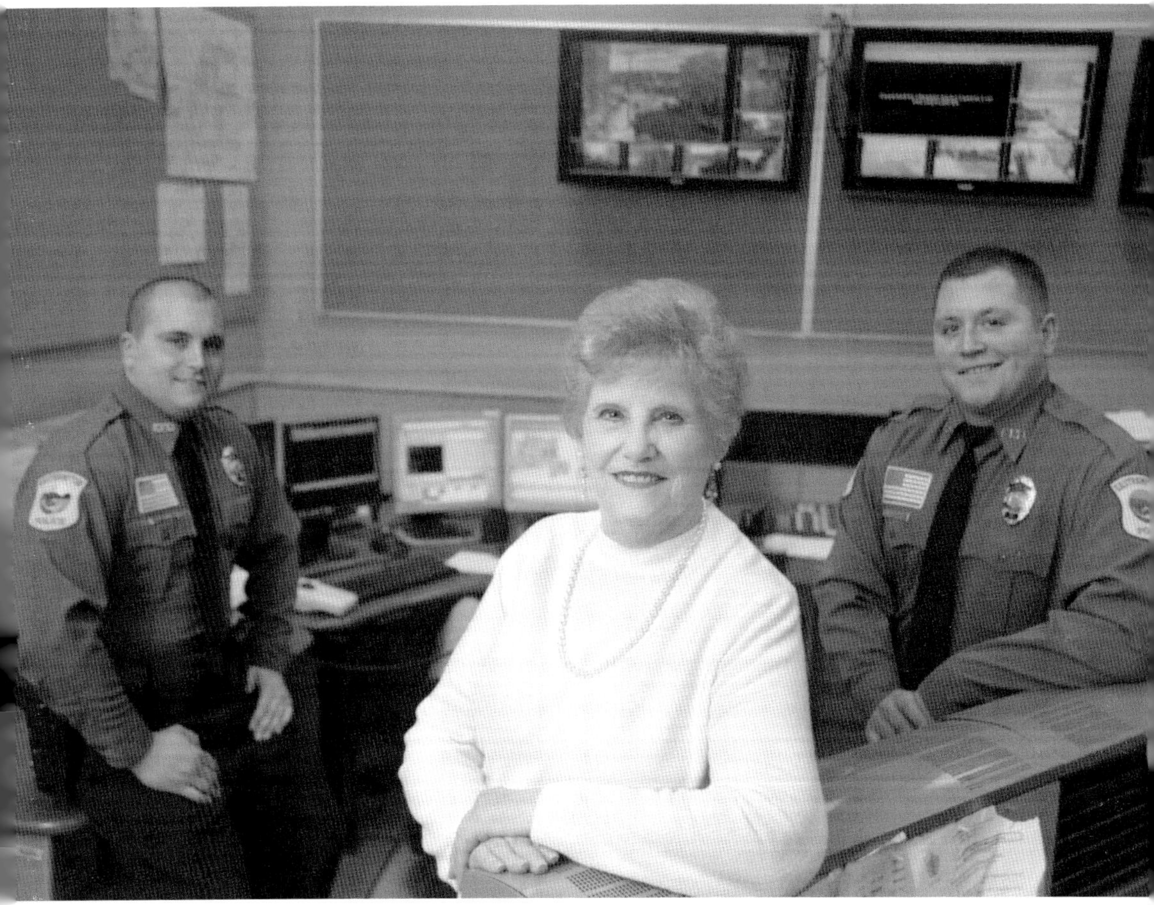

Marlene Werenski
She joined the Holyoke police department in 1971 when women were a scarcity on the force. She fostered a sense of caring and resolve for women who were in abusive relationships and had been sexually assaulted. Werenski earned the respect of fellow male officers with her top scores on firearm qualifications and with her inquisitive mind. She helped remove drug offenders in the community. Having served 25 years, she earned a Standing on Her Shoulders Award in 2013 from the Women's Fund. Today, she is a matron for the Holyoke Police Department. (Courtesy of Robert Charles Photography.)

Norman Cote

He grew up in Northampton and worked as a janitor for the Northampton School system. The children in the Northampton school system knew him as the "Snake Man" due to his amazing snake presentations that educated children about the behaviors and the environment of reptiles. He was also an exceptional long-distance runner at one time and an outdoorsman who loved to hike in the Mount Tom Range. On one of his excursions, he came across a makeshift memorial that consisted of a pile of rocks, a miniature American flag, and a note about the history of a plane crash in a plastic baggie. Tragically, a Boeing B-17G Flying Fortress bomber, which was converted for passenger transit, departed from the Newfoundland Airport, now called the Gander Airport, bound for Mitchell Field in New York. The pilot had intended to refuel at Westover Field in Chicopee. Aboard this ill-fated plane were 1st Ofc. Herman J. Valdrini Jr., Lt. Frank G. Meriam, Lt. Wilfred U. Johnson, Lt. George E. Orford, YNC Hugh J. Worth, RM2c Lee Winnard, BM2c Russell S. Scott, RM3c Alfred L. Warm, RM3c Arnold J. Simons, RM3c Ernest R. Gillis, ETM3c George R. Benfield, ETM3c George E. Fleming, S1c Arthur C. Miller, S1c Stanley P. Warshaw, S1c Gregory S. Davenport, and S2c David F. Archilles, all of the US Coast Guard. Also aboard were two civilians, Lt. Pasquale P. Coviello, an assistant surgeon with the US Public Health Service (USPHS) that was assigned to the Coast Guard, as well as Arthur Bailey of the American Red Cross. Around 10:20 p.m. on July 9, 1946, the plane slammed into the southern face of Mount Tom. An intense fire ensued, and all passengers were lost. Cote persuaded local officials to establish a permanent memorial for the 25 men. He contacted Robert Cahillane, a former director of the Veteran Services in Northampton, who took on the challenge and was the chairman of the committee of 15 volunteers who worked hard to erect a proper monument. Today, this stunning marker stands to remind people of these brave men who never reached their final destination 68 years ago, a fact that Cote and a group of local citizens (none of whom are related to the deceased) have so kindly made possible. (Courtesy of Bob Schwobe.)

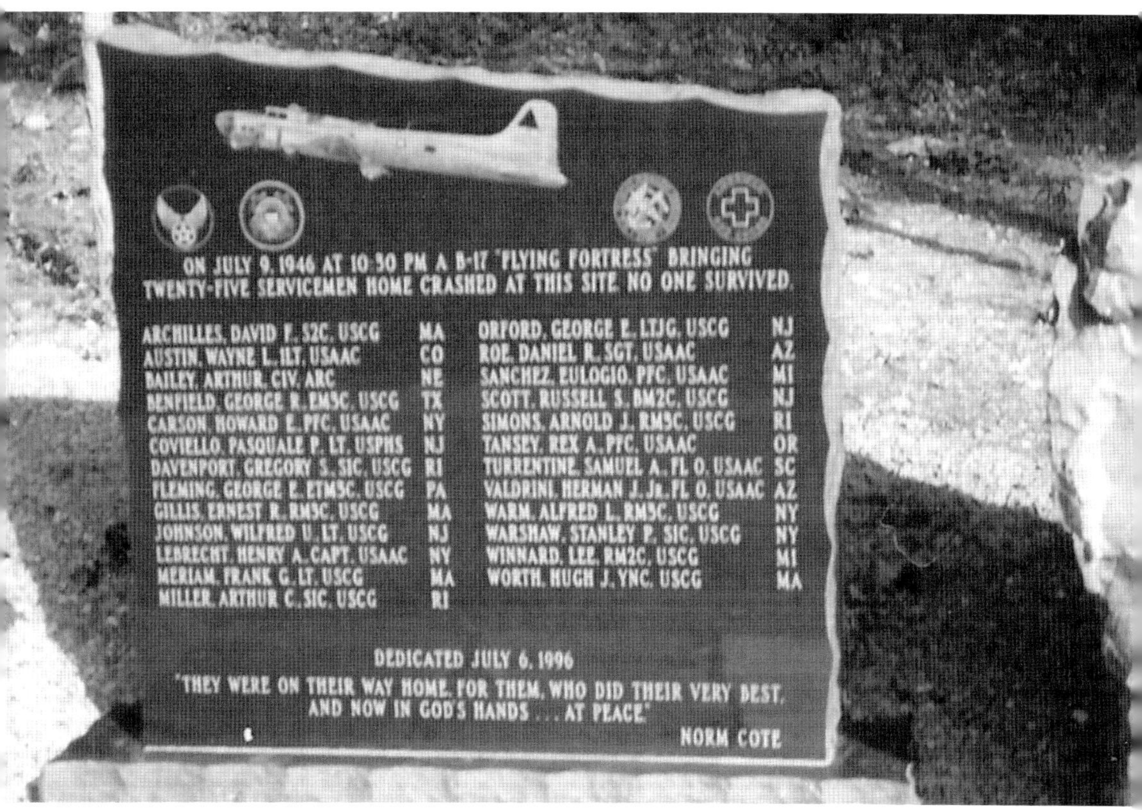

INDEX

INDEX